PERILOUS
EQUILIBRIUM

PERILOUS EQUILIBRIUM

The United States and the London Naval Conference of 1930

by

RAYMOND G. O'CONNOR

GREENWOOD PRESS, PUBLISHERS
NEW YORK

FOR

LOUIS C. HUNTER

Preface

This is a study of the London Naval Conference of 1930 within the framework of American foreign policy and naval policy. The period of the 1920's was distinguished by the desire, on the part of the public and the politicians alike, for security and disarmament. These two problems were really one, for while military force had often proved to be the final arbiter in international disputes, the reduction or limitation of armaments was considered essential to the elimination of distrust and suspicion among nations. The huge expenditures for arms and the maintenance of large military establishments were often regarded as an unnecessary waste, which could be avoided by enlightened statesmanship and international agreement.

The London Naval Treaty of 1930 constituted a formal repudiation by the United States, Great Britain, and Japan of the imperialism that had developed in these countries near the end of the nineteenth century. The treaty limited the building of all types of combat vessels and defined the relative strength of the fleets. Each nation relinquished its sovereign right to provide for its own safety in an attempt to achieve a different kind of security and seek relief from the burden of naval competition. The treaty was a concrete demonstration of the willingness of these nations to renounce aggressive force as an instrument of foreign policy, and it was the climax of a movement between two world wars for security through disarmament.

The sea that made the new world available pulled America away from its traditional isolation into the maelstrom of a wearied Europe and a rising Asia. The Navy played a significant role in this new phase of American foreign policy, and the London Naval Conference took place when the country was torn by the choice it faced. The size and composition of the armed forces constitute a political problem that rests with the government, not an exclusively technical problem to be decided by the professional expert. Yet foreign affairs and naval factors must be co-ordinated in order that national objectives can be implemented. The extent and nature of this co-ordination give rise to differences of opinion, and during the years following World War I the naval experts steadily encroached on the preserves of the statesmen.

The navy as an instrument of national policy is well exemplified by the negotiations attending a disarmament conference. The relations between the civil and military branches are brought into play. Each seeks to make its point of view prevail, and each accuses the other of a failure to grasp the full import of the issues involved, as the statesman strives for international conciliation and the professional reiterates that the fleet which exists is the fleet that wins. Often conflict rather than co-ordination occurs, and the results of the struggle are revealed in the impact on national interest and security.

This study minimizes the technical aspects of naval limitation. The details of ship construction are often a mystery to the layman, and the understanding of combat vessels is made even more difficult by the added considerations of fire power and protective armor. Tactical and strategic factors are also involved, and the testimony of experienced naval officers reveals wide areas of disagreement on all these matters. An attempt has been made to include sufficient details to explain but not confuse the story of the negotiations.

In the course of this study the author has received invaluable assistance and co-operation from many sources. Professor Thomas A. Bailey, of Stanford University, deserves special recognition for his patient advice and encouragement during the reading of successive drafts of the manuscript. Thanks are due the following who have read the manuscript in part or in its entirety: Professors Claude A. Buss; Otis Pease; Daniel M. Smith; Harold Sprout; Robert H. Ferrell; and members of the History Department "Hatchet Club" at the University of Kansas. While I have benefited from their suggestions and comments, the conclusions and shortcomings are my own. My indebtedness is also great to those who have furnished guidance to the collections of manuscript and archival material. My months of research in Navy Department files were lightened by the co-operation of Rear Admiral John B. Heffernan, Director of Naval History, and his successor, Rear Admiral E. M. Eller. Dr. William J. Morgan and Miss Loretta I. MacCrindle, of the Office of Naval History, were unstinting of their efforts in locating elusive documents. Dr. E. Taylor Parks, of the Historical Division, Department of State, displayed a kindly understanding of the scholar's needs. The Social Science Research Council generously made it possible for me to consult materials in various parts of the country. And a grant from the Research Fund of the University of Kansas was of material assistance in completing this study. Finally, I must acknowledge the contribution made by my wife and our three children. Theirs has been the greater sacrifice.

Contents

PREFACE   vii

I.   BACKGROUND OF RIVALRY   1

II.   COMPETITION AND DISAGREEMENT   11

III.   RENEWED EFFORTS FOR NAVAL LIMITATION, 1927-1929   20

IV.   ANGLO-AMERICAN CONVERSATIONS   31

V.   PRELUDE TO AGREEMENT   47

VI.   LONDON—THE ISSUE JOINED   62

VII.   JAPANESE-AMERICAN COMPROMISE   76

VIII.   LONDON—THE ISSUE RESOLVED   84

IX.   A TREATY EMERGES   94

X.   RATIFICATION   109

XI.   CONCLUSION   122

APPENDIX: TEXT OF THE TREATY   129

NOTES   145

BIBLIOGRAPHY   169

INDEX   181

Chapter I

Background of Rivalry

Sea power, however, is but the handmaid of expansion,
its begetter and preserver; it is not itself expansion.
—Alfred Thayer Mahan, 1900.

I

The modern American Navy that was involved in the controversial discussions over the limitation of armaments in the 1920's, culminating in the London Naval Conference of 1930, owed its existence to events in the United States and abroad which began in the final decades of the nineteenth century. The American empire in the Pacific began in 1867 with the annexation of the Midway Islands and the purchase of Alaska. The acquisition of this non-contiguous territory was the nation's first venture into the type of overseas imperialism that had been practised so successfully by the enterprising Europeans. By 1898, America, inspired by her victories at sea over Spain, appeared eager to assume responsibilities of which she was only dimly aware in order to follow the flag and achieve her manifest destiny. Her wealth, resources, technology, and geographical position made her virtually impervious to attack or blockage. The teachings of Admiral Mahan, who linked America's future with sea power and colonies, the efforts of Theodore Roosevelt, Henry Cabot Lodge, and others, and the enthusiasm for the new imperialism, all inspired and supported a navy that soon ranked with the leading fleets of the world and provided support for an aggressive foreign policy.

With the acquisition of colonies in the Pacific, America's interest in the Far East was no longer confined to commercial privileges. The Navy, previously committed to the protection of the American coastline and the Monroe Doctrine, found a new dimension added to its responsibilities. Maintenance of American naval power in the Western Hemisphere ceased to be the sole objective of the Navy planners, who were now obliged to direct their attention to a potential antagonist in the far Pacific. The Navy General Board, established in 1900 as a top level advisory committee of senior officers, viewed with alarm the rapidly expanding German fleet, which offered support for aggressive policies in Latin America or the Far East. Beginning in 1901, the American building program was designed with a weather eye on the growth of German naval and commercial power. The military planners concluded that the most probable cause of war would be a violation of the Monroe Doctrine by a European power. Plans for a conflict with Germany were given the highest priority, and they envisioned the course of war in the Atlantic, the Mediterranean, and the western Pacific.[1]

1

There was also danger of war in the Far East. The acquisition of the Philippines and Guam in effect blocked Japanese expansion in the south Pacific. At first the rising sun of Japan was viewed with favor by Theodore Roosevelt, who thought she could contain the imperialistic ambitions of Germany and Russia and help preserve the status quo in the Far East. The President heartily approved the Anglo-Japanese Alliance of 1902 and privately sympathized with Japan in her war with Russia. Then the balance of power was upset by the destruction of the Russian fleet at Tsushima, and the American strategists were compelled to acknowledge another probable antagonist. What had been mutual interests now became sources of potential conflict, and sights were adjusted to include the new two-ocean vulnerability.[2]

The situation, in the opinion of the General Board, demanded protection from "a European country, or from Japan, or from a European country and Japan." Since all nations realized that control of the sea would mean victory, the United States should keep its main fleet in the Atlantic to protect the Monroe Doctrine. If hostilities were to occur in the Far East, the fleet could move to the Pacific for a decisive engagement after a rendezvous with the Asiatic squadron. The American Navy, if divided, would not be effective against either antagonist, but when enlarged to a "two-ocean" standard and supported by powerful Pacific bases, or upon completion of the Panama Canal, a division of the forces would be both practicable and desirable.[3] Naval authorities did not regard the Philippines as "our heel of Achilles" in a military sense, for the islands gave the United States a strategic foothold in Asiatic waters and were a source of logistic support for fleet operations in the event of war. Then, in 1907, the impetuous Roosevelt sent American warships on a global cruise to alert other nations to the armed might of the New World, and demonstrate America's ability to support her policies and meet her naval commitments.[4]

Great Britain, meanwhile, struggling against German imperialism and commercial rivalry, faced a threat to her traditional naval supremacy. She had been for centuries predominantly a naval power, whose foreign and domestic policies depended on a fleet capable of dominating the European seas, maintaining communications with the colonies and foreign ports, and defending her interests throughout the world. Germany recognized this dependence but refused to accept it, as was revealed by the furor with which Berlin greeted Winston Churchill's designation of the British fleet as a necessity and the German fleet as a luxury.[5] To the statesmen at Whitehall, a large German navy could have no other purpose than to challenge British control of the sea in pursuance of an aggressive foreign policy.[6]

The German-British rivalry increased with the years. In 1889 the two-power standard was adopted as the basis of Great Britain's naval requirements. Calling for a fleet equal to the combined strength of the two next strongest navies in Europe, the British Admiralty twenty years later was forced to adopt a policy which required the maintenance of a 60 percent superiority over the German fleet.

The threat to British naval supremacy had other diplomatic and military repercussions. By the beginning of the twentieth century Britain had emerged from her "splendid isolation," an emergence in some degree stimulated by the feeling that her hold on world affairs was slipping. This loss of confidence in the Pax Britannica provoked a search for new forms of security, and London welcomed America's appearance as a colonial power in the south Pacific in the belief that this deeper commitment would serve as a stabilizing force in the Far East.[7] The Anglo-Japanese Treaty of Alliance, concluded January 30, 1902, helped secure Britain's flank and permitted the transfer of warships to the Mediterranean and Home fleets, but it deprived Russia of naval allies and gave Japan potential control of the western Pacific. By relinquishing naval supremacy Britain lost some of her political influence in the Far East and allowed Japan to pursue her expansionist policies with less fear of European intervention. Understandably the alliance "formed the corner stone of Japanese diplomacy for the next twenty years,"[8] but it enabled Great Britain to concentrate on the containment of Germany in European waters, and reduced her fear of Russian expansion in the Middle East and Manchuria.

The advent of World War I offered Japan the opportunity to extend her hegemony in the Far East with even less interference from a Europe embroiled in a struggle for survival. The United States, finding it impossible to retain the role of disinterested spectator, displayed an increasing concern over the progress of events in both the Atlantic and the Pacific. In the face of international chaos, and encouraged by an apprehensive President, the General Board recommended in 1915 that "the Navy of the United States should ultimately be equal to the most powerful maintained by any other nation of the world."[9] This marked a notable advance over the previous position of the Board, which heretofore had asked for a fleet capable of defeating only "probable" enemies. Requirements, the admirals explained, were based on the premise that armies and navies exist as "instruments of diplomacy." The foreign policies to which the United States was committed were: no entangling alliances; the Monroe Doctrine; the open door in China; Asiatic exclusion; military control of the Panama Canal and contiguous waters; and defense of the Philippines. The new commercial position of the United States had placed it in competition with other countries, and, the naval statesmen observed, "History shows that wars are chiefly caused by economic pressure and competition between nations and races." Thus a postwar challenge could be anticipated regardless of American involvement in the current conflict and irrespective of the victor.[10]

3

The move to set the nation's defenses in order developed rapidly and culminated in the Naval Act of 1916, which provided for an accelerated building program designed to augment the fleet by 156 ships of all classes. This legislation served a threefold purpose. First, many Americans had been frightened by the war in Europe, and the promise of a mighty navy furnished the maximum reassurance. Second, Japan's belligerent activities gave rise to misgivings over the fate of American possessions and interests in the Far East. Third, the prospect of a postwar world dominated by the enlarged and victorious sea power of Germany or Great Britain and Japan was looked on with a jaundiced eye by many Americans. The act provided for the most powerful navy in the world, and alerted the Allies to the existence of a rival whose gauntlet was flung with customary audacity into their midst at a time when they were desperately engaged in the elimination of another.

American participation in the war popularized the value of sea power more effectively than all the polemics of Mahan. The public was able to observe at first hand the importance of maintaining lines of communication and supply that spelled the difference between victory and defeat. The delivery of food, troops, and munitions was dependent on control of the sea, and the threat of invasion was always present for insular Britain if not for moated America.

The armistice found all three leading naval powers faced with problems whose solutions were inextricably interwoven with the composition of their fleets. The center of the world stage was shifting from the Atlantic to the Pacific, where even the illusion of a balance of power in the Far East had been destroyed and Japan's ascendancy had been clearly established. Great Britain still possessed the superior navy but she had virtually stopped building. America's program, if continued, would soon give her parity and eventually superiority over her recent ally. Added to Britain's woes was the likelihood that the United States or Japan would replace Germany as her rival for world trade. The exhausted British were anxious to regain their commercial supremacy and restore prosperity, which, they contended, were dependent on their traditional mastery of the sea. Sensing that the reins of world leadership were being grasped by her giant offspring, Britain refused to accept naval equality with the United States, and Wilson rejected any arrangement that would deny the freedom of the seas.[11]

In 1919 separate American fleets were established in the Atlantic and Pacific oceans. Sufficient ships finally were available and the German menace had been eliminated. More significant was Japan's emergence as the most probable enemy, strengthened by acquisition of strategic islands and removal of a powerful European rival. Increased naval forces were needed to redress the imbalance resulting from dislocations of the war, and the Wilson administration championed an extensive building program in order to meet the

4

new defense needs and induce other nations to support the President's plans for disarmament and world co-operation.[12] The growing American Navy disturbed Britain and alarmed Japan, since it appeared to be directed against their interests. The former was financially unable to compete with the United States. The latter responded by accelerating her construction program.[13]

By 1921 each of the three nations was experiencing a strong reaction against spending for armaments, and witnessing the concurrent growth of a movement for some form of limitation or reduction. Disillusion with war flourished in the wake of huge debts and a suspicion that the gains of victory were not commensurate with the sacrifices. Public opinion was not convinced that peacetime fleets should be larger than wartime fleets, and a business recession, combined with the cloudy international scene, prompted the statesmen to seek an end to competition. The Anglo-Japanese Alliance was regarded with concern by the United States and some of the Dominions, and its reconsideration stimulated Britain's desire for a diplomatic conference in the hope of eliminating a naval race with America and establishing barriers against Japanese imperialism.[14] Bankruptcy or war loomed as alternatives to agreement.

Faced with considerable domestic and foreign pressure for efforts toward a solution of the twin problems of naval competition and world tensions, the American Secretary of State, Charles Evans Hughes, persuaded President Warren G. Harding to invite delegates from Great Britain, Japan, France, and Italy to meet in Washington in November 1921 for the purpose of discussing the limitation of armaments and Far Eastern problems. Invitations were subsequently extended to China, the Netherlands, Belgium, and Portugal to participate in the sessions relating to the Far East.[15]

II

In preparation for the conference, the Navy General Board was directed to submit an estimate of the nation's naval requirements. Basing its recommendations on a comprehensive appraisal of the international situation, the Board declared that the navy was obligated to defend certain cardinal American policies, including the principle of no entangling alliances, the Monroe Doctrine, the Open Door in China, the exclusion of Asiatics, access to raw materials, the defense of possessions, and "opposition to neutralization of Pacific Islands," the latter an obvious allusion to the League mandate system which had placed former German territory in the western Pacific in the hands of Japan. Two nations, the Board claimed, were engaged in a supreme effort to gain control of remaining unexploited natural resources: Great Britain on a world-wide scale and Japan in the Far East.

The latter had taken advantage of the recent war to consolidate her position in Asia and thereby pose a greater threat to American interests. Since the German menace had been removed, the Anglo-Japanese Alliance served no purpose other than to intimidate the United States, and its continuance would demand an American Navy equivalent to that of the two nations combined. The United States alone checked British sea power in the Atlantic and Japanese sea power in the Pacific, and the naval experts were "reasonably certain that Japan would join Great Britain in any war against us that Great Britain might undertake."[16] If the alliance were discontinued, the Board concluded, the United States would need parity with her Atlantic rival and a two-to-one superiority over Japan in order to have an equal opportunity in a conflict with either nation.[17]

Armed with the findings of the Navy General Board, the American delegation, headed by Hughes and composed of Elihu Root, former Secretary of State, Henry Cabot Lodge, chairman of the Senate Foreign Relations Committee, and Oscar W. Underwood, ranking Democratic member of that committee, set about formulating the American naval program. Three plans were considered. The first, based on the tonnage of ships afloat, would have given Britain a considerable superiority. The second, based on the tonnage of ships built, building, and projected, would have granted Japan virtual parity with the United States. The third, based on the tonnage of ships built and building, gave America parity with Britain and a sizable advantage over Japan. The latter plan was adopted, and, using battleships as an "index to naval power," the General Board determined the relative strength of the British, American, and Japanese fleets to be approximately in the ratio of 5:5:3.[18]

The conference met in Washington on November 12, 1921, and Hughes continued to take the initiative, to the delight of the press and the dismay of many statesmen and most naval authorities. Following an innocuous welcoming speech by President Harding, the American Secretary of State shattered the composure of the foreign delegates by presenting them with a proposal that advocated not only limitation of naval armament but the actual scrapping of vessels as well. Both Britain and Japan finally accepted the 5:5:3 ratio in capital ships, defined as vessels displacing more than 10,000 tons and mounting guns larger than eight inches, and aircraft carriers. Italy and France agreed to a ratio of 1.67. The Japanese government had demanded 70 percent of the maximum tonnage allotted, and it accepted the reduced ratio only because the United States and Great Britain joined Japan in an agreement not to fortify certain islands in the western Pacific.[19] France had little interest in battleships, and Italy was content to receive acknowledged paper parity with her larger neighbor. That no agreement was reached on auxiliary craft, which included cruisers, destroyers, and submarines, seemed of minor importance. Secretary of State Hughes, speaking of the Naval Limitation Treaty, claimed optimistically that "this Treaty ends, absolutely ends, the race in competition of naval armaments."[20] The report of the American delegation, summarizing the results, concluded: "The limitation of capital ships, in itself, substantially meets the existing need, and its indirect effort will be to stop the inordinate production of any sort of naval craft."[21] As it turned out, the subsequent eight years were studded with efforts to stop the inordinate production of auxiliary naval craft.

The Washington Conference also witnessed the conclusion of the Four-Power and Nine-Power Treaties. The former, intended to supplant the Anglo-Japanese Alliance, was designed to bring a halt to the threat of Japanese expansion in the Far East by non-aggression pledges and a provision for consultation in the event of disputes between the contracting parties. The Treaty "substituted a four-power agreement to talk for a two-power agreement to fight," and met American and Dominion objections to the pact that it replaced. The Nine-Power Treaty guaranteed the territorial integrity of China and confirmed the principle of the Open Door, thereby terminating two decades of confusion and misunderstanding.

The accomplishments of the Washington Conference were enthusiastically welcomed in the United States by the press and the public.[22] But a similar reaction did not emerge from the corridors of the Navy Department or the decks of men-of-war. One naval spokesman, expressing an opinion shared by many of his colleagues, concluded that "America resigned to Britain the predominance in Sea Power, and gave up also her power to defend the Philippines and to accomplish our policies towards China and Russia."[23] The Navy General Board gravely observed that the conditions resulting from the Naval Limitation Treaty "will be such as greatly to lessen the power of the United States to prepare to defend its interests or unaided to enforce its policies in the western Pacific."[24] The Navy planners had furnished the American delegation with elaborate studies covering relative strength, minimum needs, and the fortification of islands, but on this occasion the civilians outranked the admirals and refused to accept their recommendations. Root acutely perceived that the outcome of the conference was "the complete negation of naval policy,"[25] a view that represented the opinion of statesman and expert alike.

The Washington treaties were well received in Great Britain. She had extricated herself from an alliance with Japan that had become embarrassing, achieved a state of equilibrium in the Far East, improved relations with the United States, and halted the ruinous naval competition.[26] But a professional judgment delivered by Admiral of the Fleet Lord Wester-Wemyss, wartime First Sea Lord, warned: "We have surrendered our naval supremacy on which up to now the whole fabric of our Empire has been founded; we have lost prestige; we have created another cause of friction with our 'French friends.' "[27] Naval limitation was a severe blow to those Englishmen who attributed Britain's greatness to her fleet and her domination of the sea. To them the treaties heralded not merely the end of an era and the subverting of a magnificent heritage, but the curtailment of a force that represented law and order throughout the civilized and uncivilized world.

Japanese press opinion was generally favorable on the grounds that international tension had been eased and the tax burden had been relieved.[28] Naval officers, as in Britain and America, were extremely unhappy. They argued that the Japanese delegates had sacrificed the beneficial Anglo-Japanese Alliance, restricted Japan's freedom of action in Asia and the western Pacific, and approved a ratio so low that it endangered her safety.[29] The French were disappointed, for they had hoped to arrive at some agreement that would provide guarantees against aggression in Europe. Italy, alone, could be smug in the added prestige that came from a conceded parity with France.

Underlying these responses to the treaties was a variety of motives, of self-interest and altruism, of short-sightedness and great perceptivity, of practical politics and mature statesmanship. Public opinion reflected a desire for peace and economy. The statesmen were of the same mind, but neither of these ends was possible without national security, which was based on good will and international agreements as well as military power. The problem of the naval expert was simple: to be prepared to win any war in which his country might become involved. In this respect his point of view was different from that of the civilians, for he thought in terms of victory rather than defense.

The conference created some problems and exposed others. It established a ratio in battleships and aircraft carriers that provided a mathematical equality for Great Britain and the United States, an arrangement which led to a lengthy and heated dispute over whether Britain thereby accepted the principle of naval equality in all categories.[30] Japan's acceptance of a 60 percent ratio in exchange for the non-fortification agreement presaged a refusal to extend this inferiority to other categories without further concessions. Limitation was imposed only on the construction of aircraft carriers and vessels exceeding 10,000 tons displacement and mounting guns in excess of eight inches. Consequently, competition was transferred to the so-called auxiliary vessels, especially cruisers, which were more suited to the needs of Britain and Japan. France never abandoned her insistence on security before disarmament, and Italy never forgot the precedent of parity with her continental neighbor. The divergent viewpoints of the admirals and the politicians in Britain, America, and Japan were to continue with varying results.

The issues presented had questioned the honor and prestige of each group, as well as their professional competence and constitutional responsibility. A degree of resentment, if not enmity, emerged which otherwise might have remained quiescent. Formerly confined within the walls of government offices, this rivalry was to burst on a bewildered public with all the force and confusion that a partisan press could muster. The clash revealed that the movement for the merging of foreign policy and naval policy had reached maturity.

It appears that in virtually every instance Hughes determined American policy and was successful from his point of view in achieving naval disarmament and international conciliation. But his decisions demonstrated an inability to grasp the significance of armament in foreign policy, namely, that successful diplomacy is diplomacy backed by force. Lacking the means of fulfillment, commitments are robbed of both spirit and substance. Hughes very properly subordinated military to political considerations, but politically he apparently was more concerned with reaching an understanding that would give the illusion, if not the reality, of a world in harmony. Unwilling or unable to resist the clamor for economy and peace through the reduction or elimination of the weapons of war, the Secretary of State sacrificed America's freedom of action, lessened her influence in world affairs, and weakened her ability to promote the national interest. It was a precarious position for a nation that had renounced the principle of collective security.[31]

Apart from the arguments of the apologists and critics was the sobering fact that new power relationships had emerged. Agreement at Washington was possible because there were no outstanding acute discernible areas of contention between the participants. But the capital ship ratio, the Four-Power and Nine-Power Treaties, and the termination of the Anglo-Japanese Alliance were a blow to Japan's pride and damaging to her prestige. After her participation in the recent war and the prospect of a free hand in the Far East, Japan might well have resented this seemingly cavalier treatment and suspected a conspiracy on the part of the English-speaking governments. Even so, by agreeing to the treaties, Japan accepted the military status of a second-class power and renounced her bid for empire in exchange for economy, good will, and security. No doubt the British and American negotiators believed they had made a good bargain, for they had secured agreements which blocked Japanese expansion, deprived her of allies, and safeguarded Western interests in Asia. The seeds of discontent sown by the apparent curtailment of Japan's ambitions were scarcely perceptible in the aura of success that suffused the outcome of the conference.

President Harding, in commending the treaties to the Senate, boasted that they involved the United States in "no entangling alliances." Yet without an entangling alliance enforcement was impossible. The pacts contained no provisions for sanctions or the use of force in the event of noncompliance, and observance depended solely on the mutual interests and good faith of the signatory nations. Unilateral coercion was impracticable because of the naval restrictions, and joint Anglo-American fleet action was neither contemplated nor conceivable. Under the circumstances the restrictions imposed on Japan were illusory, and her position in the Far East became virtually impregnable. Twenty years earlier Great Britain had made the first move to give Japan control of her surrounding seas. At Washington the United States added her blessing and was instrumental in completing the bequest.

Chapter II

Competition and Disagreement

The doctrine of naval equality, if it is to be accepted by us,
must take into consideration the whole position of the two
countries on the sea, and their respective risks and vulnerability.
—Winston Churchill, 1927.

I

The Washington Naval Conference of 1921-22 was one of the great land-marks in the history of the modern American Navy, as it marked also the histories of the other great world navies, and so one must begin with the Washington arrangements in order to understand the subsequent naval history of the United States and its principal competitors in the 1920's and 1930's. The conference, as mentioned in the previous chapter, came to an end uncertainly, so far as concerned the lesser categories of naval vessels—cruisers, destroyers, and submarines. The years that followed immediately, from 1922 until 1930, saw intense interest therefore in these auxiliary vessels.

The cruiser problem was the crux of the matter. Following the conference, Secretary of the Navy Edwin Denby directed the General Board to formulate a naval policy for the United States based on the Washington treaties.[1] After conducting extensive hearings, the Board submitted a comprehensive and detailed statement of policy predicated on the assumption that the 5:5:3 ratio would extend to all categories of vessels. Providing for a building program designed to maintain this ratio in modern, up-to-date ships, it specified that all cruisers should displace 10,000 tons and carry 8-inch guns, the maximum permitted under the treaty. The Board was anxious to obtain the greatest cruising radius and fire power possible, and identical specifications previously had been stipulated for postwar cruiser construction.[2] The President and the Secretary of the Navy approved this recommendation in its entirety, and the latter proudly announced: "For the first time in the history of our country the Navy and Congress have a definite naval policy and building and maintenance standard to work to, a standard which is proportionate to our position as a world power."[3]

Though gratified at having secured a definite policy, the Navy exponents could find little to admire in a document based on what they considered a wholly inadequate ratio. The General Board had estimated that the United States needed a two-to-one preponderance in ships in order to have an equal chance against the Japanese navy. The treaty not only reduced the margin of superiority but limited the effectiveness of the fleet in the western Pacific by the

11

non-fortification agreement.[4] Besides, warned the Board, "from a naval position that then [pre-treaty] commanded the respect and attention of the world and was potentially the greatest, we have sunk to a poor second." In order to protect America's commerce, her possessions, and her home land, which could be reached only "by way of the sea," it was imperative that the Navy be built up at least to full treaty strength in all categories.[5] Planning based on defective assumptions was preferred to planning without implementation, but events were to deprive the naval statesmen of even this one small victory.

After the Washington Conference the Commander in Chief of the Atlantic Fleet, Admiral Hilary P. Jones, wrote discouragingly of the Navy's prospects. He was depressed by the public apathy and the unco-operative attitude of the press, which was "practically unanimous in refusing to publish anything favorable to the Navy, as all papers are committed to the drastic limitation of armaments." Only the Hearst papers were sympathetic to the Navy's cause, he lamented, and their efforts, though considerable, were not unduly persuasive.[6] The Admiral's concern was not without foundation, for the general hostility of the press merely reflected the attitude that prevailed throughout the country. After World War I the nation experienced a reaction against war and a virtual revolt against militarism, in large part the result of a disillusionment as to the ideals, causes, suffering, and financial cost of the expedition to save Europe. Peace societies became increasingly popular and disarmament was advocated both for financial reasons and as a step to remove a fundamental cause of war. The public, resentful of the vast sums expended for the construction and upkeep of the huge men-of-war, encouraged an economy-minded Republican administration to curtail the building program envisaged by the Big Navy camp, which included among its more vocal adherents the Navy League and the American Legion, who vigorously urged that the fleet be raised to treaty strength without delay. A strong movement for withdrawal from world commitments and responsibilities added its voice to the clamor for retrenchment in armaments and a concentration on defense in American waters. Confronted by overwhelming demands for peace, economy, and the avoidance of entangling alliances, the administration abandoned any attempt to implement the naval policy it had endorsed.

A further rebuff was handed the military arm when Secretary of State Hughes rejected a bid for a formal and permanent liaison between the departments. At the height of the Washington Conference, Secretary of War John W. Weeks and Secretary of the Navy Denby invited Hughes to appoint an official of the State Department to sit with the Joint Army and Navy Board, which had been established in 1903 to co-ordinate operations between the two services. Hughes declined the offer on the grounds that only the Secretary or the Undersecretary of State could "speak with authority on questions of national policy," and neither was available for this duty. He later agreed to an alternative proposal to send a representative whenever matters "interwoven with the international policies of the United States" were under consideration.[7] This cool reception of a badly needed and eminently practicable effort to correlate national and military policies and achieve continuity and understanding between the departments is a startling indication of the way in which Hughes ignored the role of the armed forces in foreign affairs.

Relieved of the burden of battleship construction, Great Britain and Japan embarked on intensive building programs in the cruiser category. Japanese public opinion was made more receptive to competition by the Immigration Act of 1924, which virtually destroyed such good will as was engendered by the Washington Conference. The British program, sparked by Dominion concern over the threat of Japan and a report prepared by Earl Jellicoe on defense in the Pacific, had an adverse effect in the United States, where it had been assumed that the Washington Treaty had established parity between the two nations in all types of warships. Faced with naval expansion in the east and the west, Congress recognized the error of Hughes' optimism and enacted legislation in 1924 instructing the President to begin the construction of eight 10,000-ton cruisers prior to July 1, 1927, while at the same time providing for suspension or cancellation of the project by the President in the event of a naval agreement. Congress further displayed its reluctance to accept competition by including in the Naval Acts of 1923, 1924, and 1925 a request that the President call a conference to discuss the limitation of vessels not provided for by the Washington Treaty.

On the other hand, the Navy planners were opposed to the further limitation of naval armament, for, they contended,

As sea power comprehends combatant ships plus merchant marine plus bases, it follows that, in comparison with British sea power, for instance, if the United States and Great Britain arrive at an equality of combatant ships, Great Britain, by reason of superior strength in merchant marine and bases, remains the dominant sea power. And, therefore, every bilateral limitation in combatant ships whether in numbers, or size, or power of individual ships, further weakens American sea power relative to British sea power. With each further limitation of armament, this relative weakening will increase until, should all combatant types by [sic] abolished, Great Britain, by reason of overwhelming superiority in merchant marine and bases, would completely dominate the seas.[8]

In explaining the basis for this professional attitude, Rear Admiral William W. Phelps analyzed the disarmament question at great length and exposed a fundamental reason for the General Board's Anglophobia.

The situation sums up as follows: The United States is the present rival of Great Britain in world trade and commerce. The American protective tariff and protective coastwise laws impede British expansion of world trade and shipping. British interests for the last seven years, with the powerful backing of the League of Nations, have been slowly consolidating, and may be expected to continue the effort to consolidate a combine in which are to be included continental powers and Japan, for the purpose of breaking down, eventually, the American protective system.[9]

Confronted with what they regarded as a world-wide conspiracy guided by the Machiavellian tactics of this former ally, the admirals were convinced that America's destiny was contingent on her fleet. Equality in warships and guns could never mean equality in sea power so long as Britain retained a preponderance of merchant vessels and naval bases, and further combat limitation would merely contribute to her superiority. The politicians, on the other hand, wanted an opinion from the experts that would support their objective of a reduction in armament with its resultant economy and, from their point of view, improvement in world amity. The conflict between the civil and military branches of the government was becoming more pronounced as it approached disagreement on fundamentals rather than on technicalities.

In his efforts to promote disarmament, President Coolidge, who consistently opposed the demands of the Big-Navy bloc, accepted an invitation for the United States to attend the meetings of the Preparatory Commission in Geneva, which had been established by the Council of the League of Nations in 1925 to draft plans for a general disarmament conference. The commission, which included representatives from many small nations, was so divided over the problem of the interdependence of land, sea, and air weapons, as well as the method of limitation to be followed, that it made little progress. Nevertheless, rumors of an impending conference persisted, and the Navy Department seemed determined to avoid the charge of insufficient preparation. Questions dealing with matters of policy and including suggested answers were submitted to key officers asking for their comments and recommendations, and comprehensive and detailed reports on the outlook for disarmament were submitted by the naval attachés in Tokyo, Paris, and London.

From Great Britain came word that pacifism was popular and that the government, hailed for its recent success in the Locarno negotiations, would probably be willing to make some sacrifices in order to achieve disarmament. But, cautioned the attaché, "there are powerful elements in the British Government that will see that the British lion comes out of any conference unscathed. The great Conservative body of opinion of the aristocracy, the Admiralty, the War Office and the Air Ministry, will at the right time see that Great Britain gets a quid pro quo twice over anything that is sacrificed." Anxious to avoid public opprobrium, Britain, the report continued, "hopes to be relieved by us of the necessity of wrecking the Conference by declining to consider land and sea armaments together." Nor was she the only nation that intended to make America the scapegoat for any failure to secure a further reduction of armaments. Now that the United States participated in the meetings of the Preparatory Commission, the report warned, "there appears to be a general feeling of relief among the signers of the Locarno Treaties that with the almost certain failure of any substantial agreement there will be ready at hand a pair of broad shoulders to take the burden of responsibility."[10] Those "powerful elements in the British Government" that were determined to prevent any further restrictions on England's ability to control the sea had their counterpart in the other nations grouped around the table at Geneva, who were caught between the ideals of public opinion and what the envoys considered the realities of national interest.

The report from Paris revealed a belief that security should precede disarmament, but no reliable information was available as to the nature of any possible agreement. The Washington Treaty, which reduced France to a secondary naval power, "continues to rankle," and there was evidence that France would never again accept such a national humiliation. Her demand for a large navy, said the attaché, was due to "her historic fear of Italy which she does not dare allow to gain the lead in the Mediterranean."[11] No doubt the French authorities were also apprehensive of a resurgent Germany, whose industrial capacity and technical proficiency had launched an imposing fleet within the memories of living Frenchmen.

Japan, reported the attaché at Tokyo, had risen in recent years to the position of a great power, and her lack of natural resources impelled her to exploit other areas. China was most convenient and best-suited for this purpose, and Japan was aware of the need for sufficient military strength to pursue such a policy in the face of competition and probable opposition from other great powers. In order to maintain the necessary force, the report went on, Japan would object to any limitation of armaments that placed her in a decided position of inferiority to another nation. Public opinion now resented the Washington Treaty for what it considered an inadequate quota, and would not consent to an extension of the 5:5:3 ratio to auxiliary vessels.[12] Understandably, the size and composition of the Japanese fleet would depend on the nature of Japan's future foreign policy. The further exploitation of China would violate the Four-Power and Nine-Power pacts and evoke strenuous objections from the signatory nations. Japan would need a formidable navy to support her aggressive diplomacy and discourage an attempt at some kind of police action.

By 1927 President Coolidge was convinced that naval disarmament could be effected only by a gathering of those countries whose interests were most vitally affected by the sea. Dissatisfied with the efforts of the Preparatory

Commission, and alarmed by the growing naval might of Japan and Great Britain, he was appalled at the prospect of huge expenditures to preserve the balance of naval power. In the face of unpleasant alternatives, and encouraged by the precedent of the Washington Conference, Coolidge invited the five nations signatory to the Naval Limitation Treaty to a conference at Geneva to consider placing restrictions on the construction of cruisers, destroyers, and submarines.[13]

Japan and Great Britain accepted the invitation, but Italy refused, explaining privately that her strained relations with France made it unwise to bring up the question of parity between the two navies.[14] France declined on the grounds that land, sea, and air weapons must be considered together, within the framework of the Preparatory Commission and the League. The announcement of Secretary of State Frank B. Kellogg that nothing in the nature of a security pact would be considered at the conference probably tended to cool the ardor of the French. In order to make use of their experience and the prestige of the League to promote the success of the conference, the President suggested that the delegates be those representing the various governments on the Preparatory Commission. This arrangement, which served to place naval officers in the role of negotiators rather than advisers, was to give rise to considerable controversy.

In the United States the General Board produced a detailed study of America's naval requirements and formulated a policy that was approved by the President and used as a guide by the delegates. The capital ship ratio of 5:5:3 which had been accepted at Washington was to be applied to cruisers, destroyers, and submarines. But the Board warned of a curious paradox which added to the complexities of naval limitation.

Our strategic situation vis-a-vis Great Britain indicates that the larger the number of cruisers we possess on the basis of a ratio of 5-5, assuming that ratio to be realized, the better will be our relative situation, because Great Britain's auxiliary cruisers will then have less relative importance.

In the Pacific the situation is reversed. It is to our interest to keep the number of cruisers as low as possible so long as the cruisers of Japan and the United States are in the ratio of 5-3. This is because of the great potential threat that every existing Japanese cruiser would exercise on our essential lines of communications supporting fleet operations in the western Pacific.[15]

Thus the delegates were asked to extend the existing ratio and at the same time achieve a balance in tonnage that would be of the greatest advantage to the United States. No doubt the Navy planners were anxious that agreement be reached on a figure sufficiently low to secure administration and Congressional support for legislation to provide the ships authorized by the treaty, for the lean years following the Washington pacts were a painful object lesson. The admirals had been maneuvering a paper cruiser fleet, and

16

apparently they were reconciled to a compromise between the practical and the ideal.

Soon after London accepted the President's invitation, Mr. W. C. Bridgeman, First Lord of the Admiralty, announced the policy that was to govern the British delegates. "There are special circumstances with regard to our Navy," he said, "which are totally different from those of any other country." Britain was obliged "to maintain a Fleet equal in naval strength to that of any other Power, and provide reasonable security for safeguarding trade and communications." This was "the sacred duty placed upon the Fleet," Bridgeman added, "and one which we at the Admiralty are proud to endeavor to carry out."[16] On this clearly marked reef the conference was to founder. The need for ships to protect her commerce and unite her empire was to prevent Great Britain from granting equality in cruiser strength to the United States. But other problems arose that furnish insight into the agreement reached three years later at London.

II

The delegates met at Geneva on June 20, 1927. The American envoys were Hugh Gibson, Ambassador to Belgium, and Rear Admiral Hilary P. Jones, both of whom had been accredited to the Preparatory Commission. The British delegation was led by Bridgeman and consisted of Viscount Cecil, Vice Admiral Sir F. L. Field, and Earl Jellicoe, Admiral of the Fleet. Representing Japan were Admiral Viscount M. Saito and Viscount Kikujiro Ishii, Japanese Ambassador to France. Also present were a number of advisers, most of whom were naval officers.

The proposals and counter-proposals of the various delegations were numerous and conflicting. Initially, Britain demanded fifteen 10,000-ton 8-inch–gun cruisers and fifty-five 6-inch–gun cruisers with a maximum displacement of 7,500 tons. This proposal dwarfed the American request for twenty-five or thirty 10,000-ton cruisers mounting an 8-inch battery, for a total of 250,000 or 300,000 tons. To Admiral Jones, the British figures were "catastrophical."[17] On the assumption that the United States and Great Britain would each require 450,000 tons of auxiliary surface ships, Japan asked for "a figure of somewhat above 300,000 tons," or a ratio of at least 5:5:3.5. Not content with an increase in the Washington Treaty quota, she also wanted an allocation of 70,000 tons of submarines irrespective of the ratio.[18] And although the Japanese delegates continued to advocate a reduction in armaments rather than mere limitation, their problem appeared secondary when viewed in the light of the enormous disparity between the British and American proposals.

Nor were the two major powers able to resolve their differences. Bridgeman persisted in his stand that Britain's "special circumstances" warranted a greater number of cruisers than the United States. He not only refused to grant parity but insisted that America accept a percentage of 6-inch–gun cruisers in lieu of the 8-inch that she preferred.[19] The American delegation was reluctant to exceed a total cruiser figure of 300,000 tons, but it was willing to consider a compromise on the issue of 8-inch– and 6-inch–gun ships. When the members of the technical staff were polled as to the number of big-gun cruisers they considered necessary under the aforementioned tonnage, the total ranged from eleven to twenty-one. Admiral Jones decided that fifteen would be acceptable, although he preferred more.[20] Japan supported the American position in an effort to arrive at the lowest possible figure, but she assumed the role of mediator and attempted to bring the two nations together. Prolonged discussions brought about an imperceptible narrowing of the gap, and finally the conference dissolved without reaching an agreement.

Blame for the failure of the conference has been placed on the professional delegates, who were pleaders, it is asserted, rather than diplomats, unused to the give and take of international parleys and intent on protecting the interests of their respective services. Elihu Root observed that "in one sense, the better the naval officer, the more incapable he is of judging government policy, because the postulates on which he bases his propositions are ones on which government policy has to close the door."[21] Ramsay MacDonald told the House of Commons that "the service deputation is altogether out of place" at a disarmament conference,[22] and one authority contended that Admiral Jones "viewed the world through a porthole."[23]

Actually, however, the failure at Geneva had little to do with the composition of the delegations. Britain, by refusing to grant the United States mathematical parity in cruisers or the right to build the desired number of 8-inch–gun vessels, made agreement impossible. But even if this obstacle had been overcome the negotiations probably would have collapsed over the Japanese demands. The United States had nothing to offer in exchange for major concessions. The other nations had a preponderance of cruisers, and the American delegates were forbidden to introduce the non-fortification of naval bases as a bargaining factor to secure a more favorable ratio.[24] No doubt preliminary conversations would have ironed out many of the technical difficulties and established more practicable agenda, but it also would have exposed fundamental areas of contention and revealed the futility of a formal conference. Under the circumstances, the publicity attending the meeting at Geneva inflamed public opinion and intensified suspicions and ill feeling that otherwise might have remained dormant.

Basically, the nations were unable to reach agreement because they viewed disarmament through the colored glasses of national interest. Each was determined to maintain the force it considered necessary for its own security, and the composition of this force depended on the significance that each nation attached to sea power. For Britain, adequate sea power meant a fleet equal in combat strength to any in the world, plus sufficient cruisers to patrol and maintain the lines of communication linking the segments of her empire, each of which was not an appendage but an integral part of the whole. Australia's safety was as vital to Britain as was the safety of California to the United States. Under the conditions then prevailing, with no agreements even remotely binding the nations of the world to peaceful actions, no government in London would have dared to compromise the Admiralty's requirements for control of the sea.

Japan's concept of sea power envisioned a fleet capable of defeating whatever force might threaten her command of the western Pacific, and her admirals had established minimum needs to insure this supremacy. While slight concessions were possible in the interest of agreement, since the civil authorities still controlled the military, there were limits beyond which no politician would go. Aside from defense, national prestige was involved, and Japan's pride had been wounded by a ratio that was wryly termed the equivalent of "Rolls Royce, Rolls Royce, Ford."

American policy, while conscious of the Atlantic, was more specifically directed toward the Pacific, where possessions and interests were heavily concentrated. The great distances and the lack of adequate bases in that area led the General Board to insist on large cruisers with a maximum cruising radius. Eight-inch guns were required to offset the 6-inch batteries of other cruisers and the armament that could be mounted on merchant vessels. Fleet action, centering around the battleship and aircraft carrier supported by cruisers, destroyers, and submarines, was considered the final determinant in any contest of sea power, but the planners could ignore neither the realities of logistics nor the imperatives of commerce raiding and blockade. Then, too, America was dedicated to a navy "second to none." Parity, to her, meant at the very least equality in naval combat strength with Britain, whose bases and merchant marine made equality in total sea power a myth. American statesmen and admirals were one in their conviction that Great Britain's "special circumstances" did not entitle her to a single additional warship, or Japan's sensitivity justify a higher ratio.

Arnold Toynbee writes in a mildly satirical vein about the British and American delegates to the Geneva Conference, who believed they were being "practical" in discussing "concrete" issues like ship limitation without bothering about the "abstract" problems which the French wanted to consider, such as the question of security.[25] This is the heart of the matter, for the political issues that demanded solution made disarmament impossible. Armament is merely an instrument of foreign policy, and any attempt to regulate weapons independent of their reason for existing was doomed from the start.

Chapter III

Renewed Efforts for Naval Limitation, 1927-1929

The best President Coolidge could do on Armistice Day was
to call for more and bigger cruisers. Happily for international
peace, the law of presidential succession will spare the world
his friendly thoughts on the Fourth of July.
—Norfolk *Virginian-Pilot*, December, 1928.

I

The conference at Geneva was not without effect. Eventually, it was to
help pave the way for a subsequent meeting at London. More immediately,
however, it widened the gulf that separated the two schools of disarmament,
one advocating exclusive naval limitation and the other insisting that land,
sea, and air weapons be considered together. It also plunged Anglo-American
relations to the lowest depths since 1921, where they were to remain for the
next two years.

Britain's response to the failure consisted of a reiteration of her faith in
the practicability of disarmament and the cancellation of two of the three
cruisers scheduled to be laid down in 1927. The American response was a
peculiar contradiction of word and deed. In his message to Congress on
December 6, 1927, President Coolidge declared that "the failure to agree
should not cause us to build either more or less than we otherwise should."[1]
A few days later, Secretary of the Navy Wilbur presented Congress with a
building program that recommended the construction of thirty-three 10,000-
ton, 8-inch–gun cruisers. The Navy Bill finally passed by the House on
March 17, 1928, provided for fifteen cruisers and one aircraft carrier, but the
Senate postponed action until the following session of Congress. The administration was to need outside assistance and more favorable circumstances in order to achieve its naval program.

The Preparatory Commission at Geneva, probably stimulated by the
failure of the three-power parley, continued its efforts to reach agreement
on the method of disarmament to be followed. Great Britain advocated
limitation by ship category, and cited its successful use at Washington.
France countered with a proposal for limitation by total global tonnage,
whereby each nation was to be allotted a specific tonnage within which any
type of warship could be built. Only capital ships and aircraft carriers were
exempt, since they had been included in the Washington Treaty. The British
plan was supported by the United States and Japan, while Italy and several
smaller countries supported the French proposal. Opponents of global tonnage argued that a nation concentrating on one type of ship would provoke

competition, because, under certain circumstances, a balanced superior navy would be at a disadvantage. On the other hand, the lesser naval powers claimed that limitation by category would force them to build ships not suited to their needs and aggravate their inferior position.

In an effort to break the deadlock, separate negotiations were begun by representatives of France and Great Britain. This bilateral approach to disarmament was resented by the United States, and on at least one occasion Secretary of State Kellogg lodged a protest with the British ambassador.[2] Rumor of a pending agreement gained credence with the announcement that Britain had accepted the French contention that "trained reserves" should not be included in determining the size of armies in disarmament discussions. In exchange, France dropped her demand for global tonnage and the interdependence of armaments.[3] From these concessions there emerged the Anglo-French Naval Compromise of July 28, 1928, which stipulated that the forthcoming disarmament conference would consider restrictions on four classes of warships:

"1. Capital ships, i.e., vessels displacing more than 10,000 tons or mounting guns of more than 8-inch caliber.
"2. Aircraft carriers in excess of 10,000 tons.
"3. Surface vessels of or below 10,000 tons armed with guns of more than 6-inch and up to 8-inch caliber.
"4. Ocean-going submarines, i.e., over 600 tons."[4]

Noticeably absent from the agenda was the type of vessel best suited for the special needs of the two nations, namely, the British 6-inch–gun cruiser and the French coastal submarine.

Hoping for immediate acceptance, the British government submitted the plan to Washington, Tokyo, and Rome for approval. Kellogg sent the note to the Secretary of the Navy and asked him to prepare the "basis for an answer" which he could take up with the President.[5] Wilbur, in turn, referred the proposal to the General Board, which found it "unacceptable." Exempting 6-inch–gun cruisers and destroyers from control was comparable to the British position at Geneva, the Board observed, and constituted, in effect, no limitation. The unrestricted building of submarines displacing less than 600 tons was a potential threat to the safety of the United States, for vessels of this size could carry a torpedo having a destructive power equal to those carried by larger submarines.[6] Wilbur's reply to the Secretary of State consisted of a verbatim use of the Board report, and Kellogg's communiqué to the British and French governments used both its ideas and language in rejecting the proposal.[7] Japan did not reject the plan, but Italy's response was discouraging, since it reaffirmed her insistence on parity with France and a preference for the global-tonnage method.[8] This double rejection de-

21

stroyed the Compromise. The British Cabinet, aware that a new President would be taking office, that the Senate would be considering the Naval Construction Bill previously passed by the House, and that the speech of President Coolidge on Armistice Day offered no encouragement, decided to defer its disarmament offensive until after Hoover's inauguration and the general election in England.[9]

In his Armistice Day speech Coolidge referred to the Anglo-French understanding, and dryly observed, "It no doubt has some significance that foreign governments made agreements limiting that class of combat vessels in which we were superior but refused limitation in the class in which they were superior."[10] Tenaciously pursuing the subject, yet disclaiming any intent to compete with other countries, he urged passage of the Cruiser Bill in his annual message to Congress on December 4. With the Navy League playing a "major role" in changing public sentiment, the Senate passed the bill on February 5, 1929, and it became law with the President's signature a week later.[11]

The act provided for the construction of fifteen cruisers and one aircraft carrier, and specified that five cruisers be laid down during each of the fiscal years 1929, 1930, and 1931. The aircraft carrier was to be started by June 30, 1930. Included was a clause that authorized the President to suspend or cancel construction in the event of an international agreement in which the United States joined, to limit naval armament. Congress also placed itself on record as favoring a treaty "with all of the principal maritime nations regulating the conduct of belligerents and neutrals in war at sea, including the inviolability of private property thereon."[12] This declaration of principle concerning the "freedom of the seas" was apparently directed against Great Britain and her unrestricted and cavalier control of the sea during time of war.

The combination of a building authorization and an exhortation to disarm reveals the dilemma that plagued Congress. The legislators could not allow the Navy to deteriorate. They knew that overt inferiority in naval power weakened America's position in world affairs, they resented Britain's attitude at Geneva and her high-handed action in the Anglo-French Compromise, and they were prodded by the President and the Big-Navy Bloc. On the other hand, Congress was reluctant to sanction competition, it wanted economy, and it was sensitive to public opinion and the aggressive tactics of peace societies. Legislation that authorized building while it advocated disarmament offered a refuge from, if not a solution to, the dilemma.

The apparently contradictory position in which Congress found itself was in part due to the Kellogg-Briand Pact, which the Senate approved just before considering the cruiser bill. Condemning and renouncing war as an instrument of national policy except as a means of defense, the treaty pledged

22

the contracting parties to a peaceful solution of all matters of controversy. One newspaper whimsically inquired, "If, after just having signed a peace treaty with twenty-six nations, we need fifteen new cruisers, how many would we have needed if we hadn't just signed a peace treaty with twenty-six nations?"[13] This seemingly paradoxical action may have been an attempt to satisfy the conflicting sentiments displayed by pressure groups and public opinion, or it may have reflected the confusion that prevailed in the minds of Congressmen. Perhaps the answer was furnished by the American Legion in endorsing the principles of the pact, but, since it did not "guarantee" peace, the Legion believed that no reduction should be made in the military establishment.[14] More likely, the Senate saw no inconsistency in supporting peace by agreement while providing the means to maintain it by force. Large winnings seldom result from covering both sides of a bet, but the chances of losing are considerably reduced.

The election of Herbert Hoover in 1928 brought to office a President whose dedication to peace did not blind him to the need for weapons of defense. In his speech accepting the Republican nomination, Hoover combined an exhortation for good will in international relations with a warning of the need for adequate protection. "The experiences of the war," he observed, "afforded final proof that we cannot isolate ourselves from the world, that the safeguarding of peace cannot be attained by negative action," and he was determined to pursue a course that would lead America away from a policy that "was so isolationist that our proper responsibilities were neglected."[15] During the Senate debates on the cruiser bill, Hoover supported Coolidge in his contention that the ships were necessary.[16]

The President-elect never lost sight of his objective. While on a visit to South America aboard the U.S.S. *Utah* before his inauguration, Hoover expressed a willingness to conduct private conversations with the British Prime Minister, Stanley Baldwin, in an effort to end Anglo-American misunderstanding and promote disarmament, and he presumably authorized an American newspaper correspondent to make inquiries as to Baldwin's attitude toward such a meeting. In his inaugural address, Hoover appealed for military cuts based on the good will and avowed intentions of the nations that had signed the Kellogg-Briand Pact, and he emphatically instructed members of his administration that reduction of armaments, not limitation, was his goal.[17] The selection of Secretary of State Henry L. Stimson, who believed that the United States "could be weaned from the Harding-Coolidge policy of 'power without responsibility,'" and who was appalled at the ill feeling between Great Britain and America, provided Hoover with an experienced and enthusiastic lieutenant ostensibly devoted to the aims and ideals of his chief.[18] Signs pointed to a vigorous American effort to cooperate with other nations in preserving peace and promoting disarmament.

II

The League's Preparatory Commission, which had been in adjournment, was scheduled to open its sixth session on April 15, 1929, but the continental European nations were reluctant to continue efforts to formulate plans for a general disarmament conference until the naval powers had reached a solution to their problems.[19] The General Board recommended American participation in the sixth session, although it advised against any "informal" discussions dealing with a reduction in battleship size below the existing 35,000-ton, 16-inch–gun maximum. Also opposed was a naval holiday in capital-ship construction, on the grounds that it would be ruinous to an industry requiring highly skilled personnel, whose continued employment was essential. The Board adhered to its repeatedly expressed opinion that "the battleship is the ultimate measure of strength of the Navy and that anything that would tend to reduce the measure of strength would impair our national defense." To insure protection of the Navy's interests, Admiral Hilary P. Jones was again nominated for the position of senior naval representative.[20] The Board apparently sensed the likelihood of an imminent change in policy that would menace the Navy's position, for its correspondence reveals a vigilant effort to anticipate and prepare for any contingency. No doubt the admirals were suspicious of a new commander-in-chief who possessed a Quaker background and often spoke of peace and disarmament based on an unenforceable paper agreement, and who conceived of armaments in terms of defense rather than victory.

The instructions issued to the chairman of the American delegation to the Preparatory Commission, Hugh S. Gibson, ambassador to Belgium, were comprehensive but general. They reiterated the American contention that limitation by tonnage by categories was "the simplest, fairest and most practical method." Nevertheless, in order to facilitate agreement, the United States was willing to consider a method suggested by France at a meeting of the Commission in 1927, whereby total tonnage was combined with tonnage by categories, with provision for a change between categories through proportionate increase or decrease. America was firm in its belief that limitation, in order to be effective, must be applied to all types of combat vessels, and that the aim should be reduction in existing armaments, not merely control.[21] Hoover took advantage of Gibson's presence in Washington to join in drafting a speech which the latter was scheduled to deliver at Geneva. The President was anxious to "inject life" into the Commission's deliberations by offering a "bold and unexpected proposal," and Ambassador Gibson sailed for Europe carrying Hoover's answer to the impasse that had stalled five previous sessions of the Preparatory Commission.[22]

The Commission met at Geneva on April 15, 1929, where Gibson learned that the German delegate intended to propose that a special committee of the five principal naval powers be formed to consider naval disarmament. He was to contend that the naval problem was the main obstacle preventing the Commission from proceeding with methods of land and air reduction, and that naval reduction was of concern to the naval powers alone.[23] The British delegation, realizing that agreement with the United States was essential to further progress, was anxious to prevent any public discussions that might tear open old wounds.[24] On April 22, as the delegates settled down to resume their hitherto barren activities, the American chairman rose to address the assemblage.

America's defense, Gibson began, was primarily a naval problem, and the United States was willing to allow land disarmament to be handled by those nations most directly concerned. After reaffirming the contention that limitation by tonnage within categories was best, he conceded that the French proposal combining total tonnage and tonnage by categories would be acceptable as a basis of discussion. He then presented what came to be known as the "yardstick" formula.

My Government [he said] will be prepared to give consideration to a method of estimating equivalent naval values which take account of other factors than displacement tonnage alone. In order to arrive at a basis of comparison in the case of categories in which there are marked variations as to unit characteristics, it might be desirable in arriving at a formula for estimating equivalent tonnage to consider certain factors which produce these variations such as age, unit displacement, and caliber of guns. My Government has given careful consideration to various methods of comparison, and the American delegation will be in a position to discuss the subject whenever it comes before the commission.

Results, Gibson continued, were more important than method, which was secondary. The pact renouncing war as an instrument of national policy, he pointed out, should "advance the cause of disarmament by removing doubts and fear which in the past have constituted our principal obstacle." The United States was willing to agree to the most drastic limitation of armaments so long as all types of combat vessels were included, for a nation's naval strength was determined by that of other nations. "What is really wanted," Gibson concluded, "is a common-sense agreement, based on the idea that we are going to be friends and settle our problems by peaceful means," an agreement possible only through a "change of attitude toward the use of force in the settlement of international disputes."[25]

Hoover's desire to "inject life" into the discussions at Geneva was realized. Clarence K. Streit cabled that the address "changed the whole atmosphere here and breathed new life into the commission, which on Saturday seemed almost moribund."[26] The British, Japanese, French, Canadian, and Italian delegates made cordial replies, and Gibson reported that the reception of his speech was more favorable than he had hoped. In fact, he feared that it might give rise to "a degree of optimism that may be difficult to sustain."[27] The following day London formally endorsed both the spirit and the letter of Gibson's address, and expressed the belief that negotiations should proceed along the lines indicated.[28]

Press response in the United States was enthusiastic in its approval of the proposals, which the New York *World* considered an effort to "cut across" the "vicious circle" in which the discussion of naval limitation had become involved. The speech furnished evidence of American good will and desire to disarm, editorialized the New York *Herald-Tribune,* and the New York *Times* found "doubt and depression" giving way to hope for success at Geneva. The Brooklyn *Daily Eagle* thought that Gibson had "challenged" the other naval powers to "stop quibbling and go forward" with reduction, and to the Washington *Star* the speech signified that "statesmanship as opposed to seamanship must be the controlling factor." Widespread and generally favourable publicity was accorded the address throughout the United States, although criticism was expressed by Representative Fred A. Britten, chairman of the House Naval Affairs Committee, who called the speech a "complete surrender" and "another naval victory for British diplomacy."[29]

The British press abandoned its traditional calm in welcoming the proposals. The United States, exclaimed the London *Times,* had "taken the initiative that belongs to it," and the *Daily Telegraph* termed the speech "frank" and "radical." To the *Daily Express* it was "the most important thing that has happened in connection with disarmament since Mr. Hughes . . . rose to address the Washington Conference," and the *Daily News* hailed it as a "magnificent peace opportunity which British statesmanship cannot possibly ignore." The speech had come as a "great surprise" to the British, who welcomed it as a friendly gesture by Hoover. Perhaps the substance of Britain's response was summed up by the *Review of Reviews,* which claimed that Gibson's address "amounted to an—albeit conditional—American declaration of peace to Great Britain."[30]

French reaction was in a similar vein. The independent, semi-official *Le Temps,* of Paris, felt that Gibson's effort had "completely modified the dangerous atmosphere prevailing at Geneva," while the conservative *Figaro* found it "cause for optimism." The Republican *Journal des Débats* said that the initiative, which could come only from the United States, had been taken by Hoover, and the socialist *Populaire* approved the speech, but attributed it to the pressure of public opinion. Only the communist *Humanité* cynically observed that it was a clever speech aimed at upsetting the "Franco-British naval arrangement which is so odious to the White House."[31] On the whole, this represented a surprising degree of unanimity from a press noted for its extreme partisanship.

Newspapers in Italy expressed a difference of opinion that may not have reflected the public reaction. The *Osservatore Romano,* published by the Vatican, considered Gibson's proposals a "step in [the] advancement of peace." The Fascist *L'Impero* caustically observed that America's willingness to make concessions on land armaments was comparable to Switzerland making concessions on naval armament, and no more commendable. Gibson's contention that no other nation should have a navy larger than that of the United States was an "insincere doctrine."[32] Since all newspapers published in Italy were organs of the government, except for the *Osservatore Romano,* a greater divergence of press response was unlikely.

Japanese editorial comment was unrestrained in expressing approval. The *Jiji Shimpo* hailed the American attitude "with joy; for it means a chance for a compromise," and the *Kokumin Shimbun* felt that the Gibson offer removed "the first obstacle to discussion at a main conference." The Osaka *Mainichi Shimbun* thought the speech showed "how earnest the American Government is for the actualization of disarmament," and the *Hochi Shimbun* found that "the moral courage and straightforward statesmanship of Mr. Hoover evoke our heart-felt admiration."[33] The statesmen of Japan could look forward to newspaper support in their quest for the reduction of armaments.

III

Undoubtedly, most of the enthusiasm was evoked by Gibson's suggestion of a formula that would assess the equivalent value of ships in terms of combat effectiveness instead of relying exclusively on tonnage and gun dimension. Even the proponents of integrated disarmament, after six unproductive sessions of the Preparatory Commission, were reluctantly admitting that the dispute over methods of naval limitation was delaying the activities of the Commission, and that it was a dispute which only the naval powers could resolve. It could be further reduced to a conflict between the British desire for 6-inch–gun cruisers in sufficient quantity to satisfy her "special circumstances," and the American demand for 8-inch guns and mathematical equality in ships with Britain. The formula offered hope for a solution of the cruiser problem and a new approach to the question of parity. Obviously, the next move would have to be made by the two major naval powers, and the Commission adjourned on May 6, 1929, apparently reconciled to awaiting the outcome of future Anglo-American conversations.[34]

The formula that Hoover and Gibson suggested at Geneva was soon universally referred to as the "yardstick," a name that caught the imagination of statesman and public alike. It became the magic word that would bring an end to naval competition, make general disarmament possible, and dispel the atmosphere of mistrust between nations that remained in spite of the Pact of Paris. The response indicated a belief that the yardstick actually existed, and that it had been worked out by the President and his aides with the mathematical exactitude expected of a highly successful engineer. Unfortunately, such was not the case. Hoover and Stimson seem to have been even more astounded than Gibson by the reception accorded an idea designed to stimulate activity at Geneva. Confronted by a request from the British ambassador nearly two weeks later for clarification of the proposal, Stimson could only lamely explain that it was a "suggestion, which was not in any way completed," intended "merely to provide for the elaboration of a formula" that would permit a comparison of the "strategic usefulness" of different types of naval vessels. He offset his vagueness by stressing that the "fundamental proposition" that was "absolutely necessary" to agreement between Britain and the United States remained the issue of naval parity.[35]

The failure of the administration to consult the Navy General Board prior to offering the proposal at Geneva indicates that it had not been explored too carefully. A formula capable of equating the fighting strength of men-of-war would of necessity be highly technical in nature, and involve a careful consideration of the qualities constituting combat effectiveness. It would demand an expert knowledge of ship construction, gunnery, operational efficiency, naval tactics, and grand strategy. The Navy General Board, by training and experience, was qualified to devise such a formula. Hoover, subsequently, may have regretted that the Board's views were not obtained before he sent Gibson to Geneva.

The idea of a formula that would consider factors other than the simple statistics of guns and tonnage did not originate with the President. Secretary of State Charles Evans Hughes, who headed the American delegation to the Washington Conference of 1921-1922, presented the problem and employed the term that later was to catch the popular imagination. "One of the difficulties by which I am confronted," he wrote to the Secretary of the Navy, "is that of determining what I can perhaps best describe as a 'yard stick' by which to measure existing armaments and which can also be applied as a standard of measurement in any general plan of reduction. If you have reached any conclusions on this particular point, I would be most grateful to have your views."[36] In response to this request the Navy's elder statesmen, calling on the experience of their predecessors, replied: "The General Board can not define a 'naval unit' in such a way as to make it an accurate measure of strength of the navies of the world. It is not practicable to commute the combatant value of one class of ships into combatant value of another class for purposes of comparative measurement, even in the case of our own navy."[37] Hughes later acknowledged that the Board supplied the formula which, "slightly modified," was the basis for agreement on limitation at the Washington Conference, namely, the use of capital ships as a measure of strength.[38] Such a simple standard was a far cry from the "yard stick" that Hughes wanted, but it did provide a basis for comparison.

The Board's reluctance to commit itself to paper equations based on selected statistical data cannot be attributed solely to the traditional intractability of the alleged military mind, although the admirals probably resented this civilian effort to penetrate the screen that enveloped their technical and specialized domain. More important, the Board, conscious of its responsibilities and steeped in the vagaries of naval history, refused to bind itself to an abstract computation that ignored the realities of national defense and the unpredictability of maritime warfare. Conflict over this issue was to put an additional strain on the relations between the civilian and naval branches of the government.

An early public mention of a yardstick had been made by Allen W. Dulles, who served with the American delegation to the Geneva Conference in 1927. Writing in *Foreign Affairs,* Dulles asked that combat strength rather than tonnage alone be considered in determining parity, and he cited the French proposal to the Preparatory Commission in 1927, which had recommended that the age of naval vessels be made a factor in arriving at an evaluation of naval power. Such a formula, he claimed, would make it possible for the United States and Britain to have the type of cruisers each wanted and arrive at an agreement.[39] The publication of this article coincided with a speech by the British foreign secretary, Sir Austen Chamberlain, in which he urged that an "equation" be worked out by which the conflicting aims of the two nations could be reconciled.[40] The extent to which Hoover was influenced by these suggestions is not known, but it is clear that while the idea of a formula did not originate with the President, he was responsible for its official proposal in a form that offered the possibility of its acceptance, and at a most propitious time in the deliberations of the Preparatory Commission.

Prior to the meeting at Geneva, Britain and the United States had agreed that talks on naval questions through diplomatic channels were prerequisite to the success of any conference.[41] Then, on May 3, the British government proposed "a private and confidential exchange of views" on naval disarmament between the two countries. They were confident that a settlement could be reached based on the Gibson overtures and their impression "of the mind and purpose of the President." Such conversations, the note continued, could establish a "broad line of agreement" that would offer hope of a settlement with other naval powers, but they should be postponed until after the forthcoming general election in England.[42] Preparations for the talks were not neglected, however, for Stimson and Sir Esme Howard, the British ambassador, agreed that negotiations should be conducted by civilian statesmen rather than naval experts, because the latter would approach the problem on the basis of war between the countries, whereas the civilian "might be able and willing to take chances which the professional service man could not take."[43] The United States, which accepted the British suggestion despite Hoover's suspicion that they were "trying to drag us into something,"[44] was to be represented by General Charles G. Dawes, the new ambassador to Great Britain, who was scheduled to arrive in London after the general election. It was also decided to present the American plan first in order to place Britain in the more difficult position of having to prove the United States wrong.[45]

Lunching at the White House with Hoover and Dawes on the eve of the General's departure for London, Secretary Stimson presented agenda approved by the President:

(1) The President and I will try to produce such a yardstick which we favor from our naval advisers;
(2) We will then try to persuade the heads of the governments of Great Britain and Japan to do the same independently with their naval advisers. Each Government will then produce a yardstick from the efforts of their civilian representatives, using the Navy only as advisers;
(3) Civilian representatives of the Governments will then compare the three yardsticks and attempt to get an agreement upon a common one, the naval experts of all parties acting only as advisers in this attempt at agreement.[46]

The time had arrived for calling in the admirals, but due caution was to be exercised to prevent their intrusion into matters of policy. The margin of error, the civilian statesmen believed, had been reduced.

The luncheon must have concluded in a happy vein. Britain and America were already in agreement on so many fundamentals that it seemed as though only details needed filling in. The mutual desire for bilateral negotiation, the moral force of the Kellogg-Briand Pact, the prospects of a formula to reconcile the cruiser dispute, the relegation of naval officers to a subordinate position, and the atmosphere of good will and high intention that prevailed, all tended to dispel doubts and encourage confidence. The results of the general election in England, which placed a Labour government in power, offered even greater hope of success, for the new Prime Minister, Ramsay MacDonald, had long been the foremost spokesman of a party that stood for peace and the reduction of armament. The President and his Secretary of State probably contemplated the future of Anglo-American relations and the prospects for naval limitation with considerable optimism.

Chapter IV

Anglo-American Conversations

I said all the time, sir, that the yardstick was a certain
amount of camouflage.   —Admiral Hilary P. Jones, 1930.

I

The American emissary, General Dawes, carried the rank of ambassador,
the prestige of a former Vice-President, and the title of an army officer. He
was to conduct the conversations with the new Prime Minister, who, as one
writer has suggested, "had all that respect for the American democracy
which was often to be found in radicals bred in the nineteenth century."[1]
The Foreign Secretary, Arthur Henderson, had been appointed over the objections of MacDonald, who was determined to maintain personal control of
relations with the United States.[2] The Labour government was bent on re-
storing the amicable atmosphere that existed between the two nations before
the breakdown at Geneva in 1927 and the abortive compromise with France.[3]
Good intentions prevailed on both sides, in sufficient quantity to pave the
most arduous road to disarmament.

General Dawes arrived in London amid the plaudits of the British press,
which claimed the story "no longer a secret" that he brought with him the
formula that would make possible the reduction of naval armaments.[4] The
story remained a secret only to the General, who was to find the matter a
continual source of embarrassment. Conversations began almost immediately,
with the first meeting, a two-hour session, held on June 16. In an effort to
strip the talks of topics that would interfere with the central problem of
naval limitation, the two statesmen decided that questions such as freedom
of the seas and the rights of belligerents during wartime would not be considered. Each party claimed credit for suggesting and winning this point.[5]
The Prime Minister read and approved the speech which Dawes was to deliver to the Society of Pilgrims of Great Britain, and expressed his belief that
the Admiralty would be more "co-operative" than they had been in the past.
Impressed by this auspicious beginning, MacDonald then broached the subject of a visit to the United States, and asked Dawes for his opinion as to its
advisability. The General's reply was discouraging, for, he said, the usual
suspicion of the Senate regarding "Executive initiative in foreign affairs"
would lead that body to make the visit an occasion for "discussions of a most
demagogical and demoralizing character," which would adversely affect the
ratification of any subsequent treaty. At the conclusion of these remarks,
MacDonald wistfully observed, "It is my hope that I may sometime take a

31

trip to America, but it is decided now that it will not be until after the ratification of the disarmament agreement."[6]

Each of the participants had reason to be pleased with the results of the first meeting. It had proceeded smoothly, in a friendly and straightforward manner, with frankness on both sides. Although the Prime Minister was obviously disappointed at the cool reception accorded his remark about visiting America, nothing was said to disturb his expectation of success in solving the problems that separated the two nations.

In retrospect, it appears that the elimination from the agenda of the questions of freedom of the seas and the rights of belligerents during war was more gratifying to the Prime Minister than it was to Dawes. Experience during World War I had convinced Britain that survival depended on her ability to control the seas, and that any restriction on her actions toward neutral or enemy shipping was a direct threat to her security and safety. America's attitude, most recently reiterated in the Naval Construction Act of 1929, posed a greater danger than disarmament. That this issue would not be a part of the negotiations must have been a source of great satisfaction and relief to MacDonald and his government.

The idea of the Prime Minister's visit to the United States did not originate with MacDonald. The President's journalist emissary, Edward Price Bell, had mentioned such a trip to Stanley Baldwin before the general election. Baldwin understood this to be a legitimate, although unofficial, invitation, and he fully intended to accept it in the event his party was returned to power. When MacDonald took office, Bell, being *persona non grata,* had Constantine Brown communicate the offer to MacDonald through a mutual friend. The new Prime Minister was delighted with the suggestion and fully expected Dawes to bring a formal invitation, which London newspapers reported would be accepted.[7] MacDonald's chagrin at his rebuff by the General was soon to be exceeded only by the latter's discomfiture over the matter.

II

While Winston Churchill thundered against granting the United States "numerical" parity in naval strength, the new ambassador put the finishing touches on the speech he was to deliver at the banquet of the Society of Pilgrims of Great Britain.[8] It had been gone over with great care by Hoover and Stimson before Dawes left Washington, and was to embody their collective sentiments on the subject of naval disarmament. On the night of June 18, the General rose to announce the policy that was to govern his activities during the negotiations. Beginning with a plea for world efforts toward peace in the spirit of the Kellogg-Briand Pact, with naval reduction as the first step, he deplored the huge appropriations for ship construction, and announced his theme as "what method of procedure had best be adopted to translate a policy of naval reduction into a fixed agreement between the nations."

The problem of disarmament, the ambassador maintained, must be approached from the viewpoint of "human nature" rather than "human reasoning." The former was the province of statesmen, the latter of "experts," whose opinion, "by the law of human nature," is "not as safe in a programme which [they] . . . [formulate] as a practical interpretation of those principles applied to a partial destruction of his own navy." In order to resolve this conflict of interest, "each Government might separately obtain from their respective naval experts their definition of the yardstick and then the invitable compromise between these differing definitions, which will be expressed in the final fixation of the technical yardstick, should be made by a committee of statesmen of the nations." The conference at Geneva in 1927 failed, warned the General, because there was a "mixed commission of statesmen and naval technicians," a "method adjusted to human reasoning, but not to human nature." In conclusion, Dawes reiterated the principle of equality in naval strength between the United States and Great Britain, and appealed to the English-speaking peoples to lead the way to world peace.[9]

British press reaction to the speech was restrained, for it was considered something of an "anti-climax" after the much-heralded promise of tangible results.[10] French newspapers gave "a rather grudging approval" to the proposals, although they regarded them as of little "practical importance."[11] The Italian press was critical, and the *Messagero* claimed that the Anglo-American conversations were "merely a manifestation of the preponderance of two imperialisms," between whom war was inevitable.[12] According to the General, most of the American papers welcomed the principles stated in the speech, as did the Japanese government.[13] In Washington, Dawes provoked a more impassioned reaction. The Navy Department was "thrown into a panic" by the news that diplomats, not admirals, were to conduct the negotiations, and Senator Frederick Hale, chairman of the Senate Naval Affairs Committee, telephoned the head of the Navy League's Executive Committee to urge that immediate efforts be made to offset the effects of the speech. The League shared Hale's alarm, but felt that no immediate steps could be taken to modify the announced policy or the enthusiastic reaction of the public.[14]

As discussions with MacDonald continued, the President and his advisers attempted to devise the yardstick that Dawes was supposed to have brought with him to London. The General Board was first asked for its comments and recommendations on the Gibson proposals more than a month after they had been advanced.[15] The Board's reply was discouraging. The admirals considered it highly improbable that an accurate computation of the combat value of a naval vessel could be made, or that agreement could be reached on the weight to be assigned to the factors involved. If such a formula was absolutely necessary, the Board recommended that it should include only age and displacement of ships, because the introduction of other factors would make for complexity and disagreement on evaluation.[16]

Hoover apparently was not satisfied with this response, for he asked that Rear Admiral Hilary P. Jones, who had participated in numerous disarmament negotiations, furnish him with a "purely confidential and personal note" on an equivalent British cruiser strength based on American existing and authorized cruisers, keeping in mind "a possible conflict of the two fleets."[17] Admiral Jones submitted a lengthy, detailed study of America's naval defense requirements that emphasized the critical lack of modern cruisers and the advantage that Britain enjoyed by virtue of her numerous overseas bases and her vast merchant marine. He argued that the United States could achieve parity in sea power only by possessing a preponderance of combat vessels.[18]

Evidently this information offered no satisfactory solution, for a few weeks later Stimson suggested a yardstick that assigned a percentage evaluation to large ships as compared to smaller vessels. One ton of a cruiser of less than 5,000 tons would be rated as the equivalent of nine-tenths of a ton of a cruiser that displaced from 5,000 to 10,000 tons, and a ton of a destroyer would be equal to nine-tenths of a ton of a small cruiser.[19] The General Board response, which was incorporated in its entirety in Secretary Adams' reply to Stimson, rejected the plan and recommended against any solution based on the assumptions contained in Stimson's letter. Destroyers could not be compared with cruisers in combat value, the Board contended, for their tasks and functions were entirely different. Furthermore, it was not desirable to divide cruisers into two categories, because the United States would then be required to build ships unsuited to its needs. Any computation of equivalent combat strength was impossible, for it would be based on arbitrary evaluations of factors that could not take into account the actual conditions that might arise during conflict.[20]

This negative attitude displayed by the Navy Department must have annoyed and disturbed the President and his Secretary of State, for they had looked to their naval experts for the technical data that would enable the statesmen to fashion a formula. The unwillingness of the professionals to provide constructive criticism threw the problem back into the hands of the civilians, where it served as a reminder of the divergent viewpoints prevailing in Washington.

In London, too, there was a notable lack of progress, although the experienced Gibson had been ordered in to assist Dawes in the negotiations. To complicate matters further, the French and Japanese governments, fearing a bilateral treaty, expressed concern over the rumored visit of Britain's

Prime Minister to the United States. The British Cabinet was at odds over the effect that disarmament would have on unemployment, and MacDonald was subjected to heavy criticism on this question in the House of Commons.[21] With negotiations at a standstill, Stimson appealed to Dawes and Gibson for ways of furthering the work that had begun so auspiciously.[22] The two envoys suggested a meeting of "non-technical Governmental representatives," to be called by Great Britain or Japan, in order to exchange views and arrive at some agreement on fundamentals that would lay the foundation for a final conference. MacDonald immediately approved the suggestion and indicated his intention to call a meeting of "non-technical" representatives of the five naval powers. In the event the parley should fail because of obstacles imposed by France and Italy, the three remaining nations would meet in an effort to reach an understanding.[23] With the British government under the impression that the President and his advisers were evolving a formula that would change the problem "from one of tonnage to one of points,"[24] and with negotiations in London halted, it appeared that further delay was not only useless but harmful, for the favorable atmosphere created at Geneva was likely to dissipate in a cloud of interminable conversations.

The optimism reflected in the dispatches to Washington was not shared by the cautious and experienced Gibson, who revealed his misgivings after returning to Brussels. He had been "a good deal taken aback," he wrote, by MacDonald's assertion that while the British ship-building program of 1929 might be halted, the 1928 program could not be stopped, owing to the outstanding contracts and the adverse effect that cancellation would have on employment. Such a stand, in Gibson's opinion, would offer no prospect for reduction in armaments but merely provide for limitation based on the existing British navy and the additional ships scheduled for construction. In that event, a yardstick would only be useful for determining what America should build in order to attain parity with Britain.[25]

Further reservations were expressed by Hoover and Stimson, who were disturbed by the speed with which events in London were moving toward a conference. Adequate preparations for such a step were lacking, a situation that would give rise to public criticism, and the naval experts were not ready. The United States had no objections to a preliminary meeting confined to a consideration of methods, but it desired confirmation of the American assumption that Great Britain had agreed to accept parity between the two nations.[26]

The Prime Minister readily approved the American position and disclaimed any intention of wanting to proceed immediately to a final conference. He indicated complete agreement on the question of parity, thereby formally acknowledging Britain's acquiescence to the American claim to equality in naval strength.[27] This voluntary surrender of control of the sea was fundamental to a successful outcome of the negotiations, though the genial sacrifice of Britain's traditional maritime supremacy without firing a shot doubtless sent a tremor throughout the Empire. At the Washington Conference of 1921-22, parity had been conceded in battleships and aircraft carriers, but its denial in cruisers at Geneva in 1927 had made agreement impossible. MacDonald's acceptance of this principle was probably the most important concession made by any statesman during the negotiations that preceded the London Naval Conference of 1930.

III

Striking in the white heat of compromise, and professing a distaste for delay, the unpredictable Prime Minister urged that the two nations announce that the Kellogg-Briand Pact was "a vital and controlling fact in their negotiations," that an accord had been reached on parity, which would be measured by a yardstick being formulated, and that a date and the wording of invitations be decided.[28] The President and his Secretary of State were appalled at this recurrent haste and insisted on thorough and deliberate preparations that would cover all possible contingencies. While expressing agreement with the Prime Minister in substance, and encouraged by the accord on parity, they offered some specific suggestions of their own pertaining to the scope of a formal conference: (1) the agreement should cover all classes of combat vessels; (2) the categories should consist of capital ships, aircraft carriers, cruisers, destroyers, and submarines; (3) the "right of limited transfer between these categories" should be permitted in accordance with an agreed yardstick; (4) capital ships and aircraft carriers, already limited by the Washington Treaty of 1922, should be considered only as to the deferment of replacements; and (5) "In measuring relative combatant strength we should consider the elements of such yardstick to be (a) displacement; (b) guns; (c) age. Our general view is that protection, speed, habitability, etc., are entirely relative to the other factors and do not require special consideration."[29] The transfer of tonnage between categories would permit each nation to build the type of ship it preferred, using tonnage allotted in another category. A yardstick that ignored such characteristics as speed and armor might have been designed to facilitate its acceptance, but it disregarded two factors that could be decisive in determining the effectiveness of a warship in time of battle.

These decisions apparently had been made without consulting the Navy Department, whose views were contained in the letter from Adams to Stimson dated July 15, which strongly advised against such proposals.[30] In Washington the initiative had been taken by the civilian statesmen, who were probably impatient with, and somewhat nettled by, the dilatoriness and intractability of the naval experts. But the proposal gave the Prime Minister a clearer view of America's intentions, and a framework within which he and his advisers could formulate the British program.

While Dawes pressed for a decision on the Prime Minister's visit to the United States, MacDonald stated his intention of delaying preparations for laying the keels of two of the cruisers that were part of the 1928-1929 building program, and asked that the United States take a similar step. Hoover co-operated to the extent of a commitment to slow down preparations for commencing the construction of two cruisers. On July 24, by prearrangement, MacDonald and Hoover publicly announced their respective concessions to disarmament, and the Prime Minister proclaimed agreement on parity. Senator Claude A. Swanson, senior Democratic member of the Senate Committee on Naval Affairs, denounced the President's action, declaring it "contrary to law" and a violation of the mandate of Congress.[31] The act of 1929, under which the cruisers were being built, authorized the President to suspend construction "in the event of an international agreement . . . for the further limitation of naval armament, to which the United States is signatory." The understanding with MacDonald clearly did not meet these specifications, but Hoover doubtless believed that his action was consistent with the spirit if not the letter of the law.[32]

A few days later MacDonald summarized the situation by declaring the two nations in agreement on all issues except the yardstick, and he urged that it be hurried. He intended to advocate the abolition of the submarine, although he admitted that his position was weak because it was the naval weapon that could do Britain the most harm. His motive, he protested, was not the nation's welfare but the desire to remove this most "brutal" and "ruthless" instrument of war.[33] Stimson also professed the hope that submarines could be abolished, although he questioned that other nations would permit it. But, he warned, the elimination of submarines and the scrapping of American destroyers in order to attain parity with Britain were "predicated on drastic action with regard to cruisers by the British." There was to be no unilateral destruction of ships, and it was imperative that agreement be reached as to where cruiser strength should be "checked" prior to any conference. The determination of a yardstick to measure the relative value of ships, Stimson added, was best left to the conference.[34]

The Prime Minister was disappointed at the failure to get a yardstick, and he feared that the question of tonnage was being raised "in its old absolute form." He had hoped that they could "examine the present condition, [work] out parity within it, total the results and see what happens." MacDonald summarized the two cruiser fleets, built and building, as follows:

Eight-inch–gun cruisers: Great Britain, 15 ships, 146,800 tons; 3 projected,

30,000 tons; total, 176,800 tons. United States, 13 building, 130,000 tons; 10 projected, 100,000 tons; total, 230,000 tons.

7.5-inch–gun cruisers: Great Britain, *Hawkins* class, 4 ships, 29,400 tons. United States, none.

Six-inch–gun cruisers: Great Britain, 40 ships, 179,270 tons. United States, 10 ships, 70,500 tons.

He claimed that the 7.5-inch-gun cruisers, built in 1916, were comparable in effectiveness to 6-inch–gun cruisers, and that certain of Britain's 6-inch–gun cruisers were inferior in both armament and tonnage to the more recent American ships in that class.[35]

The introduction of figures into the negotiations was to make the Prime Minister more dependent on the Admiralty and less able to rely on his own judgment, which tended toward uncluttered generalities. His First Lord of the Admiralty, Albert V. Alexander, was a political appointee, and while loyal to his party leader, was not versed in the technicalities that surrounded naval problems. MacDonald had intended to employ the professionals solely for the purpose of arriving at a formula that would enable the civilian statesmen to dispense with their services. The American desire to exchange figures and reach an understanding on totals prior to the acceptance of a yardstick was to drive him into the arms of his experts. This eventuality he had neither foreseen nor prepared for.

IV

The rumored trip to America had not been forgotten by the Prime Minister, who had been discouraged but not disheartened by the cool reception accorded the suggestion by Dawes at their first meeting. The General was being pressed to obtain Washington's consent, and MacDonald was suffering embarrassment from queries in the newspapers and on the floor of the House of Commons.[36] Finally, on July 24, he announced publicly that such a visit was "the subject of conversation," but the following day Hoover informed the British ambassador that the presence of the Prime Minister in Washington would be worth while only in the event an agreement had been reached on general principles of naval disarmament.[37] Whether deliberate or not, the decision to make the trip dependent on a settlement was probably responsible for a shortening of the negotiations.

While the national commander of the American Legion protested any action by the President that would prevent America from "regaining" the "lost naval parity with Great Britain,"[38] Stimson summarized the position of the United States for the guidance of Dawes and Gibson in a forthcoming talk with MacDonald. Supplementing previous proposals, he recommended that the replacement of capital ships be postponed until after 1936; that the 8-inch–gun, 10,000-ton cruiser represent the "standard" in arriving at a yardstick; and that "scrappable ages" of twenty years for cruisers, sixteen years for destroyers, and thirteen years for submarines be adopted. The aim was to reach an understanding that would permit a reduction in the authorized cruiser program, and to arrive at a "theoretical tonnage" in 1936 of 200 to 250 thousand tons in the cruiser category.[39] At the ensuing meeting, agreement was reached, with minor modifications, except for the cruiser tonnage, eliminated at the instigation of the Prime Minister. MacDonald then revealed his government's concept of parity in cruisers. The United States was to be allotted eighteen 8-inch–gun and twenty 6-inch–gun cruisers to Britain's fifteen 8-inch and forty-five 6-inch, with the 7.5-inch *Hawkins* ships included in the latter group until replaced by ships mounting the smaller caliber guns.[40]

This information was received with dismay in Washington, for it envisaged a disparity of twenty-two cruisers totaling approximately 80,000 tons, a gap of impossible "yardstickability."[41] Providing for an increase rather than a decrease in naval armament, the plan added 225,000 tons of combat vessels to the existing fleets and denied the principle of parity and equality between the two navies. The proposals were reminiscent of those made at Geneva in 1927, and, to the astounded Washington authorities, they did not "offer any hope of agreement."[42] Because Dawes had been in the habit of allowing MacDonald to read most of the American despatches, Stimson expressed his and the President's "disappointment" in a supplementary telegram intended only for the General. Pessimistic in tone, the message added that "no agreement" would be preferable to one based on these extreme terms, obviously prepared by the Admiralty, which evidently had "won over" the Prime Minister to its point of view. The sixty cruisers desired by Britain contrasted with the fifty-two then in service, and if this amount was necessary a preponderance of 8-inch–gun vessels should be granted to the United States. Could it be, queried Stimson, that MacDonald had presented these figures "in order to try us out"?[43]

Emphatically not, retorted the ambassador. The Prime Minister, anxious to effect reduction, was "ground between the millstones of his own Admiralty propositions and the American proposals," and the naval experts were supported by the opposition in Commons.[44] The London *Daily Telegraph* headlined "BRITAIN'S GREAT SACRIFICE" in slowing naval construction, and told movingly of broken contracts and distressing unemployment. The Conservative leader, Stanley Baldwin, denounced the government for trying to do things too quickly, as no agreement had been reached to justify a halt in building.[45]

In America, the President found little support for compromise. His own party member, Senator William E. Borah, clamored that reduction of Britain's cruiser strength was essential to naval agreement, and asked that she follow the example of the United States at the Washington Conference and scrap some of her ships in order to achieve parity, save money, and promote peace.[46] The situation was doubly difficult, for a solution that offered any promise of acceptance involved building by Hoover and destruction by MacDonald. Strong domestic forces in both nations opposed a settlement which rejected disarmament on the one hand and security on the other. From this point it became a question of how far each leader would go in compromising his own conception of the realities of national defense and political survival, a compromise that weighed the interests of a nation against the interests of the world.

The Prime Minister was "very disappointed" that his proposals of July 29 were not acceptable to the President. Writing at some length to Dawes, he confessed to being confronted by "two predominant facts": the existence of three naval powers that could harm the Empire; and the dominions, with their special demands. If he did not observe these facts he would be driven from office. MacDonald acknowledged the difficulty of achieving both parity and American reduction, but he pleaded for continued efforts to reach agreement.[47] Hoover and Stimson were not impressed, for they thought that the Prime Minister was exaggerating both his own situation and the needs of the Empire in his effort to maintain an untenable position.[48] Stung by this charge, Gibson protested against the tenor of Stimson's despatches. Claiming that the atmosphere of the talks was excellent, he insisted that MacDonald was sincere and in no way the tool of the Admiralty, and he advocated "direct discussion" between the two leaders as the best means of solving the dilemma.[49] Washington vetoed the visit to America pending an agreement, but countered with a concrete proposal. If cruiser parity were set at 250,000 tons, to be attained by 1936, the United States would consent to a proviso that if changing world conditions should warrant, each nation could request an additional 60,000 tons.[50]

The firm attitude adopted by Washington apparently had a beneficial effect, for the Prime Minister became more conciliatory and less categorical in his demands.[51] He agreed to allow the United States a "material preponderance" of 8-inch–gun cruisers in order to make parity possible, and indicated a readiness to permit the construction of as many of these ships as America wanted so long as it did not upset the balance between Britain and other countries, notably Japan.[52] Outlining the current cruiser dispositions, he explained that the ships were operating in a "police category" rather than a "fighting category." Britain planned to scrap one cruiser each year and inaugurate a building program designed to maintain a strength of fifty cruisers, ten less than the previously established minimum. Not all was concession, however, for he reiterated the necessity for a yardstick. His information revealed that the heavily armed cruisers were "worth in a fight almost an infinity of smaller craft and guns," and Britain's geographical position posed obligations greater than those faced by the President.[53]

Stimson thought that this marked "great progress toward agreement," but he questioned MacDonald's contention as to the relative value of the 8-inch–gun, 10,000-ton cruisers. It appeared that the naval experts in the Admiralty were giving the Prime Minister information different from that given the President by the experts in the Navy Department. Under these circumstances, a yardstick, even if agreed to, might be more of a hindrance than a help in bridging the gap that separated the demands of the two nations.[54] Hoover and Stimson now realized that it was impossible to obtain an agreement permitting a reduction in American naval strength. But they believed that a settlement based on parity of fleets would remove ill feeling and suspicion between the United States and Great Britain, and create an atmosphere of good will that might promote a desire for reduction at a later date.[55]

The Prime Minister and the American ambassador resumed their conversations at Lossiemouth, Scotland, where MacDonald was observed smoking the under-slung pipe given him by the General. This was regarded as "a good augury for peace and a bad one for navies,"[56] and Dawes expected MacDonald's ten-ship reduction to evoke a similar concession from Washington.[57] Yet the State Department telegram of August 15, while conciliatory, constituted no retreat from the previous American position. The Prime Minister was disappointed at the statement concerning the inadequacies of the yardstick, but his figures, he emphasized, "go right to the bone and must be taken as the minimum to which the government at present can commit itself."[58] The finality of this assertion, while qualified as to time, indicated that further concession would either come from the United States or await a top-level conference.

Opportunely, the authorities in Washington were now fortified by information received from the General Board, which had prepared an elaborate report on the proposals advanced in MacDonald's letter of August 8. It found these proposals "somewhat vague and incomplete," detrimental to the United States, and weighted heavily in favor of Great Britain.[59] Using this material, Stimson defended his previous criticism as not being "unfair," and he objected to MacDonald's placing the four 7.5-inch–gun cruisers in the same category as 6-inch, for they were much closer to 8-inch. To create a "preponderance" of the large-gun cruisers, as suggested by the Prime Minister, would require twenty-three such craft against fifteen for Britain. Then, concluding on a hopeful note, he requested the tonnage of the proposed fifty British cruisers as of December 31, 1936, and said that if the total were 330,000 tons "we could go into a conference."[60] Whether the impatient Prime

Minister could resist this tempting bait was conjectural, but it was directed at an obvious weak spot in his armor.

In a separate telegram, the Secretary of State wired Dawes that it would be "unwise" for the two nations to attempt to reach agreement on a yardstick at that time. Such technical discussion would become prolonged, other countries would become involved, and the public would learn of the issue. The resultant controversy would be harmful to the projected conference.[61] Dawes reluctantly agreed, and voiced the fear that agreement on the formula might lead to a "yardstick drawn up to fit the settlement . . . instead of the settlement fitted to the yardstick."[62]

The much heralded yardstick had been reduced to the dimension of a footrule, a far cry from the part it was expected to play in reconciling the different cruiser needs of the two nations. The issue was not dead, for Stimson continued to refer to the formula in computing the relative tonnage of the two fleets, and its discussion was to continue into the subsequent conference.[63] The failure to communicate the formula to MacDonald was a blow to him and to the sympathetic General, both of whom had considered it indispensable to the success of the negotiations. It was an affront to the British government, and its continued use by the United States, while keeping it a secret from Britain, was scarcely consistent with the assertions of frankness and good will that emanated from Washington.

The British reply to Stimson's proposals of August 28 objected to the demand for twenty-three large cruisers, for on the basis of a 5:5:3.5 ratio, Japan would be allowed sixteen, or one more than Britain. If the United States were to accept twenty, Japan would receive fourteen, a figure that the dominions would reject. A total of eighteen was suggested. This would give Japan 12.6, or thirteen, which Japan might be persuaded to reduce to twelve.[64] Further, the proposed 330,000-ton limit would have to be raised to 339,000 tons, but the 7.5-inch–gun cruisers would be scrapped by 1936, thereby eliminating the need to consider them in the settlement.[65] The possible antagonist in the Far East could not be ignored, and superiority in other vessels would not permit less than a ship-for-ship, gun-for-gun predominance in every category. The idealistic Labour leader was not able to escape the imperatives of Empire and the traditions of a glorious past.

In Washington, these changes appeared to be so extensive that the entire situation needed reappraising. The proposal to scrap existing vessels and add new ones threw off the previous American figures that had allowed for age, and the additional 9,000 tons upset parity more than the actual weight involved. It would take time, Stimson cabled, for the Navy General Board to digest and evaluate this new offer, which made "the difficulties seem greater today than they have for a long time."[66] The introduction of the admirals into the correspondence was a confession of the inability of the civilians to solve the technical complexities presented by the evolution of the conversations from generalities to specific figures. It marked a reversal of the avowed intentions of the diplomats, who were supposed to assume greater authority and responsibility as the negotiations progressed. The American authorities had chided MacDonald for not acting independently of the Admiralty, but now they were not above citing their own professionals to justify delay and opposition to the British demands. This admission that the problem was in the hands of the General Board disclosed the reappearance of naval experts in the field of foreign policy, and, in effect, marked a new phase in the negotiations.

The Board presented a detailed analysis of the latest British position. It reiterated the belief that the cruiser category should not be divided, that total tonnage and not numbers of ships should be limited, and that the 8-inch–gun ship was best for the United States. The yardstick should not be used in determining parity, and Britain's bases and merchant marine gave her "an enormous preponderance" in sea power over America. After this forthright assertion of principle, the Board recommended acceptance of the figure of 339,000 tons of cruiser tonnage and of the proposal to scrap the 7.5-inch–gun ships. In order to attain parity, the admirals were willing to accept a total of twenty-one 8-inch–gun 10,000-ton cruisers in lieu of the twenty-three previously demanded, but they refused to settle for the eighteen proposed by MacDonald. In addition, the existing ten *Omaha* class 6-inch–gun cruisers, totaling 70,500 tons, would be retained, and eight ships mounting guns of not more than 6 inches and totaling 58,500 tons were requested.[67] Thus the Board wanted identical tonnage with Britain and three more 8-inch–gun ships than the British thought the United States should have.

V

On the morning of September 11 the American statesmen met with their naval advisers at the White House. Present were Hoover, Stimson, Secretary of the Navy Charles F. Adams, Undersecretary of State Joseph P. Cotton, and the members of the General Board. The purpose of the meeting was to arrive at a figure which represented the American concept of parity in cruisers based on MacDonald's recently professed minimum. A reading of the Board's report revealed that no yardstick had been used in arriving at the figures recommended, as the admirals understood that it had been abandoned. This was not so, retorted the President, for the yardstick was necessary and the Board had agreed to use the one that they had worked out.[68] Hoover then asked for figures based on the yardstick, and was given an amount based on a formula using displacement and age factors, which reduced the number of new 6-inch–gun cruisers from eight to five. The President next requested a computation that included the gun-caliber factor, which effected a reduction of one half a ship in the new 6-inch–gun class.[69] Upon receiving this information, Hoover asserted that the yardstick established parity at an American strength of "21 large ships, 10 Omahas and 4 new 6-inch cruisers," and several Board members assured him that this was correct. The meeting then broke up at 12:15 P.M.

At two o'clock, the General Board convened to discuss the new problem posed by the reintroduction of the yardstick. During the course of this discussion, the Secretary of the Navy entered with a dispatch to Dawes that had been prepared by the State Department. It stated that the General Board, computing parity on the basis of displacement, age, and gun factors, had arrived at an American requirement of twenty-one 10,000-ton, 8-inch–gun ships, ten of the *Omaha* class, and four new 7,000-ton, 6-inch–gun ships —a total of 315,000 tons. The Secretary said he wanted to be sure that this represented the Board's opinion as to what constituted parity. He was told that it did not. The members had understood the President to ask if this was the correct figure in applying the formula, and they had agreed that it was. They had not agreed that this was their conception of parity with Great Britain. The Secretary departed, saying that he would have to see the President. Later, Stimson arrived and discussed the matter with the members of the Board for approximately an hour, during which time it was decided that five new 6-inch–gun ships would be satisfactory. Undersecretary of State Cotton then arrived with the dispatch that Adams had read to the Board earlier in the day, and it was changed to include the figure agreed on during the afternoon exchange.[70]

The misunderstanding that occurred at the White House was the source of considerable irritation to the President, who, after being advised of the Board's rejection of the original figures in the dispatch, wrote a letter to Stimson giving his version of the conversations and professing his inability to see any cause for confusion.[71] The reason for the misunderstanding is clear, for while Hoover understood that the figures were computed using a formula conceived by the Board, he failed to recall that the Board did not agree with the formula as a means for determining parity. On the other hand, the admirals, probably resentful of the criticism that had been directed at them by the statesmen in public and in private, made no effort to clarify their position. There was no meeting of minds during these exchanges between the civilians and the naval officers. Their training and point of view made it difficult, and their responsibilities and prerogatives often made it impossible. This was the only occasion on which Hoover met with the General Board.

Following up the disputed telegram, Stimson noted that the two countries were apart only on the question of whether three of the American cruisers would mount 8-inch or 6-inch guns, or whether four or five 6-inch–

gun ships would be substituted for the three more heavily armed vessels. This point, he believed, could be left open for negotiation, and no suggestion was made that the British proposal be altered. With this narrowing of the gap that separated the demands of the two nations, and possibly to make these new claims more palatable, the Secretary of State extended the long-awaited invitation for MacDonald to visit the United States.[72]

But even this welcome news did not reconcile the Prime Minister to the American figures. The British superiority of 24,000 tons, he protested, was more than offset by the difference of six 8-inch–gun cruisers, which also provided "insuperable difficulties" in reaching a satisfactory ratio with other nations. This problem, however, could be left to the forthcoming conference.[73] Hoover was willing to discuss the matter with MacDonald in Washington, although it would be difficult, warned the Secretary of State, to secure the Senate's consent to any treaty that did not have the support of the Navy General Board.[74]

Proclaiming "THE RACE IS OFF," the London *Times* exulted that events had moved rapidly from near failure to virtual success, for the difference separating the two nations was so slight that Anglo-American conversations could be considered "completed."[75] Unfortunately, while limitation of naval armaments was promising, the President's objective of naval reduction was not. The proposed cruiser tonnage for the British fleet amounted to an increase of 39,000 tons over the existing total, and America would have to build 215,000 tons by 1936 in order to reach her allotted figure.[76] This anomalous situation, whereby negotiations directed toward disarmament had led to a tentative agreement to increase armaments, was a far cry from the intentions of the statesmen and the high hopes of the public. Only by disregarding the advice of the naval experts could reduction be effected, and each nation refused to take this necessary step. Stimson blithely urged MacDonald to do so only a few days after he had explained why such action was impracticable for the United States, although Dawes with some exaggeration claimed that the existing accomplishments were the result of overriding the admirals.[77] In England, the Admiralty occupied a position of influence and prestige considerably greater than that held in America by the General Board, which was exclusively advisory in nature and existed only by order of the Secretary of the Navy. The Prime Minister's reluctance to overrule the recommendations of his naval experts irritated the impatient Dawes, whose suspicions of professional motives never abated.[78] The role of the Admiralty was considerable, if not decisive, although whether it was "helpful," as claimed by MacDonald's first lord, depends on one's attitude toward disarmament.[79] Neither government gave any evidence of freeing itself from the imperatives defined by the admirals.

With the visit of the Prime Minister scheduled for October, preparations were hastened for the subsequent five-power conference. Great Britain, it was agreed, would issued the invitations and act as host. On October 7, notes were handed to the French, Italian, Japanese, and American ambassadors at London. Representatives of their respective governments were invited to gather in the British capital during the first week in January, 1930, to consider an agreement on naval limitation. The agenda were to include those categories not embraced by the Washington Treaty and a modification of the battleship-replenishment program. The British government, the invitation emphasized, had found "no inclination in any quarter to set up new machinery for dealing with the naval disarmament question," but it hoped this meeting would provide a "text" to "facilitate the task of the League of Nations Preparatory Commission and of the subsequent general disarmament conference."[80] In their notes of acceptance, each nation professed an interest in efforts to reduce the burden of armaments. France, Italy, and Japan asked for an exchange of views in preliminary conversations, and the remaining months were to find the United States confronted with a conflict of viewpoints that placed the Anglo-American differences in an entirely new perspective.

Chapter V

Prelude to Agreement

> But the way we get it, a Quaker is undertaking to show a
> Scotchman how he can save money on his Navy.
>> —Dallas *News*, October, 1929.

I

The Prime Minister and his party sailed from England on the morning of September 28, 1929. A personal visit from Stanley Baldwin, leader of the Conservative party, and a telegram from the King wishing MacDonald "Godspeed" revealed the importance with which the trip was regarded. Echoing Britain's enthusiasm, the American press auspiciously hailed the meeting as "an augury without precedent in modern times" and "a long step toward sanity."[1] French papers were not so sanguine. Opinion ranged from "suspicion" on the part of the *Temps* and the *Journal des Débats*, to "virulent hostility" in the case of the *Matin*.[2] The enthusiastic welcome accorded the visiting dignitary in New York and Washington was marred by a "stag" dinner given by Stimson in honor of the Prime Minister to which the latter's daughter was not invited. Though the incident "stirred" capital society, it did not appear to dim the luster of the meeting with the President.

Conversations between the two leaders were carried on in an atmosphere of informality and amicability from October 4 to October 10. No agenda had been prepared, and each of the participants presumably intended to confine the discussion to a consideration of naval limitation and the general improvement of Anglo-American relations.[3]

MacDonald attacked the naval problem by proposing a reduction in maximum battleship displacement from 35,000 to 25,000 tons, and in gun caliber from 16 inches to 12 inches, with an increase in scrappable age from twenty to twenty-six years. Hoover demurred. He was anxious to avoid building any battleships before 1936, and many naval officers had warned him that the airplane would eventually make the large craft obsolete. The Prime Minister retorted that his own naval advisers objected to a reduction in the number of battleships, and with this impasse a change in capital-ship limitation became impossible.[4] Thus each statesman cited his experts in support of his inability to agree with the other, an ironic twist that was to become more pronounced as the talks continued.

The knotty cruiser problem was given a new approach. Explaining that the General Board was more amenable to flexibility in the age factor, the President suggested that the British might retain some old cruisers for police duties in order to narrow the gap separating the two nations. In spite of the promise of this significant concession, or because it was unacceptable to either or both nations, the two leaders agreed to postpone attempts to settle the cruiser question on the grounds that it might be resented by other countries. Hoover accepted MacDonald's offer to reduce destroyer tonnage to 150,000 tons, although the figure was contingent on a reduction in submarine tonnage by other nations, especially France. The United States was willing to scrap submarines in excess of 50,000 tons and grant Japan 70,000 tons in this category, but this concession was to be "held in reserve" for bargaining in the event of any controversy with Japan over the cruiser ratio. Hoover and MacDonald decided that the latter would present his Admiralty with a proposal to reduce the total tonnage of aircraft carriers from 135,000 tons to 120,000 tons, and establish a minimum-unit displacement for these vessels in order to prevent them from being placed in the cruiser category. Transfer between categories would be limited to 10 percent of the tonnage allotted, although it was realized that France would probably ask for more. Admittedly, this was a delicate matter, for it could serve to upset the arrangements that had established parity between America and Great Britain.[5]

The entire problem of naval limitation was disposed of without final agreement on any issue, although some understanding was reached on method and approach. The experts were neither overlooked nor overruled, and a settlement was left to the formal five-power conference. Actually, the two leaders realized that a decision on specific items was not practicable, even if it was possible, though both had expected the personal touch to produce more tangible results.

The explosive question of "freedom of the seas" was raised by Hoover. Many people, he said, took the view that a solution of this perennial subject was a prerequisite to the establishment of satisfactory relations with Britain, and the matter must be discussed in order to pacify those who, like Senator Borah, believed that it was linked with disarmament.[6] The British envoys were reluctant to deal with this controversial issue, which for the previous two years had been the subject of an exhaustive study by the Committee of Imperial Defense. To obtain British support, it had to be presented "just right," and the term "freedom of the seas" was forbidden because of its association with criticism of the British navy. A semantic compromise which substituted "rights and immunities at sea during war" was recommended as being less inflammatory.[7]

Convinced of the impracticability of general concessions, the President urged that ships carrying food be exempt from capture during war, and that an agreement covering belligerent rights contain such a provision. Unable to agree, the two statesmen decided to refer the entire matter to a group of jurists at a later date, and include the food-ship proposal in a press release at the conclusion of the Prime Minister's visit. Yet this item was deleted upon receipt of a series of emphatic messages from London, a decision which "clearly chagrined and disappointed" both Hoover and Stimson.[8] This episode furnishes further evidence that MacDonald, in his efforts to placate the American statesmen, advance disarmament, and improve Anglo-American relations, was willing to make concessions that his government would not accept.

In elaboration of his efforts to reduce friction, the President offered a plan to divide the world into eastern and western hemispheres. If the British maintained no naval bases in the Western Hemisphere that would be a "menace" to the United States, the latter would agree to maintain none in the Eastern Hemisphere that would be a "menace" to Britain.[9] Once again defeat came from London, where the Chiefs of Staff, in vetoing the suggestion, contended that it would impose restrictions on British possessions and leave the Americans free to do what they liked in their own.[10] This matter, decided MacDonald, would have to wait until he had returned home.[11]

Hoover continued on the offensive by proposing an amendment to the Treaty for the Renunciation of War aimed at enforcement. The suggested amendment provided that in the event of an international dispute a committee, consisting of members from both aggrieved and impartial nations, would be appointed to attempt a reconciliation.[12] MacDonald expressed interest in the proposal, but he thought that it might conflict with the Covenant of the League of Nations. After a fruitless discussion, the two leaders decided that each government would give further consideration to the question of whether such a step was desirable and the method by which it should be handled.[13]

In a joint statement issued at the conclusion of the conversations, Hoover and MacDonald reiterated their faith in the Kellogg-Briand Pact and in the new atmosphere of trust and confidence for which it was responsible. They announced virtual agreement on major problems of naval disarmament, and expressed their conviction that the forthcoming conference would end "all competitive building between ourselves with the risk of war and the waste of public money involved." The part each nation was to play in the promotion of world peace was different, for "one will never consent to become entangled in European diplomacy and the other is resolved to pursue a policy of active cooperation with its European neighbors," but they shared the same objective.[14] It was an innocuous document, designed to avoid controversy at home and antagonism abroad, but it contained nothing new, and its generalities reflected the failure of the participants to reach agreement on a solution to the problems outstanding between the two powers.

"The symbol of a great page in history," was a typical American newspaper reaction to the meeting.[15] MacDonald's personality and his sincere and moderate public utterances won the affection of the public and the press, and both internationalists and isolationists found cause to rejoice. While the Newark *News* observed that once more "Washington is something more than the capital of a self-isolated United States,"[16] the New York *Herald-Tribune* warmly applauded Hoover's avowed abstention from European diplomacy.[17]

In England, the press treated the MacDonald visit with warmth and enthusiasm. The joint statement was greeted with acclaim, not for what it said but for its being a document without precedent in Anglo-American relations. The Prime Minister's prestige was higher than it had ever been, and Conservatives feared that their party would be labeled "pro-Continent" and the Labour party "pro-American."[18] Though MacDonald received some criticism for granting parity to the United States without obtaining a revision of the war debts in exchange,[19] most of the British press reflected a later appraisal, which regarded the visit as MacDonald's "greatest contribution to foreign policy" during his second period in office.[20]

Comment in the French newspapers was skeptical. They thought the meeting accomplished little of a "concrete nature," but admitted that it may have created better "feelings." There was an expression of "relief" that the joint statement did not disclose the existence of an Anglo-American *rapprochement,* and the *Temps* felt that the real significance of the document lay in the fact that the two statesmen were able to sign a paper containing a common agreement.[21] The Rome *Tevere* noted ominously that the meeting presaged a mighty alliance directed toward world domination.[22]

The meeting defies analysis in terms of specific accomplishments, for in this respect it could be considered a failure. In other respects, and these may have been more important, the visit was a success, for MacDonald made himself popular with the President, the Secretary of State, and the American public. The talks were conducted in the same candid spirit that had characterized the exchanges in London with General Dawes, and each of the participants was brought to a deeper awareness of the sincerity and good will of the other. Topics ranged from naval limitation to freedom of the seas, naval stations, and the strengthening of the Kellogg-Briand Pact, with a resultant clarification of each nation's position. The high hopes of both leaders were not realized. MacDonald was clearly over his head in much of the negotiation, and his eagerness for tangible results often overcame his caution. In his ignorance and enthusiasm he made concessions that were completely unrealistic from the official British point of view, and he was forced into the humiliating position of having to modify his stand. But friendship and trust replaced hostility and suspicion, and the improvement in

Anglo-American relations which Hoover and MacDonald sought became a reality.

II

Sporadic conversations were conducted with representatives of France, Italy, and Japan during the period of Anglo-American negotiations. Hoover and MacDonald were especially careful to avoid offending Japan, whose strategic location, naval strength, and participation in previous conferences gave her a key position in disarmament deliberation. The Japanese delegates to the Geneva Preparatory Commission had welcomed the Gibson proposals, including the yardstick, and on June 11 Ambassador Katsuji Debuchi asked if the United States had plans for a naval conference. Stimson evasively replied that the attitude of other nations must first be determined, but he was anxious to know what the ambassador thought of having Great Britain, Japan, and the United States work out a formula along the lines suggested by Gibson. Debuchi was under the impression that this would be done by America, although both he and Stimson were of the opinion that there would be little hope of agreement if negotiations were left to the naval experts. Another question, said the ambassador, about which "Japanese opinion was very sensitive," was the 5:5:3 ratio. Satisfactory for capital ships, it failed to provide the number of auxiliary vessels needed in Chinese waters due to the "present troubled condition." Stimson sidestepped the issue by reminding Debuchi that the immediate concern was over formula rather than ratio and numbers, which would be discussed later.[23]

On the following day, the Japanese ambassador in London, Tsuneo Matsudaira, called at the British Foreign Office to inquire about the status of Anglo-American naval conversations. Advised that nothing had been done pending the arrival of General Dawes, he was assured that Tokyo would be kept informed on all developments in the negotiations, and Japan's representatives would be consulted regularly.[24] Matsudaira was not allowed to participate in the meetings between Dawes and MacDonald, however, for fear that his presence might give rise to the rumor that a conference was in progress in the absence of France and Italy.[25] This exclusion was resented by certain groups in Japan, and an article in the semi-official *Diplomatic Revue* (*Gaikō Jihō*) suggested the possibility of a forthcoming Anglo-American peace instead of a world peace.[26]

The Japanese government expressed its willingness to co-operate with other nations in an effort to reduce naval armaments in the interests of economy and peace,[27] but the Tokyo naval experts were skeptical of the yardstick and believed that differences over technical details would make its acceptance unlikely.[28] Japan would not consent to the abolition of the submarine, and she was opposed to having the question of ratios brought up

51

in the Anglo-American conversations.[29] On August 12, Matsudaira told Dawes that his government favored a reduction in all categories, but a ratio of 10:10:7, he insisted, was essential.[30] This demand was confirmed on August 27, when Matsudaira and Debuchi notified MacDonald and Stimson, respectively, that the new ratio would apply to all categories except capital ships.[31] At the time of the Washington Conference, Debuchi explained, relations with the United States were strained and the Shantung question was a source of irritation. Furthermore, the Anglo-Japanese Alliance was in existence, and it provided Japan with an ally. Now the situation had changed, for America and Japan were friends, but the latter had no allies. Japan considered herself a powerful and independent nation on an equal footing with other world powers. As such, she was entitled to parity with the United States and Great Britain, but she would settle for no more than a higher ratio.[32]

MacDonald crucially questioned whether the ratio would be applied to British or American figures in the event the United States were granted a greater number of 8-inch–gun cruisers. The ratio in both cruiser categories, he was informed, would apply to the American figures, which would give Japan less than 50 percent of the British strength in 6-inch–gun ships. The Japanese ambassador saw no reason why Japan should not have more of the heavily armed cruisers than Britain, but MacDonald indicated that such an arrangement would not be acceptable.[33]

Japan, concerned lest she be presented with a *fait accompli* without having had the opportunity to justify her own needs on political and technical grounds, protested the exclusiveness of the Anglo-American conversations and expressed the desire to become a participant.[34] The request was not granted, but on September 24 Stimson furnished Debuchi with the cruiser figures of the two nations. The Japanese ambassador hoped that America would accept fifteen and Britain twelve 8-inch–gun cruisers, and he reiterated Japan's contention that the 10:10:7 ratio was essential. Stimson insisted that the 5:5:3 ratio which applied to capital ships should apply to all classes, although he was embarrassed to present this argument to a nation that already possessed a greater number of the larger-caliber cruisers.[35]

Great Britain indicated a willingness to follow the American policy on the 10:10:7 ratio, but MacDonald was anxious to avoid giving Japan the impression that she was being opposed by the two nations in concert.[36] London was faced with the complex problem of meeting the American demands for big-gun cruisers and at the same time preventing Japan from having enough of these ships to jeopardize British interests in the Far East. To further complicate the issue, the ratio was based on tonnage, not on numbers of vessels, and some of the Japanese 8-inch–gun cruisers displaced less than 10,000 tons.[37] The situation became so delicate that Dawes was cautioned to refrain from discussing the ratio question with Matsudaira in order to prevent misunderstanding and confusion.[38]

The Japanese request for a higher ratio was based on reasons as sound from her point of view as they were unsatisfactory to Britain and America. Auxiliary vessels were needed in Chinese waters, and the long Japanese coastline demanded ships for patrol purposes. Except for the Exclusion Act of 1924, the years since the Washington Conference had seen a marked improvement in Japanese-American relations, and a lessening of suspicion and mistrust. The United States, Tokyo thought, should be willing to accept a higher ratio because Japan was less likely to pursue a policy that would threaten the interests of her Pacific neighbor. The ending of her alliance with Britain had left Japan standing alone, and, like her former ally, she was not able to depend on her domestic supply of food and raw materials.[39]

Japan, at this time, was nearing a turning point in her history. During World War I, when the European nations were engrossed in conflict, she had been able to develop a huge foreign trade with a comfortable excess of exports. The resumption of peace and the return of European competition saw her lose this favorable balance of trade and fall back on colonial outlets for her industrial surplus.[40] Population increased rapidly, and unemployment rose as Japan appeared to have reached the limits of industrial expansion. In the nineteenth century a nation faced with this situation could find relief through imperialism, but the Western powers had denied this solution to Japan at the Washington Conference. Only China appeared to offer the opportunity which Japan so desperately sought, but the economic exploitation of this huge and politically chaotic nation was bound to meet with resistance from the Western powers and Russia. Under the circumstances, many Japanese resented the obstructionist tactics of the Occidental statesmen, who seemed dedicated to the maintenance of a status quo designed to destroy Japan's prosperity and deny her the role of a great power. The urgent domestic distress was forcing the moderate internationalists into the camp of the extremists, who added the emotional appeals of nationalism and racial exclusion to the realities of economic disintegration.

Another pressure against concession was a public opinion that had been encouraged to believe that the application of the Washington ratio to auxiliary vessels would be a threat to Japan's security. Since 1922 the Japanese press had carried warnings to this effect by politicians and naval experts, and the authorities found themselves in the position where a retreat would reveal deception on their part and result in a loss of influence and prestige.[41] The claim for a 10:10:7 ratio, which bore the slogan "With menace toward none, security for all," was not advanced for the purpose of bargaining. It was a position from which the Japanese statesmen did not intend to withdraw.[42]

The Japanese press welcomed the invitation to a conference at London, and urged that naval limitation be approached from a political viewpoint and remain aloof from the pressure of naval experts.[43] To head the delegation the government appointed Baron Reijiro Wakatsuki, a prominent statesman who enjoyed the confidence of the major parties in Japan. En route, the delegates stopped in Washington, where they met with the American delegation on December 17 and 19. The affable Wakatsuki conferred with Hoover and Stimson, but the conversations, though friendly, did not lead to any concessions on the ratio.[44] The purpose of the stopover, from the Japanese point of view, was to improve relations with the United States and attempt to reach an understanding on naval matters prior to the conference.[45] The American authorities regarded the visit as a means of smoothing the ruffled sensibilities of the Japanese government, a move that had been agreed to by MacDonald while he was in Washington.[46] In this respect the meeting may have been a success, but no agreement on naval limitation emerged. The controversy was merely postponed.

III

The French government, from the time of Gibson's speech at Geneva, was concerned over the possibility that naval disarmament would be effected independent of the League Preparatory Commission. At Gibson's suggestion, Britain assured the French authorities that no such move was contemplated. Discussions between the five naval powers, the Foreign Office explained, were intended to permit a resumption of the work of the Commission, which had been halted by disagreement on naval matters.[47] None the less, as the Anglo-American conversations proceeded, French apprehension increased. When MacDonald announced the establishment of the principle of naval parity between the United States and Great Britain, his words were received by the Paris press with "considerable caution" because of the suspicion that this equality would eventually serve to curb French armament. The *Journal des Débats* viewed the agreement as a "cheap and easy way" for America to gain naval supremacy, for the British Empire required such a dispersal of the British navy that it would be no match for the more concentrated forces of her rival.[48] Disarmament, according to the Paris *Temps,* was no road to peace, for it could only follow the achievement of security, and conversations of the type being carried on in London were useless.[49]

On September 20, the French ambassador presented Stimson with informal notes protesting the extent of the Anglo-American discussions. The French government had understood that the talks were to deal with methods and categories, not with actual figures, which were to be left to a general conference devoted to a reduction in land, sea, and air weapons.[50] This conference, insisted the French ambassador in London, was to be conducted

54

under the auspices of the League of Nations. He added that the French naval authorities were alarmed at the failure to consider the new developments in naval construction which enabled Germany to build ships possessing the displacement of a cruiser and the guns of a battleship. These technological advances cast doubt on the validity of the method of limitation by categories and made the previous French concept of limitation by global tonnage more realistic.[51] France allegedly did not fear the activities of the United States or Great Britain, but she was ever aware of the danger in a possible alliance between Germany and Italy. "General security" remained the most important problem, and to promote this security France asked that the Kellogg-Briand Pact be amended to provide for consultation between members in the event of any violation of its provisions.[52]

The French authorities were pleased with the results of the MacDonald visit, which they considered a great contribution to international conciliation. They were particularly relieved by the joint statement issued by Hoover and MacDonald at the conclusion of their talks, for there had been a suspicion in some French quarters that America and Britain intended to arrive at a naval agreement which would be forced upon Europe.[53] France continued to express her understanding that the London parley was not to be in any sense final, an understanding that was constantly repeated by the French diplomats and the French press.[54] Stimson confided to the British ambassador that it might be necessary to treat the London conference as only tentative so far as France was concerned, but he thought that the other nations might reach a settlement that would be binding among themselves.[55] Further obstacles to agreement were provided by the French government's refusal to grant parity in naval strength to Italy, and by its insistence that submarines be retained because of their defensive capability.[56] The French Premier, André Tardieu, discussed the new German cruiser threat with the American ambassador, and deplored Italy's insistence on parity, which he was inclined to attribute to the ratio concept established at the Washington Conference in 1922.[57]

The entire problem was recapitulated in a note of December 20, in which the French government announced its views on the forthcoming conference. Acknowledging that the naval disarmament issue was delaying the work of the League Preparatory Commission, France maintained that the meeting at London was for the purpose of formulating "principles and methods" by which disarmament could be effected at a subsequent convention. The Kellogg-Briand Pact was not a satisfactory basis for disarmament, for it did not "guarantee" security, and a political agreement was a necessary preliminary to any armament treaty. Nevertheless, France intended to approach the conference with sincerity and in the spirit of co-operation. The note questioned the application of mathematical formulas by categories and reaffirmed the conviction that limitation by total tonnage alone or in combination with a system of transfer between categories would be more desirable. The amount of naval tonnage required by France was in direct proportion to her land and air armament, and her needs would depend on the extent to which other nations would join in a "guarantee of security" to implement the provisions for action against an aggressor contained in article XVI of the Covenant of the League of Nations. As a step in this direction, France suggested the possibility of a treaty of mutual guarantee and non-aggression between Mediterranean naval powers, to include those not invited to the conference. Concluding, the note expressed confidence in the ability of the five world naval powers to reach an agreement that would lead to a conference on general disarmament. This, France believed, was the only way to approach the problem of peace through the reduction of military strength.[58]

The note was not made public until December 27, but its contents quickly became known. The position taken by Premier Tardieu and Foreign Minister Aristide Briand that decisions made at London must be approved by a general conference received the enthusiastic approval of the Chamber of Deputies, the press, and the populace.[59] News of the declaration was received with dismay by the British press, which thought it a "chill wind" that presaged trouble for the forthcoming parley. The British authorities regarded the note with "misgivings," and public sentiment in England was firm in its refusal to assume further obligations to provide military support in the event of aggression.[60]

The publication of the complete text of the memorandum evoked "nothing but warm praise" in the French papers, some of which expressed the hope that the delegates would not retreat from this position, and the debates in the Chamber of Deputies preceding a vote of confidence revealed strong support of the government's program.[61] The British authorities were not interested in a Mediterranean pact, but they thought that an agreement providing for "consultation" in the event of hostilities, similar to article I of the Four-Power Treaty, would be of some assistance in reaching a naval understanding.[62] In Washington, the French note reinforced the belief that France would not be a party to any treaty formulated at London. She had taken such an extreme and dogmatic stand that drastic modification seemed improbable.[63]

The new American ambassador, Walter E. Edge, was able to allay Tardieu's suspicion that the United States and Britain intended to present France with a completed agreement, but the Premier was unyielding in his demand for security and for final action on disarmament by the League of Nations.[64] Pressure against compromise was exerted in the press and through the political opponents of the government by the Big-Navy group, headed by the minister of Marine, George Leygues, and Captain Jean Françoise Darlan, and backed by the steel trust.[65] The almost unanimous approval given the December 20 note by the French Parliament made it difficult for Tardieu to modify his position, although he was anxious to co-operate with America and Britain.[66] Fundamentally, however, the atmosphere at Geneva was more conducive to a settlement on French terms, for she could count on support for views that were not shared by the great naval powers. At issue was the question whether disarmament and world peace would be based on the moral force of the Kellogg-Briand Pact or the military commitments of the League Covenant. Rumors circulated that France would relax her demands, but as the conference approached, no reliable indication of a change in her official position was forthcoming.[67]

IV

Italian policy during the preliminary conversations was less complex but no less firm than that of her northern neighbor. The London Naval Conference of 1930 took place during what has been called Mussolini's phase of "international conciliation," although Franco-Italian tension continued.[68] Italy, Mussolini confided to the American ambassador, had refused to participate in the Geneva Conference of 1927 because she had been granted parity with France at Washington in 1922 and was determined not to give it up. The Fascist government could scarcely accept less than its predecessor had won. Yet the Italian press joined that of France in intimating that Britain and America would offer an agreement which the other nations would be forced to accept or assume the blame for a conference failure.[69] Naval equality for Italy, some authorities contended, was exclusively a question of prestige, for her financial position did not permit competitive building.[70] But she justified her demands on the grounds that imports were more vital to Italy than they were to France, and on the basis of the precedent established by Anglo-American parity.[71]

Rome vacillated on the submarine question. Foreign Minister Dino Grandi professed support of Britain's desire for the abolition of undersea craft, only to reveal later that a difference of opinion among the Italian naval experts prevented a commitment. The British ambassador was not alone in his suspicion that this indecision might be a deliberate effort to promote Anglo-American pressure on France to accept parity with Italy.[72]

The demand for naval equality prevented Franco-Italian conversations from making any progress, and they were discontinued prior to the conference.[73] Rome saw little possibility for agreement at London, and the apathy of the Italian authorities was reflected by the people, who took slight interest in a matter that seemed to affect their pride but not the actual size of their navy.[74]

In the United States preparations for the forthcoming Conference had continued. Undersecretary of State Cotton urged that the Navy General Board not be permitted to prepare a report, for, he contended, their advice in 1927 for the meeting at Geneva had furnished a too "rigid" set of instructions which inhibited agreement.[75] He found an ally in Assistant Secretary of the Navy for Air David S. Ingalls, who favored air power rather than equality in ships as a means of attaining naval parity.[76] This heretical viewpoint made little impression. Airplanes were considered useful for scouting and spotting purposes, and the new carriers *Lexington* and *Saratoga,* first employed in the fleet problem of 1929, had not demonstrated their full capabilities.[77] Stimson held a series of conversations with individual members of the General Board, who presented their views on the functions and value of the various types of combat vessels and furnished the secretary with information calculated to make him an amateur technical expert.[78]

The selection of delegates was simplified by an official request from Britain that no "technical experts" be nominated by the participating nations. The United States readily acceded to this request and indicated that experts would serve only as advisers.[79] Stimson was appointed to head the American delegation, which consisted of Ambassador Dawes, Secretary of the Navy Adams, Senator Joseph T. Robinson, Senator David A. Reed, Ambassador to Belgium Hugh S. Gibson, and Ambassador to Mexico Dwight W. Morrow. Certain senators criticized the appointment of Senator Reed, a Republican and seventh ranking member of the Foreign Relations Committee. Actually, he was selected after Senator Borah had declined a position on the delegation, presumably because the crusty Idahoan did not want to be in the position of having to defend a treaty that he might not like.[80] Some Senate opinion held that Senator Claude A. Swanson of Virginia, ranking Democratic member of the Foreign Relations and Naval Affairs Committees, should have been chosen as a delegate.[81] But his forthright criticism of the President's action in suspending construction of the new cruisers probably prevented Hoover from making the selection.

Heading the list of advisers was Admiral William V. Pratt, Commander in Chief of the United States Fleet, who had played an active part in the Washington Conference of 1921-1922. Admiral Hilary P. Jones was included, both for his experience and as a concession to those naval personnel who were "incensed" at Hoover's apparent disregard of the General Board.[82]

All told, it was a strong delegation, sincere in the desire to reach an agreement that would be a contribution to disarmament and world peace, and be acceptable to the Senate and the people of the United States. The major problem was whether sincerity, ability, and experience could overcome the obstacle of national interest, both at home and abroad.

The American delegation first met in Washington on December 11.

Stimson briefed the delegates on background and outstanding issues, and spoke pessimistically of the possibility of reaching agreement on a yardstick, which involved so many "imponderables" that only adroit "bargaining" could bring about its acceptance.[83] Other sessions followed as the delegates prepared for a vigorous effort at London. No commitments, the nation was assured, would be made that might threaten national security, and any reduction in America's fleet would have to be accompanied by an equivalent reduction by the other naval powers.[84] An air of optimism was added by the news that Washington had agreed to sign the World Court statutes, which would require Senate ratification of membership in that tribunal. The announcement was regarded as a contribution to the success of the coming parley, for it was proof of America's intention to co-operate with other nations in the quest for peace.[85]

Conversations between the United States and Great Britain continued, but they were almost exclusively confined to the proposed agenda. Stimson hinted that an understanding on the status of the Singapore base might induce Japan to accept a lower ratio, but this tactic, which had proved effective at Washington in 1922, was vetoed by MacDonald, who adamantly refused to allow the bastion to become a "bargaining factor" in the negotiations.[86]

The Secretary of State was strongly opposed to the delegates making opening speeches that included their proposals in any detail, for, he believed, a modification or compromise would be difficult after definite positions were made public. He also objected to the British desire for private plenary sessions on the grounds that they were not practical because they were never private. MacDonald accepted these suggestions, and declared that no method of procedure would be adopted without the approval of the United States. Opening speeches, he agreed, should be confined to generalities, and he thought that they would be. But he could not control the delegates from other nations, and, since "the reason for the ass' bray is that the ass is built that way," an accident was possible. The Prime Minister had found that in conferences of this kind it was best not to establish a firm and detailed plan of procedure, for the "moods and nature" of the situation would determine the way in which matters should be handled.[87]

V

Rumor, speculation, and controversy increased as the date set for the conference grew near. The suspicion that armament manufacturers had influenced the negotiations at Geneva in 1927 led the Washington authorities to take precautions to prevent any such activity at London. A lawsuit brought by a hired observer, William B. Shearer, for his efforts at Geneva furnished an object lesson which the administration did not hesitate to exploit.[88] Disarmament remained unpopular among many Britons for its effect on shipyard work and unemployment, which were major problems in depression-plagued England.[89] Naval reduction and parity with America were denounced by distinguished British naval officers in speeches and in the press on the basis of Britain's greater needs and responsibilities.[90] Adding to the outcry, the British journalist and naval expert, Héctor C. Bywater, wrote that the controversy over the 8-inch–gun ship was absurd, for these vessels were "doomed" by the more heavily armed new German cruisers.[91] Resolutions opposing a reduction of the British fleet and a consideration of the "pernicious doctrine" of freedom of the seas were unanimously adopted by the overseas branches of the British Navy League and the Navy Leagues of Canada and South Africa. This development assumed greater significance as the dominions exerted more pressure on the home government in naval matters.[92]

MacDonald's political position was precarious, for he faced two parties that could remove him from office if they so desired. The King's decision to speak at the opening of the parley strengthened MacDonald's hand, and the three major parties were committed to parity with the United States, but the Prime Minister was willing to accept a lower standard of parity than either of the two opposition leaders. When asked why the British cruiser demands had been reduced from the seventy-two deemed necessary at the Geneva conference to the recent figure of fifty, First Lord Alexander explained that the Admiralty had consented to the new total as a result of the Kellogg-Briand Pact and the general improvement in international conditions. But Viscount Bridgeman, First Lord of the Admiralty in the former Conservative government, maintained that the situation had not altered appreciably since 1927, when the higher figure was insisted on by the Admiralty.[93] Adding to MacDonald's problems, the British Conservative press began to weaken in its support of his position on naval disarmament. This change was attributed to a fear that the Labour government, under the "pacifist" Prime Minister, who had already reduced naval requirements, might be willing to accept figures so low that the nation's defenses would be endangered.[94]

The Japanese press was reported to have lost its early "faith" in the efficacy of the Hoover-MacDonald conversations, a faith that had been replaced by a feeling that the nations were reverting to "the old game of politics." A general belief prevailed that the 10:10:7 ratio was a menace to no one, and that it should be granted on the basis of simple justice.[95]

In Italy, the *Poglio d'Ordini* caustically observed that "it may come to pass that the reef of Franco-Italian parity may sink the little ship of the London argonauts seeking peace. The possibility of such a happening does not perturb us in the least."[96] The Spanish government, worried lest she find herself excluded from a treaty affecting the nation's security, lodged a protest against the discussion of a Mediterranean pact unless Spain was represented.[97]

In the midst of this less than auspicious news, and as the Navy Department announced an acceleration of construction work in response to Hoover's desire to help business, the United States delegation sailed from New York.[98] The huge group of delegates, advisers, professional assistants, and clerical personnel was sped on its way by a fanfare of publicity and a warm and sober message from the President. Reservations had been obtained for forty-three rooms at the Ritz Hotel and twenty-three rooms at the Mayfair to provide living accommodations and office space for the staff.[99]

The obstacles which stood in the way of agreement were not so numerous as they were enormous. Britain and the United States were separated by 30,000 tons of cruisers, but the relative value of 8-inch–gun and 6-inch–gun cruisers was a question that neither statesmen nor experts had been able to settle. Japan was determined that the capital-ship ratio of the Washington Conference should not be applied to auxiliary vessels, and the United States was equally determined that it should. Italy insisted on parity with France, which the latter refused to consider. The French clamored for security before disarmament and demanded that any final settlement be made within the framework of the League of Nations. It was obvious to participants and spectators alike that success would depend on concessions, either mutual or unilateral. But there was little evidence of the spirit of compromise among the statesmen, the naval experts, the press, or the public.

Chapter VI

London—the Issue Joined

There are no technical difficulties in the way of the conference. We should sail for home with an agreement within two months.   —Admiral William V. Pratt, January 9, 1930.

I

According to Arthur W. Page, the American delegation "lit in London runnin'."[1] The delegates were anxious to begin their task, and Stimson, freshened and fortified by the ocean voyage, immediately opened discussions with MacDonald in an effort to consolidate the position of the two nations before the conference opened. The Prime Minister, who appeared tired, complained that he could not be sure from one day to the next whether he would remain in office, but he was convinced of the need for talks with his American colleague in advance of formal negotiations.[2]

The two statesmen disagreed on the Japanese position. MacDonald believed that Japan was firm on the 10:10:7 ratio. Stimson, on the other hand, felt that Japan would not insist on this ratio because she needed financial relief from the expense of replacing her battleships. Stimson intended to refuse to discuss this question until the ratio of auxiliary vessels was settled. The two men agreed to resist the Japanese claim and use the issue of battleship reduction to exert pressure.[3]

The Prime Minister, annoyed at France's actions, declared that he was unable to give the guarantee that she wanted in her proposed Mediterranean pact. Stimson believed that France would be satisfied with a consultative treaty, and MacDonald showed Stimson a draft in the form of the Four-Power Treaty that had been signed at Washington in 1921. There was no mention of the United States being a member of the contemplated pact.[4]

Italy was being even more difficult than France, the Prime Minister complained, because she wanted some of the French colonies. Stimson offered little assistance in these Continental squabbles, for he was not interested in either French or Italian naval strength except for the effect it might have on the British. As for battleships, the United States was willing to reduce their numbers but not their size. MacDonald took the opposite stand, and he explained that the Admiralty was adamant on the subject.[5] Thus, the two statesmen were able to agree only on joint opposition to the programs of other nations. They were unable to resolve any of the problems that separated the United States and Great Britain.

Stimson lunched with members of the Italian delegation on January 19.

The discussion was friendly and naval technicalities were avoided, but Stimson felt that a cordial personal relationship was established.[6] Dino Grandi, the Italian Foreign Minister, observed that his country regarded America as "the hope of the white race," for "Europe was decadent."[7] There is no evidence of Stimson's response to this information or whether he was influenced by this apparent attempt at flattery.

The American Secretary of State was more optimistic about the chances for the conference after a talk with Tardieu and Briand. The former appeared to be sincere in his desire for a successful outcome, and he made a significant concession by withdrawing French objections to the parley's reaching final agreement independent of the League of Nations.[8] It was only later that Stimson realized the crucial split between British and French public opinion on the questions of military assistance and the role of the League.[9]

Stimson could regard his pre-conference activities with satisfaction. He had gained one important concession and had consolidated his position with Britain in opposition to the claims of Japan. His relations with the heads of other delegations had been cordial, informal, and promising. Stimson's early reports reveal a confidence and self-assurance that must have been gratifying to the President. Dawes, on the other hand, was more conscious of the underlying obstacles to agreement, but he was no longer in a position to communicate directly with Washington on disarmament. The General felt that the atmosphere of friendship and good will merely disguised the unyielding sentiments of all the delegates. Each thought that his own unassailable position must be accepted by the others.[10] Dawes was not normally pessimistic, but his experience in the preceding six months made him aware of the gap between intentions and performance in naval disarmament.

II

Gathering in London were many of the world's most illustrious statesmen, and Hugh R. Wilson, writing some ten years after the event, nostalgically observed that it was "the last of the great conferences done in the tradition of the Congress of Vienna."[11] Premier André Tardieu led the French delegation, which consisted of Aristide Briand, Minister for Foreign Affairs; Aimé-Joseph de Fleuriau, ambassador to Great Britain; George Leygues, Minister of Marine (attended to April 14); Jacques-Louis Dumesnil, Minister of Marine (delegate from April 14); René Massigli (delegate to February 11); and Henry Moysset (delegate from February 11). Two cabinet crises in Paris during the course of the conference were responsible for the changes in the composition of the delegation.

Prime Minister MacDonald headed the British delegation, which included Foreign Secretary Arthur Henderson, William Wedgwood Benn, Secretary of State for India, and First Lord of the Admiralty Alexander.

Separate delegates represented the Commonwealth of Australia, the Dominion of Canada, the Dominion of New Zealand, the Union of South Africa, India, and the Irish Free State.

The Italian delegation consisted of Dino Grandi, Minister of Foreign Affairs, Admiral Giuseppe Siranni, Minister for the Navy, Antonio Chiaramonte Bordonaro, ambassador to Great Britain, and Admiral Alfredo Acton, Senator of the Kingdom.

Japan was represented by Reijiro Wakatsuki, member of the House of Peers, Admiral Takeshi Takarabe, Minister of Marine, Tsuneo Matsudaira, ambassador to Great Britain, and Matsuzo Nagai, ambassador to Belgium.

Both Italy and Japan had disregarded MacDonald's request that no naval officers be appointed as delegates, but in each case the person concerned was occupying a civilian position in the home government and no objection was made by the other nations.

The first plenary meeting of the conference was held on January 21 in the Royal Gallery, House of Lords. London was blanketed by an unusually heavy fog that delayed many of the delegates. King George V welcomed the delegates and expressed his hopes for the success of the conference. Stimson then suggested that MacDonald be chosen chairman, a suggestion that met with approval after it had been seconded by Tardieu. Arrangements had been made beforehand for MacDonald's selection without consulting the Japanese or Italian envoys. The American delegates belatedly recognized the mistake in ignoring two nations that were noted for their sensitivity, and the Americans resolved to be more careful in dealing with matters of protocol and prestige.[12]

The British Prime Minister, taking the chair, traced the background of the conference and outlined the reasons for its being called. He spoke hopefully of the prospects for disarmament as an approach to security and peace. In conclusion, he emphasized the importance of the sea to the welfare of Great Britain and maintained that "our Navy is no mere superfluity to us. It *is* us."[13] MacDonald was careful to observe his own admonition against making any demands, but he clearly indicated Britain's unique and almost exclusive dependence on sea power.

The heads of the other delegations spoke briefly. They confined their remarks to general statements concerning their nations' interest in disarmament and peace and their hope for the success of the conference. The chairman then terminated the proceedings and announced the next meeting for January 23.[14]

At the second plenary meeting MacDonald announced that the heads of delegations had agreed on the procedure for the conference. Two types of meetings would be held: plenary sessions of all the delegations to ratify recommendations of committees, and a "working committee" to be composed of delegations. Any subcommittees that were required to deal with particular matters would be appointed as the need arose.[15] Subsequently, a "First Committee" was appointed to consider questions on the agenda. Alexander was designated as chairman and members were chosen from the various delegations. The First Committee established two other committees: a "Committee of Experts" to discuss and make recommendations on technical matters referred to it by the First Committee; and a "Committee of Jurists" to prepare a treaty regulating the conduct of submarines during war. Theoretically, a problem on the agenda would be considered by the First Committee or referred to one of the other committees. After the subcommittee resolved the question it would report its findings to the First Committee, which in turn would make its own report to the delegations assembled in plenary session. In actual practice, the issues resolved by these committees were primarily, but not exclusively, of a minor and technical nature. The First Committee was reluctant to handle certain questions, such as those involving matters of "high principle," which it thought should be dealt with by the heads of delegations.[16] Some items referred to the Committee of Experts were returned on the grounds that they were matters of policy which the committee was unable or unwilling to consider.[17] Most of the basic and significant problems were decided at meetings of the heads of delegations after being hammered out by the delegates in private and often lengthy conversations.[18]

After MacDonald had revealed the procedural arrangements, he suggested certain rules that should govern publicity. Committee meetings should be conducted in private. After each sitting a communiqué should be issued that had been agreed on by the representatives of the delegations present. These communiqués were not to prevent the delegates from expressing themselves to the press, but they were to be guided in their remarks by the official release. The delegates agreed unanimously to observe these restrictions.[19] The news-hungry correspondents were to complain about the dearth of information, but their success in gathering bits of material, often distorted, was to be a constant source of irritation to the delegates.

The delegations were then asked to give their "general views" on naval disarmament. These were not to include their program or any details concerning their demands, which were to be expressed in private conversations between the delegates. These "general views" were intended to explain the interest of each nation in naval armament and clarify the relationship between its position and its requirements. The delegations were seated in alphabetical order, with America first, and the speakers were called on in this sequence.

Stimson declined to elaborate on the position of the United States, for, he said, it was "well understood," and repeating it would serve no purpose.[20]

Australia's representative pointed out the geographical factors that affected his country and the importance of the sea for the world trade which supported and welded together the British Commonwealth.[21]

Tardieu presented his country's case in elaborate detail. Including the coastline of France and the extent and size of her overseas possessions under geographical factors, he claimed that the total vulnerable coastline was smaller only than those of Great Britain, the United States, and Japan. Actually, Tardieu asserted, France needed a two-ocean navy for protection against Germany in the north and Italy in the Mediterranean. Economically, France depended on trade with her colonies, and militarily, the lines of communication with the empire must be maintained.[22] Stirring and impassioned in the traditional Gallic manner, the speech impressed some observers as having been designed primarily for home consumption.[23] Nevertheless, the fundamental French obsession with security was presented in a clear and dramatic statement which left the unmistakable impression that naval parity with Italy was out of the question. Also implied was the impracticability of the limitation of weapons in a single category, especially for a nation whose two most likely antagonists occupied the same land mass that she did.

MacDonald emphasized three points: first, that England was an island; second, that the British Commonwealth made a dispersal of naval forces necessary; third, that the navy occupied a special place in the minds and hearts of the British people.[24]

Grandi acknowledged the relationship of armaments to a nation's security, but he considered this a relative factor that depended on the armaments of other nations. Italy, "to all intents and purposes," was an island, dependent on other lands for vital imports. She was, however, willing to accept a reduction in her navy "to any level, no matter how low," so long as no other Continental nation exceeded that level.[25] The allusion to France was unmistakable.

Wakatsuki made a general statement to the effect that reduction in armament must depend on the circumstances and the situation peculiar to each nation, and on the reasonable assurance that another nation or combination of nations would not be a threat to its existence. He made no effort to justify Japan's position or to indicate any factors that would make her case unique.[26]

The New Zealand delegate described his country's position in the Pacific, and her dependence on trade. New Zealand's defense needs, he emphasized, were based on her position as an integral part of the British Commonwealth of Nations.[27]

MacDonald concluded the meeting by observing that all the delegations had been heard from and that their frank and friendly attitude held promise for the future of the conference. After noting that members of the press were in attendance and might make news if it was not furnished them, he adjourned the meeting. The delegates were now free to apply themselves to the task ahead.

III

The actual negotiations began with a series of conferences between the heads of delegations. Sir Maurice Hankey, general secretary of the Conference, had prepared a list of suggested topics which he submitted to the delegates for their consideration in arriving at the agenda. Several days of formal, informal, and intra-delegation discussions followed, and it seemed to Dawes that "life [was] one long debating society."[28] The heads of delegations spent three and one-half hours settling an argument between the French and the Italians over a question of precedence, but the agenda for the conference were finally approved.

The agenda were divided into two sections, one containing "General Questions" and the other "Special Questions." Listed under General Questions were:

France
(1) The system of global tonnage.
   The French Delegation's transactional proposals.
(2) What classification is to be adopted?
(3) Transfer—the amount and conditions thereof?

Great Britain
   The system of limitation by categories.

Italy
(1) Determination of ratios.
(2) Determination of levels of the total tonnage of the several countries.

Under the heading "Special Questions," section "A" listed ships not regulated by the Washington Treaty, i.e., cruisers, both of the 8-inch– and 6-inch–gun type, submarines, and destroyers. Each category was to be considered in relation to gross tonnage for each nation, the maximum tonnage of each ship, the number of ships to be allotted to each nation, and the life of the vessels. Submarines and destroyers were also to be limited by displacement and gun caliber, and activities of the underseas vessels in regard to merchant ships were to be regulated. Other questions concerned the characteristics of ships to be exempt from limitation and the conversion of merchant vessels into warships. Under section "B," the Washington Treaty categories were listed, and questions were raised concerning a modification of the provisions that governed battleships and aircraft carriers.[29]

The third plenary meeting convened on January 30 to consider the agenda, appoint the necessary committees, furnish material for the press, and give the delegates an opportunity to continue their informal sessions. After MacDonald opened the meeting and mentioned the agenda, Grandi pointed out that the two items submitted by the Italian delegation raised questions of both principle and fact. The first was the determination of ratios between navies. The second was the maximum tonnage to be allotted each of the five nations. Until these matters were settled, Grandi warned, Italy could not agree on method or on any of the problems connected with disarmament. MacDonald adroitly announced that the Italian questions would be deferred.[30]

Gibson, speaking for the American delegation, reviewed the work of the League Preparatory Commission, where certain nations had supported the opposing methods of limitation by categories and limitation by total tonnage. These two schools had been deadlocked until the French delegate, in 1927, proposed the "transactional" or compromise scheme whereby the two methods were combined. Total tonnage was divided by category, and transfer of tonnage was permitted between certain categories. In April 1929 the United States had accepted this suggestion as a basis for discussion without relinquishing the belief that limitation by categories was more desirable. The United States, Gibson reiterated, was willing to consider the French plan because the American government believed that the technicalities of naval disarmament were less important than the attitude of the nations in attacking the problem.[31]

Tardieu complimented Gibson on his presentation of the French proposal, and he agreed that it was important for the conference to settle on a method, but limitation by categories, in his opinion, was more suitable for nations possessing large navies. Limitation by tonnage was more flexible and better suited to the needs of nations having smaller fleets.[32]

Speaking for Great Britain, Alexander stated a preference for the category method, a preference shared by Japan and the United States. Britain was willing, however, to consider a modification of limitation by global tonnage for other nations, provided that proven measures were taken to safeguard or limit the transfer of tonnage between categories.[33]

The third plenary session again revealed the shortcomings of public discussion. There were no debates, only speeches that reaffirmed the established positions of the various nations. The delegates were reluctant to make offers or demand concessions that might provoke unfavorable reactions at home or leave them vulnerable to criticism in the press or from their colleagues. The First Committee, with the two subcommittees which it later appointed, was designed to take care of the technicalities, of which there were many, and much of the paper work. Other matters, it appeared, were too important to be entrusted to duly constituted, formal gatherings.

The American ambassador in Tokyo reported considerable Japanese interest in the conference. All of the speeches at the opening session were re-ported in full by the press. Before the dissolution of the Diet, the opposition made an unsuccessful attempt to force the government to state that the 10:10:7 ratio was essential to Japan's security. Disagreement over the ratio existed with-in the inner circles of the Tokyo government, where some statesmen claimed that acceptance of the lower ratio would lead the conference to a successful conclusion and enhance Japan's world prestige.[34] Castle believed that the demand for a higher ratio stemmed from Japan's concept of great naval battles such as Tsushima and Jutland, in which it appeared that a 10:7 superiority in ships would virtually assure victory. The United States was regarded as the likely antagonist in a conflict over China.[35]

The French press was elated over the early developments. France had been placed in a subordinate position at the Washington Conference. At London, Tardieu was successful in securing a position of equality with the greater naval powers.[36] But newspapers attacked the method of limitation by categories, which, they contended, was meaningless in view of the tech-nological advances being made in ships and weapons. The American dele-gation was blamed for delaying the conference by its insistence on imprac-ticable methods and particular types of ships.[37]

Early reports in the Italian press consisted of moderate and factual ac-counts submitted by the correspondents attending the conference. Then, on January 30, the Rome *Tevere* published an editorial claiming that the con-ference was confused, that France was trying to destroy it, that Grandi had frustrated Tardieu's attempts to humiliate Italy, and that MacDonald feared the conference would fail and bring about the downfall of his government. The French transactional proposal was ridiculed, and the Italian newspapers asserted that principles such as ratios and maximum tonnage must be de-termined before methods could be discussed.[38]

IV

During the early days of the conference, the American delegation was engaged in the formulation of a plan for presentation to the other nations. On January 26 a tentative proposal, which had been prepared without con-sulting the naval advisers, was circulated within the delegation. The experts raised strong objections to a proposed reduction in the number of 8-inch–gun cruisers, but Admiral Pratt stated that Senator Reed was merely interested in having the naval officers put the ideas into "proper language."[39] Appar-ently, the American delegation accepted the General Board recommenda-tions of September 11, 1929, as the basis for America's naval requirements until February 3, 1930. On that date, Stimson, Adams, Reed, and Morrow met with MacDonald and Henderson to discuss parity in cruisers. The two leaders agreed on the impossibility of finding a "scientific" yardstick, and

MacDonald refused to discuss equivalents in terms of 8-inch- and 6-inch-gun cruisers. He insisted that the Admiralty would never consent to America's demand for twenty-one 8-inch-gun cruisers, but if the United States would accept fifteen of these ships MacDonald could concede almost any number of the 6-inch-gun vessels.[40] The American delegates may have decided to depart from the General Board figure after this meeting, but obviously some of the delegates had had a similar figure in mind before the Prime Minister's positive assertion of the Admiralty's position. He probably suggested fifteen cruisers for bargaining purposes, assuming, rightly, that the Americans would select a compromise figure.

The following day Stimson called a meeting of the delegates with Admiral Pratt and Admiral Jones. Stimson commented on the uselessness of the yardstick, and Jones replied that it could be effective only when applied to existing tonnage when ship characteristics were known. The cruiser question was then discussed in considerable detail, with the two admirals embracing opposite points of view. Pratt argued for eighteen 8-inch-gun cruisers and five additional 6-inch-gun ships. Jones insisted on the General Board figure of twenty-one of the more heavily armed vessels. At the conclusion of the discussion the delegates voted unanimously to accept the lower figure.[41]

The meeting of February 4 was in reality a mere formality. It was probably designed to assuage the feelings of Admiral Jones and some of the other naval experts and to forestall criticism at a later date. For several days the delegation had conducted hearings in which the naval advisers were asked to testify and answer questions.[42] The delegates pored over detailed analyses of the comparative values of the two types of ships, which had been prepared by the various navy bureaus and the technical experts accompanying the delegation. Ballistic figures to demonstrate the penetrating and explosive power of the respective shells, data on the effectiveness of the two guns at various ranges and under different conditions, cruising radius, armor, cost per ton, and seaworthiness—all were reported on and considered before a decision was reached.[43] The naval advisers could not agree among themselves, although the majority favored the heavier guns. According to Dawes, the delegates were also split, but the minority finally accepted the figure of eighteen 8-inch-gun cruisers because they believed that without it the conference would fail.[44]

The delegates were in a difficult position. They were forced to decide which of two alternatives presented by the naval experts should be adopted as the American program. They had been exposed to a mass of data and testimony that failed to establish unanimity among the experts, who had devoted their lives to these problems. Furthermore, the delegates were subject to pressures that the professionals could ignore. The latter made recommendations; the former made decisions. This responsibility was coupled with the repeated assertions that diplomats, not naval officers, were to dominate the conference. Compromise, the spirit of the Kellogg-Briand Pact, and success had all been emphasized by the President. Technical arguments were reduced almost to the point of absurdity by the realization that the formula for agreement was the figure of eighteen, not twenty-one.

The General Board gave its final word on battleships just before the delegation departed for London. In case a modification of the Washington Treaty was to be considered, the Board recommended a reduction in numbers whereby the ratio in ships would be 15:15:9. The United States would scrap three battleships, Great Britain five, and Japan one. But the post-war British battleships *Rodney* and *Nelson* made it "just, fair, and necessary," that the United States lay down two battleships and Japan one, to be completed in 1934, at which time the United States would scrap two and Japan one. The Board refused to consider a battleship "holiday" until parity with Britain had been obtained by eliminating the "handicap" of the *Rodney* and *Nelson*. A reduction in the size of battleships was not acceptable.[45] In order to illustrate the disparity, a hypothetical battle situation was conceived in which the *Rodney* and *Nelson* with two other British battleships were pitted against four of America's finest vessels. The two newer ships could sink all four of the American ships while the latter were eliminating two of the British.[46] The vaunted "backbone of the fleet" was not to be minimized or sacrificed in any negotiations if the professionals could help it.

Stimson, on the evening of February 4, submitted the new plan to Hoover for his consideration. The proposals had not been communicated to the British or the Japanese in detail, but conversations with the delegates of those nations had revealed that such a plan might be acceptable. Under its provisions the United States was allowed eighteen 8-inch–gun cruisers, Great Britain fifteen, and Japan twelve. Total cruiser tonnage would be 327,000, 339,000 and 198,655 respectively, with America and Britain having the option of duplicating the cruiser fleet of the other. As for destroyers, Britain and the United States were granted 200,000 tons each, and Japan 120,000 tons. Submarine tonnage was established at 60,000 for each of the Atlantic nations and 40,000 for their Pacific neighbor. Battleships were to be reduced immediately to a unit total of 15:15:9. No new battleships were to be laid down until 1936, except for one vessel to be built by the United States in order to compensate for the two modern British battleships. Stimson's message also mentioned replacements, aircraft carriers, and vessels exempt from control.[47]

Hoover "heartily approved" these recommendations the following day, and that evening Stimson presented the proposal to MacDonald, and Reed made it known to Wakatsuki.[48] Only details concerning capital ships were withheld, because the American delegation wanted first to determine the prospects for agreement in auxiliary vessels.[49] Messages were sent by Senator

Robinson to Senator Swanson and by Senator Reed to Senator Frederick Hale, chairman of the Naval Affairs Committee, explaining that insistence on twenty-one 8-inch–gun cruisers would make agreement impossible.[50]

The American proposal was a categorical denial of Japan's claim for a 10:10:7 ratio. The Japanese delegates were disappointed and their naval advisers were discouraged, for they believed that the proposal offered little hope of obtaining their demands. In Japan, the plan provoked an indignant reaction in naval circles, and the press was stirred to resentment.[51] Complaints ranged from the discourteous treatment of Japan by America's unwillingness to consider her needs, to the accusation of the Tokyo *Nichi Nichi* that Japan was being treated like a "peddler." An editorial in the Tokyo *Hochi* wryly suggested that England and the United States try to apply the Washington ratio to France and Italy, while the Tokyo *Jiji* observed that the Americans were motivated by the fear of Japan as a threat to their security.[52]

On February 6, Stimson learned that portions of the American proposal, which was supposed to remain confidential, had leaked to "hostile newspapers." After discussing the matter with MacDonald and Wakatsuki, he issued a statement to the press which consisted mainly of general information, although he did include the figures on proposed American and British cruiser strength. Stimson explained that no offer had been made to the French or the Italians, for their problems were not so directly related to those of the United States. The announcement was well received by the press in England and America. The Italian press welcomed the proposal as the first forward step that had been taken at the conference, a step that supported the Italian viewpoint of figures first and methods later.[53] The following day Stimson issued a notice to all members of the delegation, enjoining them to refrain from discussing any details of the proposal with correspondents or other unauthorized personnel.[54]

V

The British government outlined its position in a memorandum released February 7. Describing Britain's place in the world and the need of sea lanes for her existence, the paper asserted that disarmament was of vital importance in reducing competition, improving friendly relations with other countries, and lessening the chances for war. International agreements to reduce armament were necessary for world security. In regard to the current conference, Britain preferred limitation by categories, but she was willing to consider percentage transfer between types.

The memorandum proposed that fewer battleships be allowed, and that unit displacement be reduced from 35,000 to 25,000 tons. Gun caliber should be lowered from 16 inches to 12 inches, and age should be increased from twenty to twenty-six years. A plea was made for an agreement that would eventually eliminate the battleship, which was both expensive and "of doubtful utility." Aircraft carriers were to be limited in unit tonnage and in caliber of guns, and vessels of this category under 10,000 tons were to be included in the total tonnage assigned to that class.

As for cruisers, those mounting 8-inch guns could remain at a maximum displacement of 10,000 tons, but 6-inch–gun ships should be limited to 6,000 or 7,000 tons. The age of all cruisers was to be fixed at twenty years. The previous demand for fifty vessels totaling 339,000 tons would remain constant, provided that the size of units was satisfactory.

The size and total tonnage of destroyers would depend on the conclusion of an agreement restricting submarine warfare, but the British proposed that destroyer leaders be limited to 1,850 tons and that other vessels of this type be limited to 1,500 tons, both mounting guns with a maximum caliber of 5 inches. Britain desired a total of 200,000 tons in destroyers, but this figure could be reduced if the submarine programs of the other nations were pared.

Submarines, the memorandum asserted, should be abolished. If this was not possible, then their size and numbers should be restricted so that they could be employed only for defensive purposes, and attack on merchant vessels should be limited by treaty. Other auxiliary ships, not subject to limitation, should be specified, and each nation should publish figures annually to reveal the number of vessels built and under construction.[55]

A conference on February 11 between the British and American delegates convinced Stimson that an agreement between the two nations would be "easy" unless Japan and Italy introduced complications. He intended to stand fast on cruisers, but he was willing to withdraw the claim for a battleship replacement if Britain accepted the American demand for eighteen 8-inch–gun cruisers. Stimson continued to prevent a discussion of capital ships on the grounds that the question of auxiliaries should be settled before opening negotiations for changes in the Washington Treaty.[56]

The French government fell on February 17 because of a financial crisis, and the conference was adjourned to allow the French delegates to return to Paris and the other delegates to be relieved of pressure from journalists. Stimson took advantage of the delay to continue negotiations with the British. MacDonald had been attacked so vigorously in the press and by the opposition parties for accepting fifty cruisers that he warned he might have to increase his demands, and the British press reacted unfavorably to the American request for a new battleship. The Prime Minister was also plagued by the threat of New Zealand and Australia to build ships of their own if the ratio between British and Japanese ships should not be satisfactory.[57]

In spite of these obstacles, a tentative agreement was reached, contingent only on possible French demands. The figures were those of the American offer of February 4 with two exceptions: the request for a new battleship was dropped and there remained a question as to whether the American cruiser total would be 320,000 or 327,000 tons. The United States was authorized to modernize old battleships, and even Pratt and Jones were agreed that this modernization would constitute parity in capital ships. Both nations decided to delay pressing Japan for a settlement until after the forthcoming national elections in that country in the belief that concessions would be more likely after the vote.[58]

The cruiser dispute was resolved within a few days by splitting the difference at 323,500 tons. The figures for destroyers and submarines were to depend on the demands of Japan and France, but both Britain and the United States agreed to try and reduce these categories from the totals prescribed in Stimson's proposal of February 4. The American delegation unanimously approved the tentative agreement.[59] The harassed MacDonald may have been encouraged to compromise by the criticism of segments of the British press, which belabored him on the one hand for sacrificing Empire security and on the other for failing to bring about agreement on armaments.[60]

Stimson proudly claimed that one of the major objectives of the Hoover administration had been realized, namely, the elimination of friction between the United States and Great Britain over the cruiser issue.[61] This controversy had clouded Anglo-American relations since the abortive Geneva Conference in 1927, and its removal was a significant accomplishment. A more sobering thought, which must have occurred to Hoover and his envoys, was how little actual progress this tentative agreement represented in terms of disarmament. The conference had been in session for more than a month. During that time a contingent settlement had been reached between two nations which had begun negotiations six months earlier, and between whom all but minor differences had been resolved. The measure of success was qualified by the magnitude of the task that remained. Noteworthy, too, was the fact that the crucial concession was made by the United States in accepting eighteen 8-inch–gun cruisers instead of the twenty-one that had been considered a minimum requirement. The irony of the situation was apparent to those who recalled that MacDonald had suggested the lower figure in a letter to Dawes on August 30, 1929.

The subject of freedom of the seas was not introduced at the conference. A White Paper issued by the British government in defense of signing the optional clause of the World Court statutes claimed that Britain was not abandoning her historic position on this question because in the next war there would be no neutral nations.[62] As the London Conference opened, a high-ranking British naval officer warned that an agreement on freedom of the seas would mean the "destruction of this country."[63] The American and British delegates agreed that the question should not be raised at London. MacDonald explained in the House of Commons that the conference was not the place for a discussion of this problem, and that there was sufficient subject matter without it.[64] Senator Reed pointed out that such negotiations would have delayed the settlement of naval limitation.[65] The outcome of the Hoover-MacDonald conversation on rights and immunities at sea during war was still fresh in the minds of the statesmen.

Chapter VII

Japanese-American Compromise

The London Conference has at least succeeded in reducing
its aims.   —*Publisher's Syndicate*, March, 1930.

I

Efforts to reach agreement on a modification of the Washington Treaty provisions concerning aircraft carriers were to prove more time-consuming. The General Board had concluded that lowering the total carrier tonnage would be a greater disadvantage to America than to any other nation, since she would conduct a naval war farther from her home bases than would either of the other four naval powers.[1] MacDonald proposed that the Washington Treaty figure of 135,000 tons of aircraft carriers for the United States and Great Britain be reduced to 100,000 tons, provided that the other nations retained the previous ratios. Stimson objected to a reduction on the grounds that so much American tonnage was "frozen up" in two 33,000-ton ships.[2] Rear Admiral W. A. Moffett, the American naval air expert, was willing to approve a reduction in carrier size from a maximum of 27,000 tons to 25,000. He was not willing to increase the scrappable age from twenty to twenty-six years, because the United States was handicapped in the number of carriers by possessing the two huge converted battle cruisers. He applied the same objection to the proposal to reduce total tonnage from 135,000 to 100,000 tons. The United States, he asserted, needed ten carriers. Under the higher figure only seven were possible, while Britain could have nine. At 100,000 tons Britain could possess six and the United States four.[3] When the Japanese delegates refused to accede to the British suggestion for a reduction in total carrier tonnage, the matter was deferred pending the solution of other problems.[4]

One might assume that aircraft carriers should have been the subject of more controversy than cruisers. That they were not indicates that the role of aircraft in sea power was not fully understood or agreed upon. The highly publicized experiments of the Army Air Force in the aerial bombing of warships had failed to convince the partisan services of the decisive nature of air power.[5] New methods of warfare are traditionally slow of adoption, and, as an official historian points out, "The seven years between 1926 and 1934 would see carrier aviation revolutionize Fleet concepts of naval warfare."[6] The translation of technical and tactical innovation into practice, policy, and politics was to proceed even more slowly.

The delegates also may have reasoned that limitations had been imposed

76

by the Washington Conference, and that efforts should be concentrated on categories which lacked controls. At London the ratios and tonnage of these vessels were not changed, but the installation of flying decks on existing capital ships was prohibited, and their installation on cruisers was restricted to 25 percent of the total tonnage of that category.[7] Aircraft on these vessels were to be few, and were to be employed for scouting and spotting purposes. In addition, the construction of carriers displacing less than 10,000 tons was prohibited.

Negotiations with Japan were complex, difficult, and exasperating. Soon after the conference began, Senator Reed was designated to represent the American delegation in conversations with the Japanese envoys.[8] Stimson and his colleagues considered the Japanese proposals "extreme," and Dawes argued that the introduction of the battleship into the American proposal for bargaining purposes was a mistake because it had encouraged other nations to adopt similar tactics.[9] The Americans felt that Japan was not justified in asking for an increase in the cruiser ratio, but Stimson was willing to consider a compromise in the submarine category. The Japanese delegates were to be notified that an increase in the 8-inch–gun ratio was not possible, and that no modification of the Washington Treaty would be made unless a prior agreement was reached on auxiliary vessels.[10]

The delicacy of the negotiations was aggravated by a dispute between the Japanese civilian delegates and their experts over the relative fighting strength of the two types of cruisers and the number of each that a fleet should possess in order to be most effective.[11] Some Japanese authorities regretted that the higher ratio had been submitted so categorically, for now the public was convinced that it was necessary for Japan's security and it had become an important political issue in the pending election. The Japanese Foreign Minister, Baron Shidehara, explained that Japan did not contemplate a war with the United States, for even the larger ratio would not permit an attack on the Philippine Islands or on the American mainland, but in the event of a conflict it would give the Japanese navy a "sporting chance" in the western Pacific. France had urged Japan to join her in opposing a compromise on submarines, but Shidehara declined because he felt that it would divide the conference into opposing groups.[12]

On January 29, the army adviser to the American delegation, Lieutenant Colonel Charles Burnett, in a conversation with Ambassador Matsudaira, brought up the question of a possible amendment to the existing Immigration Act. Matsuidaira said he hoped that it could be passed, for he thought that the exclusion policy would prevent any "real friendship" between the two nations. In the course of the discussion, Burnett implied that a successful agreement on naval limitation might have a beneficial effect on the immigration issue.[13] Two weeks later Stimson wrote Hoover that the Japanese had suggested "indirectly" that they would be satisfied with the establishment of a quota system which included a prohibition against Japanese labor. Senators Reed and Robinson were of the opinion that such an amendment would pass the Senate so long as it was not part of the naval treaty. Stimson did not consider the proposal "politically feasible," but he thought that it would contribute more to a solution of the problem of American-Japanese relations than anything else. Stimson carefully explained that the matter was not being discussed at London, and that he was mentioning it to the President only for the latter's consideration.[14]

The brief evidence here available indicates that an American, not a Japanese, had broached the subject. Burnett had served in Japan and was well known to many of the Japanese statesmen. He may have been selected to sound out the Japanese delegates through Matsudaira, or he may have done so on his own initiative. There is no evidence that the Japanese envoys proposed a modification of the immigration law in exchange for an agreement on naval limitation, nor is there any reason for believing that such a *quid pro quo* would have succeeded. Hoover, no doubt, would have rejected it, and Congress certainly could not have been bound by it. Such an understanding could not be kept secret and its disclosure would have destroyed any prospects for American acceptance of either the quota or the treaty. The impracticability of the suggestion must have been apparent to the President, for there was no encouragement from Washington.

II

At a meeting on February 17 of the American, British, and Japanese delegates, Senator Reed complained about Japan's insistence on a ratio of 8-inch–gun ships based on the larger American figure rather than the lesser number allotted to Great Britain. Wakatsuki replied that, although Japan was not expecting war with the United States, there were only two nations on the borders of the Pacific, and it was only natural that Japan should compare her fleet with that of the United States. A 60 percent ratio had been accepted for capital ships on the condition that fortifications in the Pacific would not be augmented. At the present conference there was no basis for accepting a figure lower than 70 percent of America's most powerful cruisers, and Japan could not agree to a lower figure. Reed argued that the American fleet was dispersed in the Atlantic and the Caribbean, as well as in the Pacific. He contended that the American people would be disturbed by Japan's insistence on strengthening her fleet, and that the Senate probably would not ratify such a treaty. Wakatsuki retorted that the Japanese people could not understand why the higher ratio was refused if the United States had no hostile intentions. Japan, he repeated, could accept no other figure. Henderson disavowed responsibility by observing that the British delegates were merely spectators. The meeting ended in a friendly atmosphere but with no settlement.[15]

Behind the stated imperative of the ratio, the Japanese envoys were carefully nurturing a movement for the neutralization of the Philippine Islands. A mutual covenant was envisioned, whereby the United States would agree not to use the Philippines as a base against Japan in exchange for a commitment not to attack the islands. While Stimson acknowledged the impropriety and impracticability of the suggestion under the circumstances, he was aware of the inherent danger in the situation for both nations.[16] Among Army authorities, a conviction had been developing that the islands could not be defended and actually constituted a military liability.[17] The Navy, on the other hand, thought in terms of an offensive war in which the fleet would engage the Japanese forces in the western Pacific. From the standpoint of logistics the Philippines and Guam were of the utmost importance, as both nations realized. The pattern at Washington eight years earlier was not to be repeated, for concessions at London were confined to ships.

The British Foreign Secretary's blithe assertion of neutrality during the Japanese-American conversations must have been as transparently false to the negotiators as it was to Henderson. In many respects the British were more concerned about the cruiser ratio with Japan than was the United States. MacDonald had made this quite clear in his earlier exchanges with Dawes, and the American agreement with Great Britain was contingent on a satisfactory settlement with Japan. No doubt an effort was still being made to avoid the appearance of concerted action against the Japanese program, but under the circumstances the United States ostensibly assumed not only the responsibility for conducting the negotiations but any blame for recalcitrance as well.

The election in Japan on February 20 that Stimson claimed had delayed negotiations resulted in a clear victory for the government, which was now expected to move decisively in the prosecution of its domestic and foreign policies. Reed and Matsudaira now met frequently and informally in a determined effort to break the deadlock. As a concession to Japan, Reed suggested staggering the construction of America's 8-inch–gun cruisers in order to keep the ratio lower until the expiration of the treaty in 1936. At this point Japan introduced a new complication by demanding 105,000 tons of destroyers as against 150,000 each for the United States and Great Britain. The American delegation thought that Japan should receive a maximum of 90,000 tons. Stimson expressed annoyance at the attitude of the Japanese delegates, who, he complained, held "stubbornly" to a position which the United States could not accept.[18]

Hoover indicated his consent to an agreement granting Japan a 70 percent ratio in 8-inch–gun cruisers so long as she would possess a 60 percent ratio when the treaty expired, provided that she accept 52,000 tons of submarines, 70,000 tons of destroyers, and a satisfactory ratio in 6-inch–gun cruisers. The difference between the two navies, the President believed, would be sufficient to ensure America's control of the Pacific in the event of trouble.[19] As a desperate but unsuccessful measure, the American delegates warned the Japanese that a refusal to accept a lower ratio in 8-inch–gun cruisers and a reduction in submarine tonnage would lead to a cancellation of the non-fortification agreement at the expiration of the Washington Treaty.[20] Threats were beginning to replace concessions as the conference dragged on.

In Japan, Foreign Minister Shidehara confided to Castle that he, personally, was in favor of accepting the American offer, but he was afraid of navy opposition. Castle cautioned the American delegation against any discussion of fortifications because it would be regarded by the Japanese as a threat, which would jeopardize disarmament negotiations and endanger peace in the Pacific.[21] Kikujiro Ishii, a distinguished Japanese statesman who had headed his country's delegation to the Geneva conference in 1927, complained that the opposition of America and Britain to Japan's claim for a higher ratio was a denial of the Kellogg-Briand Pact. In his opinion, the refusal to allow Japan sufficient naval armament for her defense implied that the United States and Great Britain visualized a conflict that would result in Japan's defeat.[22] This Japanese protest was partially echoed by the San Francisco *Union*, which asserted that "the Kellogg treaty is such a perfect guarantee against war that the Powers are about to decide that they can get along with just a few more war-ships than they had when they signed it."[23] Neither nation had a monopoly on cynicism and disillusionment.

III

Within a few days Stimson was able to report definite progress in the negotiations. The existing strength of the Japanese navy in large-caliber cruisers would be in excess of 70 percent, while the treaty was in effect, because of the contemplated staggering of the American building program. Only 20,000 tons remained to be allocated. The United States wanted Japan to retain this amount in overage cruisers, with no provision for replacement, in order to satisfy public demand for a 70 percent ratio. The Japanese delegation asked that this tonnage be spread over other ship categories, a suggestion which the American delegates were not willing to accept because of objections from the Navy, the British Admiralty, and the Dominions. Unless Japan conceded this point agreement appeared unlikely.[24]

The Japanese delegates, probably in an effort to quell dissension in their own delegation, continued to make offers which they knew the American envoys could not accept.[25] On March 12 Stimson was ready to make preparations for a two-power treaty with Great Britain. He was apprehensive that

MacDonald might be removed from office, and he thought that announcement of the treaty would be a good "tactical maneuver" to counteract the delays caused by the French and Japanese. Also, the American delegates feared that Japan was exploiting her position as the key to a three-power pact in order to gain further concessions. France, it appeared, was urging Japan to remain firm on the submarine issue.[26] The following day, MacDonald and Stimson decided to go ahead with the treaty unless Japan accepted the American position. Parity was to be established in auxiliary vessels and competitive building between the two nations would cease. The Washington Treaty was not to be modified unless Japan joined in an agreement covering all categories.[27] Hoover reluctantly acknowledged that a two-power treaty was better than no treaty. But he greatly preferred a three-power pact, and he was willing to make some concession to obtain Japanese participation, even at a later date.[28]

Within hours of the decision to proceed with a two-power treaty, agreement was reached with Japan. Wakatsuki and the majority of his delegates accepted the following figures: 8-inch–gun ships, 108,400 tons; 6-inch–gun ships, 100,450 tons; destroyers, 105,500 tons; and submarines, 52,700 tons. The settlement gave Japan a 60 percent ratio in 8-inch–gun cruisers, 70 percent in 6-inch, 70 percent in destroyers, and parity in submarines. In addition, Japan reserved the right to demand at the expiration of the treaty that she be allowed to replace her lighter 8-inch–gun cruisers (the *Furutaka* class) with 10,000-ton ships in 1943. The United States, in turn, reserved the right to contest the claim. By this agreement Japan was restricted to the larger-caliber cruisers which she possessed or was building; she was allowed only 2,000 tons of additional 6-inch–gun ships; her destroyers were reduced by 17,000 tons; and her submarines were reduced to the tonnage that she would reach by 1936 through scrapping overage vessels. Hoover cabled his approval of the settlement.[29]

According to Wakatsuki, the Japanese envoys reluctantly accepted a compromise rather than assume responsibility for the failure of the conference.[30] Admiral Takarabe, delegate and Minister of Marine, and the Japanese naval advisers objected to the terms of the compromise, but the Admiral signed the telegram to Tokyo recommending the settlement because he was unwilling to be held accountable for the delegation's returning to Japan without a treaty.[31]

After a week had passed with no reply from Tokyo, the American delegates became uneasy. Secretary of the Navy Adams notified Rear Admiral Pringle and Captain Smyth that Japan might demand further concessions. He expressed the hope that the American experts would support the delegation in opposing any change. The two officers voiced their ignorance of the terms of the settlement, but Adams gave them no details.[32] Two days later, at a meeting of all the naval officers, Rear Admiral Arthur J. Hepburn told Admiral Pratt of the conversation and asked if he knew and would tell the terms of the agreement. Pratt replied that he had been kept informed but had been asked to remain silent. Reed and Stimson, he volunteered, were the only delegates familiar with the details. The talks were begun by Reed and Matsudaira, but Stimson later took charge and was responsible for the suggestion of a delay in the construction of three of the American 8-inch–gun cruisers. Pratt had been advised regularly and had approved of each step. His main reason for doing so was that he doubted if Congress would furnish the money for the kind of program that the Navy wanted. On March 31, Adams asked each officer if Japan could be given any more concessions. All agreed that no more concessions were possible, and some thought that too many had already been made.[33]

Stimson was probably wise in not letting the naval experts know what was being offered. The terms of the settlement were much closer to the original demands of the Japanese than they were to the first American proposals. Japan was given her 70 percent ratio in 6-inch–gun cruisers and destroyers. She was granted equality in submarines. The figure of 60 percent that Japan accepted in 8-inch–gun cruisers would not be achieved until after the treaty expired. During the life of the treaty Japan would have more than a 70 percent ratio of the more heavily armed vessels because of the postponed American construction program. A wag might have commented that if Stimson had been any more successful the United States would have had no building program at all.

IV

Although the Japanese delegates had accomplished more than might reasonably have been expected under conference conditions, the authorities in Tokyo encountered numerous obstacles in securing approval for the agreement. The propaganda campaign begun by the navy party before the conference started had been very effective in persuading the public that America was a potential enemy and that a higher ratio in ships was of the utmost importance.[34] The chief of the Japanese Naval Staff, Admiral Kato, complained that the plan "is just like offering us the crumbs and telling us to eat them."[35] The Admiral told Prime Minister Hamaguchi that the low ratio in large-caliber cruisers and the prohibition of new submarine construction before 1936 made the proposal unacceptable. He thought that Japan should be given parity in all categories, but since she had asked for only a 70 percent ratio the concessions should be made by the United States.[36] Tokyo newspapers opposing the compromise referred to it as the "American proposal," and Stimson strongly objected to the unfairness of the term because the settlement exceeded any offer made by the American delegation.[37]

Premier Hamaguchi finally broke the deadlock by declaring that the agreement had to be accepted from the standpoint of the nation's foreign policy, even though the naval authorities considered it unsatisfactory as a defense measure. In spite of a personal appeal to the Emperor by Admiral Kato, the government approved the compromise.[38] The Japanese reply was presented to the American and British delegations on April 2. A week later all details had been settled and a three-power treaty, at least, had become a reality.[39]

The achievement of an equilibrium in naval power between the United States and Japan was both complicated and simplified by the domestic and foreign problems of the two nations. In Japan, the parliamentary political parties were in control of the government, but a series of diplomatic misfortunes, from the frustrations of the Versailles Treaty through the unsuccessful Shantung venture of 1927-1929, gave added weight to the machinations of nationalist and military groups for a more adamant and less cooperative foreign policy. In the United States, Hoover may have been viewing Japan as a factor for peace in the Far East. Just as Theodore Roosevelt, three decades earlier, had regarded Japan as a stabilizing force against the imperialism of Czarist Russia, so might Hoover have looked on Japan as a bulwark against Communist aggression. After all, Japan had signed a treaty which acknowledged the territorial integrity of China, and she had given every indication of fulfilling her international obligations. Russia had not, and the actions and ideology of her government posed a threat to the status quo. Concessions to Japan in the field of naval armament were probably the most effective contribution that the President could make toward the containment of a nation dedicated to world revolution.[40]

Chapter VIII

London—the Issue Resolved

We sit till we settle.—Secretary of the Navy Charles Francis Adams, March 1930.

I

While the representatives of the United States, Great Britain, and Japan debated the question of comparative naval strength, the conference continued its regular deliberations in an effort to solve the problems common to all five nations. The fourth plenary session met on February 11 in order to allow each delegation to present its views on submarines. Alexander, in presenting Britain's case, argued that the undersea craft should be abolished:

(1) In the general interests of humanity.
(2) In consideration of our view that these vessels are primarily offensive instruments.
(3) In order to secure a more substantial contribution to disarmament and peace.
(4) In view of the very important financial relief to be obtained.
(5) In consideration of the conditions of service of the personnel and the undue risks which can be abolished.

In the event abolition should fail, Britain would attempt to limit submarines in size and numbers in order to restrict their use as offensive weapons. She would also suggest an agreement to regulate the attack of submarines on merchant vessels.[1]

Stimson made a strong appeal for the abolition of submarines. He pointed out that ton for ton the submarine was the most expensive warship. It was "a weapon particularly susceptible to abuse," and the record showed that such abuse had brought the United States into World War I. The elimination of these ships would help to prevent involvement in future conflicts.[2]

In opposition, the French delegate defended the undersea vessels on the basis that:

(1) The submarine is a warship like the others.
(2) The submarine is a defensive weapon which all naval powers cannot do without.
(3) The use of the submarine should be, and can be, regulated like that of any other warship.

Developing each of these points at some length, he concluded by declaring that while France could not accept the abolition of the submarine, she was willing to enter into an international agreement to regulate its use.[3]

The Italian position was presented by Grandi. The submarine, he said, was "the weapon of the less against the more powerfully armed," and its abolition would favor the stronger naval powers. But Italy was willing to sign an agreement regulating its use, and she was not against its elimination as a matter of principle. If all the other nations agreed to the abolition of the submarine, and such an agreement promised to "exert a decisive influence" on disarmament, then Italy would be willing to accept it.[4]

Takarabe concurred in condemning the more deplorable aspects of submarine warfare, but he regarded the submarine as merely another weapon that could provide Japan with a less expensive defense. The Japanese delegation was willing to subscribe to a treaty that limited the activities of these vessels in time of war.[5]

France and the United States submitted two resolutions proposing a study of the submarine problem, and these were turned over to the First Committee for consideration and the preparation of a report.[6] The First Committee referred the resolutions to the Committee of Experts, which divided them into three parts:

Part   I. The question of the abolition of the submarine.
Part   II. The legal aspect of submarine warfare.
Part III. The question of the limitation of the unit size of the submarine.[7]

Part I was returned to the First Committee as a policy matter outside the jurisdiction of the Committee of Experts.[8] The First Committee was unable to reach agreement on the question of the abolition of the submarine, and the conference ended with the issue not resolved. Part II was referred to a Committee of Jurists.[9]

The Committee of Experts failed to agree on the unit size of submarines and the gun caliber. The United States and Great Britain favored 1,800 tons as the maximum displacement, but Japan insisted on 2,000 tons because of the heavy seas surrounding the Japanese islands. The French delegates wanted to establish two classes of submarines: one having a limit of 1,800 or 2,000 tons, the other a limit of 3,000 tons. France professed a need for the larger vessels to protect the lines of communication with her colonies, a task that could be performed only by a ship with a large cruising radius and suitable living conditions for the hot climate in which it would be operating. The problem was referred back to the First Committee for solution.[10]

The French representatives were also responsible for disagreement on the size of guns. The 5-inch–caliber limitation was accepted by all the other members of the committee. France believed that 6-inch (155 mm.) guns should be allowed, since that was the minimum cruiser authorization and a submarine operating alone should be able to protect itself in the event it was unable to submerge. This question was also referred to the First Committee.[11]

The First Committee reached a compromise on the size of submarines whereby the maximum-unit displacement was set at 2,000 tons, but each of the nations represented at the conference was permitted to maintain three submarines not to exceed 2,800 tons. An exception was made in the case of an existing French submarine displacing 2,880 tons.[12] The maximum caliber of guns was set at 5.1 inches (130 mm.), except for the larger submarines, which could mount 6.1-inch (155 mm.) guns. France was allowed to retain 8-inch (203 mm.) guns on her oversized 2,880-ton vessel.[13]

The drafting of a declaration to impose restrictions on submarine warfare was both simplified and complicated by previous efforts to solve the problem. A treaty for this purpose signed at the Washington Conference had been ratified by all the nations except France. Conversations at London revealed that France would not accept a treaty which provided for the trial and punishment of anyone who violated the established regulations, or which prohibited submarines from destroying the commerce of signatories to the treaty.[14] Stimson asked for opinions on an agreement from the State Department and from Elihu Root and John Bassett Moore, the latter an authority on international law and a former counselor of the State Department.[15] As the discussion at London continued, the Washington authorities contributed to compromise by conceding that the inclusion of articles concerning punishment and exemption from submarine attack was not especially significant in an agreement to regulate the use of undersea craft.[16]

On March 19, Stimson submitted for consideration a British revision that seemed to meet the French objections to portions of the Washington Treaty.[17] This British version was, with minor word changes, adopted by the Committee of Jurists and eventually approved in formal session. The declaration stated:

The following are accepted as established rules of international law:

(1) In their action with regard to merchant ships, submarines must conform to the Rules of International Law to which surface war vessels are subject.

(2) In particular, except in the case of persistent refusal to stop on being duly summoned, or of active resistance to visit or search, a warship, whether surface vessel or submarine, may not sink or render incapable of navigation a merchant vessel without having first placed the passengers, crew, and ship's papers in a place of safety. For this purpose the ship's boats are not regarded as a place of safety unless the safety of the passengers and crew is assured, in the existing sea and weather conditions, by the proximity of land, or the presence of another vessel which is in a position to take them on board.[18]

Thus the British and American desire to impose limitations on submarine warfare was accomplished, and French objections were overcome by the elimination of offensive clauses.

II

Destroyers were limited to 1,850 tons displacement, but this maximum was to apply to "flotilla leaders" that were not to exceed 16 percent of the total destroyer tonnage. The remaining tonnage was to be utilized in the construction of ships having a maximum displacement of 1,500 tons. Guns of a maximum caliber of five inches were permitted on craft of this type.[19]

The question of ships that were to be exempt from limitation caused a considerable amount of dissension. Purpose, size, speed, armament, and protection were the major characteristics that entered into the discussions. The Committee of Experts finally settled on two categories of vessels that would not be subject to limitation. "Exempt vessels" were those which conformed to certain specified restrictions as to displacement, speed, armament, protection, and purpose.[20] "Special vessels" were those possessed by the various nations which did not come within the regular categories of combat vessels or the stipulations regarding exempt vessels.[21]

The French delegates wanted the tonnage of the "special vessels" to be included in the total tonnage allocated to each nation. The other delegates wanted it to be separate, and the matter was finally referred to the First Committee without recommendation.[22] Here it was agreed that special vessels would not be included in the total tonnage, but any replacements of the existing vessels in this classification would be charged against one of the combatant categories unless it met the restrictions of the "exempt" class.[23] The tonnage of the special vessels agreed to by the Committee of Experts amounted to: Great Britain, 49,561 tons; United States, 91,496 tons; Japan, 80,660 tons; France, 28,644 tons; Italy, 11,960 tons. This ingenious compromise, whereby the proponents of each solution found a degree of satisfaction, encompassed minelayers, destroyer tenders, submarine tenders, seaplane tenders, monitors, gunboats, despatch vessels, and even old cruisers.[24]

Rules for the disposal of warships were adopted by the First Committee on April 12. The regulations were compiled under five headings:

(i) by scrapping (sinking or breaking up);
(ii) by converting the vessel to a hulk;
(iii) by converting the vessel to target use exclusively;
(iv) by retaining the vessel exclusively for experimental purposes;
(v) by retaining the vessel exclusively for training purposes.[25]

Regulations for the age and replacement of vessels were established and agreed to by the First Committee on April 12, and provided:

(a) For a surface vessel exceeding 3,000 tons but not exceeding 10,000 tons standard displacement.
(i) If laid down prior to 1st January, 1920—16 years
(ii) If laid down after 1st January, 1920—20 years

(b) For a surface vessel not exceeding 3,000 tons standard displacement.
   (i) If laid down prior to 1st January, 1921—12 years
   (ii) If laid down after 1st January, 1921—16 years
(c) For submarines—13 years.

The contracting parties were required to notify the other nations when a vessel was laid down and also furnish other details concerning each new ship.[26]

Nothing was said about inspection or surveillance to insure compliance with the restrictions of the treaty. In fact, the subject was not even discussed at London. The observance of solemn agreements between sovereign nations rested on the honor and good faith of the signatories.

III

France had come to the conference with a set of demands that made naval disarmament almost incidental. The enthusiasm with which the press, the politicians, and the people had greeted the memorandum of December 20 promised little in the way of concession from Tardieu and his fellow-delegates. The French naval requirements were set forth in a statement on February 12. Reaffirming the principle of interdependence of armaments, it pointed out that the French fleet was smaller than it had been in 1914, and reminded the other delegations that France had not built 70,000 tons of battleships allowed her under the Washington Treaty. Her requirements in auxiliary craft were:

8-inch–gun cruisers	100,000 tons
Old cruisers having guns of over 6.1 inches (155 mm.)	24,850 tons
Cruisers or destroyers having guns of less than 6.1 inches	258,597 tons
Submarines	99,629 tons
Total tonnage	483,076[27]

A press release the following day contained the foregoing figures and an offer to "examine favorably" any plan for a security pact that would make France's demands relative to the needs of others.[28]

Actually, all of France's requirements were set within the framework of security. The military alliance of 1919 with Great Britain and the United States died of inaction in the Senate. In 1924 the Geneva Protocol for the Pacific Settlement of International Disputes was formulated with the aid of Arthur Henderson and his Labour party colleagues, but it was rejected by a British Conservative government the following year.[29] The Locarno Pact, or Treaty of Mutual Guarantee, was concluded in 1925. It was the British Conservative answer to the French demand for security, and Britain's commitments were less specific and less comprehensive than they were under the unsuccessful Geneva Protocol. France was dissatisfied with the vagueness

88

of Britain's obligations in the Locarno Pact. She was also disappointed with the Kellogg-Briand Pact, which provided no machinery for the solution of disputes or any means of censuring or punishing an aggressor nation. The negotiations with France at the London Naval Conference were to revolve about her quest for security and her contention that political guarantees were a necessary prelude to disarmament.

The French figures announced on February 12 were objected to by the British delegation as being too high. Neither the public nor Parliament, it was protested, would support an agreement that provided for scrapping British ships and, at the same time, enlarging the French fleet. But Briand argued that a larger fleet was demanded by the people and the government, who were disturbed by the new German "pocket-battleships," which combined the speed and displacement of a cruiser with the fire power of a capital ship.[30] One French delegate privately admitted, however, that the increase was dictated more by a fear of Italy, whose actions under Mussolini made her more of a threat than Germany.[31] MacDonald and Henderson thought that France should formulate her needs in the light of the security offered by the Covenant of the League of Nations, the Locarno treaties, and the Kellogg-Briand Pact. Also, the British statesmen contended, since Italy demanded parity with France, a large French navy would give rise to a large Italian fleet. Britain would then have to raise her own requirements because of her espousal of the two-power standard, whereby she maintained a fleet equal to the next two strongest navies in Europe.[32] The American delegates avoided entering the controversy, though they believed that France was justified in asking for a ratio in auxiliary vessels higher than the 1.67 figure of the Washington Treaty.[33] Actually, of course, the United States was vitally interested, because a settlement resulting in an increase in Britain's figures would upset Anglo-American negotiations.

The French government fell on February 17 over a financial issue and the conference was adjourned. Tardieu soon returned to power and appointed a new delegation which arrived in London on March 6. Briand retained his position as Foreign Minister and member of the delegation.

The American delegates, the London correspondent of the New York *Times* reported, had been careful to avoid giving the impression that the United States would participate in any political pact to reduce armaments by giving assurances of security.[34] By the middle of February the French authorities were circulating the information that Tardieu would agree to a 10 percent cut in his naval demands in exchange for a pact that provided for consultation in the event of war, and a 20 percent cut if other countries agreed not to supply an aggressor nation with munitions and supplies.[35]

When the French government fell, rumor circulated at London that the United States might be willing to consider an amendment to make the

Kellogg-Briand Pact more effective. America's participation in a consultative pact, the *Christian Science Monitor* predicted, would be the "key" to the success of the conference. The Washington *Post* warned that naval disarmament could not justify the nation's involvement in a guarantee of foreign territories. Such a proposal was similar to the commitment contained in Article X of the Covenant of the League of Nations, which, it claimed, had been rejected by the American people. In Washington, administration spokesmen were exercising "extreme caution" in discussing the question of security or consultative pacts in the negotiations at London.[36]

IV

With the high French demands and the fall of the French government, a feeling of pessimism swept over the conference. Tardieu explained privately to Stimson that the figures could be reduced, but by this time they had already provoked considerable resentment in the British press. Stimson was worried lest the French demands force MacDonald to raise his requirements to a figure that would make agreement with the United States impossible. Britain suggested a consultative pact, but France insisted on a security agreement. Briand spoke to Stimson about an amendment to the Kellogg-Briand Pact, but the American Secretary of State understood that it should be discussed apart from the naval conference. Stimson insisted that he had not encouraged anyone to believe that the United States would enter a consultative or security pact embracing the Mediterranean.[37]

Walter Edge, American ambassador to Paris, arrived in London on February 25 and reported that France was sincere in her efforts to reach agreement. In his opinion, she would first try to persuade Britain to join in a Mediterranean pact. If that failed, an attempt would be made to obtain America's assistance in amending the Kellogg-Briand Treaty.[38] On February 25 French delegate René Massigli delivered the draft of a suggested Mediterranean pact to the British Foreign Office. He was curtly informed that opinion among the delegates held that little purpose was served in giving France any further guarantees, since her excessive naval demands indicated that she paid little attention to those which she had obtained.[39] Hoover, concerned over French recalcitrance, suggested that the American delegation consider a three-power treaty with a clause providing for additional building in the event of naval competition from a nation not a party to the treaty.[40]

France was absolved from responsibility for conference delay by the Paris *Le Temps,* which blamed the inadequate preparations of America and Great Britain. The French press achieved virtual unanimity in insisting that France should not reduce her naval figures unless she received adequate security guarantees, and in accusing Italy of wanting parity solely for prestige.[41]

The French delegates were in a difficult position, and their plight stemmed from factors beyond their control. France had leaned heavily on England as a guarantor of European security during the 1920's, especially in regard to potentially dangerous and revisionist Germany. Yet the two nations were in basic disagreement over policy toward their recent enemy. France desired a weak nation incapable of threatening the peace. Britain, on the other hand, felt that prosperity at home and abroad was dependent on economic recovery in Germany. Thus the political safety pursued by France was jeopardized by the economic objectives of Britain. France also gained the impression that the British were engaged in a gradual withdrawal from their Continental commitments in favor of a *rapprochement* with the United States, and while a new threat had emerged in the Mediterranean, an Anglo-American attempt was being made to reduce France's naval requirements at the same time they were being forced upward by Italy.[42]

In Washington the administration was worried about the growth of a movement, encouraged by French propaganda and certain American correspondents, for a presidential statement of policies regarding the Kellogg-Briand Pact. Officials diagnosed the development as a French attempt to force Hoover to offer American political assurances for peace. In the event he refused to do so, France could blame him if the conference should fail. American "peace groups" urged that the nation join a security or consultative pact which might save the conference, and the increased publicity accorded the controversy had begun to intensify and divide public opinion.[43] Agitation for more effective disarmament was also carried on by the League for Independent Political Action, of which John Dewey was a member, and a student committee from twenty New York colleges and universities. Leaflets written by Dewey, Reinhold Niebuhr, and others were distributed.[44] Raymond B. Fosdick and James T. Shotwell were among the leaders of a group of prominent men and women which advocated American participation in an agreement to confer in the event of a dispute that might lead to war.[45]

Hoover was disturbed by repeated assertions that Stimson was in favor of the President's expanding the Kellogg-Briand Pact and that the delegation was split over the issue. Hoover assured the Secretary of State that he did not believe these reports, but he was apprehensive about their effect on public opinion. On his own part, he was not inclined to modify the pact in order to gain a reduction in the French demands. Furthermore, he asserted, his political opponents, both Democrats and "certain independent Republicans," would use for their advantage any declaration by him of an intent to expand the pact.[46]

The same day that Hoover conveyed his concern over a modification of the Kellogg-Briand Pact, Stimson cabled that agreement might become possible only through the conclusion of a political agreement which offered security. The Italian delegates refused to retreat from their position on parity with France, but they stated privately that they would accept less if a Mediterranean pact were concluded. MacDonald was willing to negotiate a consultative pact for the Mediterranean, but France declined on the grounds that it would add nothing to the Covenant of the League of Nations. Stimson notified both Great Britain and France that the United States would not participate in either a consultative or a security treaty, but privately he hinted that an amendment to the Kellogg-Briand Pact would not be too objectionable if Briand was willing to accept it as the basis for a reduction in his naval requirements. The Secretary of State forwarded a draft of a proposed naval armament treaty to Washington which contained a clause providing for consultation of the contracting nations in the event that a "change of circumstances" should affect the naval requirements of one of the parties.[47]

The President proposed certain changes to the draft in order to make it clear that the consultation would be solely for the purpose of discussing a change in naval programs. He was anxious to avoid any impression that the treaty was in the nature of a "Holy Alliance of the Allied and Associated naval powers." He indicated a willingness to discuss, independent of the naval treaty and if suggested by France, an agreement by "all nations" to investigate outstanding controversies. A pact to consider "coercive sanctions" or one restricted to the major naval powers was out of the question.[48]

The American delegates agreed with the President's attitude, which Stimson explained to MacDonald. The Prime Minister assured Stimson that Britain would not aid France's efforts to secure American commitments.[49] MacDonald, at this point, favored a Mediterranean pact similar to the Four-Power Treaty, "and possibly a little bit further," but a guarantee of military action was an impossibility. He and Stimson felt that an attempt to include sanctions in the Kellogg-Briand Treaty would force Britain and the United States out of the pact.[50] Hoover and Senators Borah and Swanson thought that ship concessions to both Japan and France were preferable to entering a political pact that provided for consultation or guarantees.[51] Senator George H. Moses of New Hampshire announced that he favored a consultative agreement, but outspoken opposition was voiced by Senators Borah, Swanson, Hiram W. Johnson of California, Simeon D. Fess of Ohio, and David I. Walsh of Massachusetts.[52]

On March 7 Briand mentioned an amendment to the Kellogg-Briand Pact to Stimson, who retorted that the treaty had nothing to do with naval disarmament.[53] The French Foreign Minister dropped the subject, but he revived it two days later with MacDonald and Henderson. Briand understood that Stimson believed a move to give France more security would be possible after a naval treaty had been ratified by the Senate. This position, in Briand's opinion, was not logical, for the United States could not be unconcerned about European affairs, and action prior to hostilities was certainly preferable to waiting until they occurred. MacDonald, after agreeing with Briand, went on to explain that the American attitude was determined by a "progressive element" in the Senate which would defeat a treaty that included a provision for a consultative arrangement. The Prime Minister expressed the hope that some statement in the preamble of the naval treaty which acknowledged an interest in the maintenance of world peace might be approved by the United States and give France the assurance that she required.[54] It would appear that MacDonald was ignoring his promise not to assist France in obtaining American commitments, but his mild solution offered nothing more tangible for Briand than the pact that carried his name.

The negotiations apparently had reached a dead end. Britain's agreement with the United States was contingent on a settlement with France, and the latter was unwilling to reduce her naval demands without a political guarantee of her security. The French position was disturbing in that it jeopardized the attainment of a five-power treaty. It was calamitous in threatening to prevent a three-power agreement and causing the conference to fail.

Chapter IX

A Treaty Emerges

You can't blame the French for asking for security. Look
what a mess Uncle Sam got in by lending money without it.
—Austin *American*, April 1930.

I

Speculation over efforts to satisfy the French demand for security reached
such proportions that Stimson wrote a long letter to the President explaining
the situation. His reason for not wanting to join in a consultative pact, he
pointed out, was not one of principle, for the United States had been and
was a party to this type of agreement. Stimson's objection in this particular
case rested on the assumption that if France reduced her naval requirements
in exchange for such a pact, she would expect aid from the United States in
the event of an emergency. Under the circumstances, MacDonald was con-
tinuing to explore the matter and the American delegates were endeavoring
to help him without exerting any pressure that might lead to a misunderstanding over obligations or responsibility. The Prime Minister was at odds
with his Foreign Office, for the latter, headed by Henderson, was willing to
participate in an agreement to provide France with broader guarantees.[1]

In an effort to clarify the situation, Stimson called a press conference on
March 11 and explained the reason for America's refusal to participate in a
consultative pact. The United States, he added, did not want to find itself
in a position similar to that in which Sir Edward Grey, the British Foreign
Minister, found himself in 1914. By a previous arrangement with France
which carried no commitments, Stimson explained, Grey had moved the
British Mediterranean fleet to the North Sea and the French had moved
their Channel fleet to the Mediterranean. With the German declaration of
war, France demanded that Britain protect her north coast because she had
shifted her forces to the Mediterranean as a result of the British concentration in the North Sea.[2] Stimson's example was most pertinent, for the war
plans of the French General Staff had been based on the support of the
British fleet, although the two nations had only agreed to consultations in
the event of a threat to peace.[3]

The response of the Paris press was mixed. The Paris correspondent of
the London *Times* reported that the announcement was received with "disappointment and regret," for it meant that the objectives of the conference
could not be realized.[4] The New York *Times* cited several Paris newspapers
to the effect that Briand had not been expected to gain acceptance of his

94

proposals at London; hence no one was disappointed that he had failed. France was now free to construct a fleet that would meet her needs.[5]

In the United States, Stimson's announcement that America had rejected the French scheme "gave relief to a good many Senators and joy to others."[6] An outspoken denunciation of the American decision was voiced by Raymond Leslie Buell, who ridiculed the idea that a consultative pact would constitute an "entangling alliance," and recalled that a similar concession at Washington in 1922 had made naval reduction possible.[7] The British press revealed overwhelming opposition to granting France additional promises of security, and newspapers speculated as to the next move of the French delegates.[8]

Opinion in Italy was changed from optimism to pessimism by the American attitude. The Italians had hoped to benefit from the conclusion of a consultative pact, for they had expected that it would enable France to grant them naval parity. As this possibility was eliminated, the Italian press resumed its attacks on the French position.[9]

II

The conference reached a low point during the days following the Stimson announcement. Briand complained that France could not reduce her requirements until she knew what Italy wanted. Grandi persistently refused to furnish figures and just as persistently reaffirmed Italy's claim for parity with France. Briand spoke pessimistically of a public opinion that could "throw the Government out in forty-eight hours" if the delegates relaxed in their demands.[10] MacDonald complained that the high French figures were a preparation for war, not peace, and that her program was designed to force an increase in world armament.[11] On March 16 Tardieu flatly stated that a reduction in French naval requirements would be possible only if a political pact were concluded which gave France additional security assurances. Since the United States could not be a party to such a pact, he placed full responsibility on Great Britain.[12]

The realities of the French position were discussed fully and frankly by Tardieu and Aubert in a series of conversations with Dwight Morrow. Uppermost in their minds was the uncertainty of British policy toward Europe, which had changed from a post World War offer of a military alliance to an apparent desire to escape League commitments. French fears of a British withdrawal from the Continent were heightened by the increased efforts toward Anglo-American co-operation. In the light of these more recent developments, it was imperative that the attitude of the United States toward European affairs be clarified. American participation in a consultative pact would demonstrate that she was not trying to pull England out of the European system, and it might encourage England to provide France with adequate assurances of security. As for Italy, France could never accept parity because her responsibilities extended beyond the Mediterranean to the North Sea and the Far East.[13]

The British press continued to give MacDonald little encouragement to satisfy the French demands. *Time and Tide* ridiculed the idea that political pacts should precede disarmament and spoke caustically of the willingness of an America separated from Europe by 3,000 miles of ocean to have Britain guarantee peace. The *Nation and Athenaeum* suggested that MacDonald consent to a consultative pact, provided that the United States be a partner, and the London *Daily Herald* averred that no British government would consider an agreement that committed Britain to military action in a war that she had no part in starting.[14] The *New Statesman* diagnosed the conference as "sick of the palsy,"[15] and the Italian press carried the analogy to its extreme by singing "dirges" over the parley, which it considered dead.[16]

But within a very short time the problem of consultation was to pump new life into the conference. The attitude of the American delegation had been made clear by Stimson's statement to the press, which Dawes believed had put an end to speculation about America's participation in a consultative pact.[17] Briand and Tardieu realized that such action was out of the question, Stimson reported on March 17, and it was "no longer an issue" at London.[18] Two days later the British Prime Minister dined with Briand as the latter was preparing to return to Paris. MacDonald came away convinced, as he told Stimson, that France was bent on becoming the foremost military power in Europe, capable of defeating both Germany and Italy; that events in Europe were heading toward such a conflict; and that France was intent on becoming the economic center of Europe.[19] Stimson may have assumed that MacDonald had become reconciled to a disarmament treaty without France, until, on the night of March 22, he received a telephone call from a highly excited Prime Minister, who had heard from the British ambassador in Paris that "the French had quit the conference."[20]

To Stimson, it seemed as though "we were on the brink of a precipice." The conference was in danger of collapsing in a bad frame of mind, and he resolved that every attempt should be made to eliminate any misunderstanding that could be preventing a settlement.[21] He immediately advised Hoover that certain circumstances might warrant American participation in a consultative pact, so long as sufficient safeguards were inserted to insure against misconceptions.[22] Then, without waiting for further word from Washington, Stimson arranged a meeting with MacDonald and Henderson, where he brought up the subject of pacts and insisted that it was time the discussion came out into the open. He reviewed the French attitude and the consultative clause in the Washington Four-Power Treaty, and pointed out the difficulty of measuring such a commitment in terms of ships and the implication of assistance in time of trouble. He then declared that if some other nation gave France the security that she demanded, the United States would be willing to consider a consultative pact.[23]

Hoover, meanwhile, had been disturbed by persistent reports that the American delegation was divided over the issue of a consultative pact and that the failure of the United States to support such a pact was disrupting the conference. Agitation reached the point where the administration was barely able to prevent the Foreign Policy Association from calling a meeting in New York to protest what some called America's isolationist policy. In a final effort to dispel the confusion, the President made a statement to the press, not to be attributed to him, denying that any of the nations participating in the conference had suggested that the United States join in a consultative pact. The other nations, he asserted, were aware that the United States could not enter an agreement that called for military assistance, and the consultative pacts mentioned by certain groups would not effect a reduction in naval armament.[24]

Stimson denied that the American delegates were responsible for the rumors, which he labeled "nonsense." But it did appear that MacDonald was modifying his position on a security pact, and Stimson assumed that in this new atmosphere the President would be willing to consider a consultative agreement if it were properly qualified.[25]

The Washington authorities now realized that the rumors were well founded, and Cotton, following a discussion with Hoover, cabled Stimson some observations on the subject of consultation. An agreement similar to the Four-Power Treaty was not satisfactory, because it would draw the United States into areas that were not its concern. If the agreement were broadened, then other nations would be drawn into questions affecting the Western Hemisphere, a situation which the United States could not permit. Also, such a treaty might be interpreted as an attempt by the five naval powers to dominate the world. Consequently, any pact that the United States could be a party to would be so weak as to be meaningless. Cotton did not actually say that the President forbade a consultative pact, but the inference was unmistakable.[26]

In view of the rumors that the American position in regard to a consultative pact had changed, and prior to receipt of the above message from Cotton, Stimson issued a dramatic statement at midnight on March 25. Denying any change in the attitude of the delegation, he maintained that the only objection to negotiating such a pact was the possibility that it might be understood as implying an obligation to provide military aid to another nation. In the event security were furnished by some other agreement that would remove the need for any further commitment, the United States would be willing to consider a consultation pledge.[27]

This announcement was probably the most startling event of the conference. "Utter confusion" prevailed in Washington at the news of Stimson's position, for there had been no indication that the administration was willing to accept a consultative agreement.[28] Senators Borah and Shipstead attacked the Stimson announcement on the grounds that "a consultative pact is a security pact in disguise."[29] The New York *Times* printed the statement on the first page and editorialized that it was an encouraging development, for discussion of the political questions could be resumed with some hope for the future of the conference.[30] The chairman of the Foreign Policy Association greeted the Stimson declaration as a move to save the conference, and the president of the National Student Federation of America offered the services of 400,000 students in order to promote the plan.[31] The Washington correspondent of the London *Times* reported that Stimson's midnight statement was not having a good reception in the American press. This response, he asserted, was not inspired by objections to the policy but was merely a reflection of the "bewilderment over the circumstances in which it was produced and uncertainty as to its meaning and scope." Official sources revealed that the administration did not know the statement was to be made and was not in agreement with its contents.[32]

The London *Daily Telegraph* suspected that the announcement was an attempt to persuade Great Britain to offer France the guarantees that she demanded, guarantees that the British government should not and could not give.[33] In general, the London newspapers were skeptical of the Stimson declaration. They understood it to mean that Britain would first have to agree to a security pact, which was not popular, and their Washington correspondents were reporting confusion in the capital over the failure of the State Department to clarify the situation. The British weeklies were more optimistic. *Time and Tide* thought that the Stimson proposal was "oxygen for the Naval Conference." The *Saturday Review* said that "the patient is understood to survive," and both the *Nation and Athenaeum* and the *Week End Review* felt that the conference had been revived after nearly dying. The Paris correspondent of the Manchester *Guardian* reported that the French press attached little or no importance to the Stimson announcement, but French official circles thought that it cleared the atmosphere at London and promised to speed a decision.[34]

The impact of the press statement on the authorities in Washington was considerable. Administration spokesmen were reluctant to comment on the proposal, for they, too, were unaware of its implications and uncertain as to its scope. Senators Swanson and George added their opposition to American membership in a consultative pact. As the controversy mounted, a short-lived resolution was introduced in the House of Representatives authorizing Hoover to include a provision in the naval treaty providing for consultation of the signatories in the event of a threat of war. The sponsors of the resolution hoped that it would assist the President, and they believed that the nation could not expect to be a party to a treaty that offered advantages without accepting some responsibility.[35]

The President was quick to express his disapproval of Stimson's action. Hoover had consistently maintained that a political agreement should not be made a part of the naval treaty, for in his opinion the Kellogg-Briand Pact was the political foundation for disarmament. Stimson's telegrams had indicated a constant refusal to consider a consultative pledge that did not directly concern a possible modification of the terms of a naval limitation treaty concluded at the London conference. On this basis the President had made a strong statement to the press, only to find that Stimson had changed his views. Hoover was disturbed about the "inconsistency of the present situation," and he cautioned the Secretary of State to notify Washington before making any new commitments. The President then suggested a pact whereby the nations signatory to the naval treaty would agree to consult in the event of any disagreement among themselves, with a protective clause stating that the United States would not discuss any military or coercive measures.[36]

Stimson replied to this admonition with an account of the background and development of the discussions concerning France's desire for a security pact, MacDonald's refusal to accede to it, and the opposition of Henderson and the Foreign Office to the Prime Minister's course. French apprehension had been aroused by MacDonald's attitude of semi-isolationism, and MacDonald had been annoyed by the methods of the French diplomats and the French press. On March 22 a five-power agreement seemed impossible. But on March 24 Henderson had apparently persuaded MacDonald to change his mind, for he authorized the British Foreign Minister to telephone Briand in Paris and invite him to London to discuss mutual security. When Briand accepted the invitation, the French press began to circulate inaccurate and exaggerated reports of the changed situation. Stimson issued his statement in order to counteract these accounts, which had already reached London. Stimson apologized for not notifying the President before issuing the statement, but, he explained, the announcement had enabled the British to modify their position.[37]

Unfortunately for the Secretary of State, the record and his personal diary do not support his account. Stimson had told MacDonald on March 24 that the United States would consider a consultative clause in the naval treaty if the question of security was met by other nations. This drastic shift, in all probability, was an effort to encourage the Prime Minister and provide support for greater British concessions toward France. The following day, when Stimson was visiting MacDonald, Henderson asked what steps should be taken to bring Briand back from Paris, where he intended to remain until he was notified that Britain was ready to discuss a political pact. MacDonald appeared undecided, and turned to Stimson as if for advice. The latter absolved himself from any responsibility, though he did remark that a decision would have to be made soon. Then, to quote from Stimson's dairy, "MacDonald finally, half under his breath, muttered to Henderson that he had better telephone to Briand to come. As I remember it, Henderson at once left the room, and I heard nothing more about that proposition."[38]

The position that Stimson adopted on the 24th was an abrupt change in policy, and there is no indication that it was made in response to a modification of the British position. On the contrary, the events of the 25th indicate that MacDonald must have gained hope from the new American attitude, and Henderson undoubtedly used this information to persuade Briand that it was worth his while to return to London. This assumption is borne out by the rash of rumors that erupted from Paris on the evening of the 25th and led Stimson to issue his famous midnight statement. It would seem, therefore, that the impetus for renewed conversations with France came from Stimson, not Henderson, and not as a result of the former's dramatic press release.

For several days the American delegates labored in an effort to produce a consultative agreement that would satisfy Hoover, MacDonald, and the French authorities.[39] During this period, the anxious Japanese and French ambassadors called on Cotton to inquire about America's decision on a consultative pact. The Undersecretary's reply to the Japanese ambassador was that no decision had been made; to the French ambassador, that he had not given the matter any thought.[40] No doubt Cotton, who had probably thought of little else, found the subject painful and his position as intermediary exceedingly uncomfortable.

Finally, the President resolved to settle the issue, and on March 31 he sent a personal message to Tardieu and Briand. Delivered by Stimson, it outlined the position of the United States in international affairs, its desire to promote peace, the part played by the Kellogg-Briand Pact in the quest for security, and the significance of disarmament in furthering this quest. The message was an attempt to assure France that naval disarmament in the spirit of the Kellogg-Briand Pact would serve her desire for security more effectively than a political consultative agreement.[41] The French Foreign Minister told Stimson that he appreciated the message and that he was aware of America's inability to make commitments. He also thanked Stimson for the latter's announcement of the previous week, which Briand claimed had served to break the deadlock between the French and the British. No further reference was made to a consultative pact with the United States.[42]

In retrospect, it appears that France was primarily interested in American participation in a consultative pact because of the effect that it would have on Great Britain, for it certainly would have provided her with little additional security. British efforts for an understanding with the United States had been accompanied by a tendency to withdraw from the Continent. In fact, American objections to the Geneva Protocol on the grounds that it seemed to be "an unfriendly European concert," were partially responsible for its rejection by Great Britain.[43] The recent indications of Anglo-American friendship had made French authorities even more uncertain of the extent or reliability of British involvement in European affairs. A commitment to consult would place the United States in the position of endorsing collective-security measures and thereby encourage Britain again to turn its face toward Europe. The assurances that France needed could come only from England, but Tardieu and Briand felt that they must come via the United States.

III

Negotiations between France and Britain continued, with the former attempting to obtain military assurances from MacDonald and the latter endeavoring to reduce the French naval demands. Italy continued to aggravate the situation by her persistent refusal to accept any settlement that did not provide for naval parity with France. "The position of Italy is one of sitting silent on the sidelines," Stimson reported on February 16, and two weeks later he could only say that "the Italians remain noncooperative."[44] Grandi, when reproached, protested that he "would be shot at the first station across the frontier" if he relinquished the claim to parity with France that Italy received at the Washington Conference.[45] British and American representatives believed that the French problem could be solved either by a security pact or a reduction in Italy's demands. Neither avenue was promising, but no alternatives were available.

In an effort to break the deadlock, MacDonald ordered the British ambassador in Italy to appeal directly to Mussolini for a specific program in place of the monotonous insistence on parity, and Tardieu urged concerted Anglo-American action at Rome in an effort to modify the Italian demands.[46] But the British ambassador pointed out that neither he nor his American colleague could see Mussolini without giving the impression that they were trying to circumvent Grandi, and both envoys believed that such a move would be a diplomatic blunder. The British government finally abandoned the attempt. Stimson, throughout, was anxious to avoid complicity in the effort to influence the Italian government. His role was to offer assistance to all parties and take no sides.[47]

Grandi made his final offer on April 9. His government, he said, would agree not to exceed the tonnage of war vessels "possessed at any given time by the strongest European continental Power."[48] During the course of the negotiations Italy never retreated from these original demands and France never abandoned her refusal to accept them.

Spain, though not represented at the conference, may have influenced the outcome through her concern over a Mediterranean pact. Before the conference began, the Spanish ambassador advised Cotton that his government had notified the other nations of its sensitivity in this area. The United States, the Undersecretary replied, had not considered this question in connection with the conference, and all that he knew about it was what he had read in the newspapers. America's interest in such a pact was "minimum."[49] MacDonald, in his conversations with France, explained that he could not consider a Mediterranean agreement, for he had assured Spain that he would not do so. But he was willing to discuss the subject at a later meeting of the Mediterranean countries.[50] Thus one means of providing France with the security she sought was ruled out in advance by a unilateral commitment with a nation not a party to the conference. Yet MacDonald should not be singled out for blame, for France alone approached the parley from a political rather than a naval point of view.

A five-power treaty rested on Britain's ability to convince France that she should reduce her figures and reach agreement with Italy. In turn, France's willingness to compromise depended on the extent to which Britain would assure her of military assistance. As the conference passed into its third and final month, MacDonald, propelled by the vision of failure and the diverse pressures at home and abroad, made a final desperate effort to achieve success. In so doing, he revealed the dilemma of a national leader torn between international objectives and the realities of party politics and public opinion.

On the same day that MacDonald authorized Henderson to ask Briand to return to London, he announced in the House of Commons that he would not extend Britain's commitments under the Covenant of the League of Nations and the Locarno treaties.[51] In a statement on March 30, he denied the possibility of any further military commitments on the grounds that Britain could not bind herself to fight in a war that arose from a situation over which she had no control.[52] In the face of these public utterances, discussions were being held by British and French representatives led by Henderson and Briand which resulted in a re-definition of Annex F of the Locarno Agreement. These proposals to reinterpret Britain's existing obligations were, on April 7, rejected by the Cabinet and leaders of the Conservative and Liberal parties, and the Prime Minister was forced to modify the phraseology.[53]

The final British offer was presented to Briand on April 8. The French

Foreign Minister felt that MacDonald's terms were evidence of good will but they were not sufficiently committal to change the situation. France's naval requirements were based on those of Italy, he added, and her claim for parity could not be accepted.[54] France must possess a superiority of 240,000 tons over the Italian navy, the French Minister of Marine told Alexander.[55] And on April 10 negotiations ended. MacDonald, Briand, and Grandi agreed to continue conversations after the London parley was completed in an effort to reach agreement between France and Italy.[56]

IV

The five-power treaty was a victim of Italian pride, French fears, British caution, and American isolation. These barriers to agreement were, for the time, insurmountable. To avoid loss of prestige, the arrogant Mussolini felt that he could not accept less than parity with France. Tardieu and Briand could not grant parity to Italy because of public opinion and the dual threat of Germany in the Channel and the North Sea and Italy in the Mediterranean. MacDonald was prevented from furnishing France with adequate safeguards by public opinion and an adamant domestic political opposition. In effect, Britain was afraid of being drawn into a Continental war as she had been in 1914; France was afraid that she might not be. In any event, British guarantees would only have effected a reduction in the size of the French naval demands, not an acceptance of parity with Italy.

The American position, in some respects, was the weakest of all. Clearly, the Kellogg-Briand Pact was not a sufficient basis for disarmament, for it contained no obligations or commitments on the part of any nations to furnish military aid, apply sanctions, or even to consult in the event of aggression. Few nations could afford the luxury of reducing the security provided by armaments without obtaining a compensatory amount of protection from some other source. Yet Hoover was inflexible in his determination to avoid any agreement that implied American responsibility, imposed limitations on her freedom of action, or provided an excuse for other nations to interfere in affairs traditionally American.

There is little doubt that Stimson's indiscreet announcement that the American delegation would be willing to discuss a consultative pact injected new life into the conference. Qualified though it was, it indicated to the delegates and to the public that America was sincerely interested in effecting agreement, and that she was not totally resolved to divorce herself from European problems and ignore the difficulties faced by other nations. A three-power agreement might have resulted without the Stimson offer, but this is questionable. Britain had indicated that she could not accept the figures in her tentative agreement with the United States unless France reduced her demands. The new atmosphere following the Stimson declaration was apparently responsible for the willingness of France and Italy to continue their efforts to reach an agreement, and the prospect of these further negotiations induced Britain to go ahead with the three-power treaty.[57]

V

On April 10 Stimson cabled that the delegation had reached a final agreement with Great Britain and Japan, and that an effort was being made to include France and Italy in certain portions of the treaty. Hoover sent his congratulations on a job well done.[58]

Dwight Morrow was appointed chairman of a special committee to prepare the final treaty. This committee, aided by various assistants, met repeatedly during the period from April 13 to April 21. The group began working on a draft prepared by one of the British advisers, who in turn had used a draft provided by Captain Smyth and Commander Train.[59] The fifth plenary meeting was called on April 14 in order to approve reports submitted by the First Committee and the Committee of Experts, which, according to MacDonald, furnished the "raw material" for the treaty.[60]

The sixth, and final, plenary meeting was held on April 22. The delegates agreed that a portion of the treaty dealing with method, i.e., limitation by category or by global tonnage, should be referred to the Secretariat of the League of Nations with the request that the matter be called to the attention of the Preparatory Commission. It was then decided that the present conference should take the place of the naval disarmament conference scheduled for 1931 by the Washington Treaty. The next conference on naval disarmament would be held in 1935 unless events should make it unnecessary. The title of the present conference was to be "The London Naval Conference," and the treaty was to be known as "The London Naval Treaty of 1930."[61]

The heads of the various delegations made friendly and conciliatory remarks about the results of the conference. Briand took the opportunity to include a plea for security before disarmament, and Wakatsuki explained that only the time limit on the treaty made it possible for Japan to accept certain of the figures.[62] The pact was then signed by the delegates in alphabetical order, and Briand made a gracious speech praising the work of MacDonald as chairman, after which he presented MacDonald, on behalf of all the delegates, with the gold pen used for signing the treaty. The British Prime Minister responded with appropriate remarks and assured the delegates that the conference was merely adjourning. Discussions were to continue among Great Britain, France, and Italy in the hope of achieving a five-power treaty.

VI

The treaty consisted of five parts. Parts I, II, IV, and V were agreed to by all five nations. Part III contained the agreement among the United States, Great Britain, and Japan.

Part I concerned capital vessels and modified portions of the Washington Treaty of 1922. A "holiday" was provided whereby the signatories agreed not to lay down any battleships during the period 1931-1936, and provision was made for a reduction in the number of these vessels. Great Britain was to dispose of five, the United States three, and Japan one. France and Italy were permitted to construct the ships that they had failed to build in 1927 and 1929 as authorized at Washington. The construction of aircraft carriers displacing less than 10,000 tons was prohibited.

Part II contained the restrictions that applied to the construction of submarines, exempted vessels, the communication of building information, the disposal and conversion of overage vessels, and the special vessels not included within the regular categories.

Part III consisted of the details of the agreement among Japan, Great Britain, and the United States. It included the "escalator clause," which authorized any of the parties to build additional vessels if the "national security" of that party was threatened by the building of a nation not signatory to this section of the treaty.

Part IV contained the restrictions governing submarine warfare.

Part V provided that the treaty would be effective until December 3, 1936, except for Part IV, which would remain in effect indefinitely. The treaty was to be ratified by each nation. When the United States, Japan, Great Britain, and specified members of the British Commonwealth of Nations had deposited their ratifications at London, the treaty would become effective for those nations. Parts I, II, IV, and V would become effective for Italy and France when they deposited their ratifications.[63]

VII

The French delegates, according to the special correspondent of the London *Daily Express,* rejoiced at having adhered to the provisions of the memorandum of December 20, especially in regard to their naval claims and their refusal to accept parity with Italy. The immediate reaction in Paris on hearing that France would not be a party to the treaty was one of relief, for there had been apprehension that no agreement would be reached and that France would be blamed for the failure. A three-power treaty and the prospect of continued negotiations with Italy was considered promising. French opinion concluded that "Britain no longer rules the waves," according to the Paris correspondent of the London *Morning Post,* while France remained with her hands untied. Not unpopular was the belief that Italy was responsible for preventing a five-power pact by her unreasonable insistence on parity with France. Most of the French press, the New York *Times* reported, thought that the conference marked an advance in the right direction, although it had not accomplished all that had been expected.[64]

Press response in the United States was mixed. Comment in the eastern states was voluminous, and, except for the Hearst papers, generally favorable. Editorial reaction in the central states and in the West was characterized by apathy and indifference, in contrast to the enthusiastic welcome accorded the Washington Treaty in 1922. Opposition to the treaty was most stridently expressed in the East by the Hearst New York *American,* and in the Middle West by the Chicago *Tribune.* Each of these newspapers maintained that Japan and Great Britain had won a victory over the United States by modifying its navy to suit their own.[65] The *Literary Digest* concluded that "newspaper editorial opinion is on the whole favorable, altho not so unanimously enthusiastic. The idea that half a loaf is better than none is widely prevalent."[66] The majority response was probably expressed by the New York *Times,* which editorialized that while the treaty was not all that had been hoped for, it was a real contribution to peace and good-will.[67]

The British press reflected the dissatisfaction with which it had treated the proceedings in London. The London *Morning Post* was extremely critical of the treaty, which would "make more trouble than it is worth," and MacDonald was blamed for having prevented a five-power pact by provoking France and Italy. British opinion was interpreted by the *Sunday Graphic* as being relieved that no further European guarantees had been made, and the journal maintained that Britain's attitude toward the Franco-Italian dispute should be one of "friendly detachment." MacDonald's "original blunder" in not having preliminary conversations with the authorities in Paris, instead of those in Washington, was blamed by the *Saturday Review* for the failure to achieve complete success, although it admitted that the outcome was better than nothing at all. The London *Daily Telegraph* saw the treaty as an advance in the effort to disarm and as a contribution to Anglo-American friendship, but it cautioned the Prime Minister against partiality or political commitments in the forthcoming conversations with France and Italy.[68]

Picking up the French theme, the London *Post* editorialized that security, not economy, was the aim of naval policy, and the Manchester *Guardian* warned that a "sense of security and mutual confidence" between nations did not exist in sufficient quantity to make disarmament possible. The London *Daily Herald* complained that the treaty merely limited, not reduced, naval armament, but the London *Times* felt that the delegates were so conscious of the shortcomings of the conference that they did not realize the "magnitude of their own achievements." Aside from the agreement by three

106

great powers to limit all categories of warships, a spirit of friendliness and co-operation pervaded the conference and helped to improve relations among the five participants. The *Week-End Review* denounced the American policy of "isolation," which "lacks moral courage," but it did admit that the conference represented a step in the right direction. Criticism was directed at the Prime Minister by *Time and Tide* and the *Saturday Review* for not facing the question of security, which, they contended, must precede disarmament. The *Economist* and the *Spectator* praised the treaty and pointed out French short-sightedness in expecting that a political pact would provide security. On the whole, British press response was qualifiedly favorable.[69] And it tended to reflect party lines much more closely than the American press.

Italian delegates Grandi, Sirianni, and Acton were given an enthusiastic welcome on their return to Rome after the conference. The newspapers featured their arrival and hailed their firm stand on parity with France.[70] The Italians felt that the conference was responsible for aggravating the ill feeling that had prevailed between France and Italy, for the former had blocked Italy's reasonable claims. France was accused of having made a five-power agreement impossible by her refusal to accept parity and her demand for "a crushing naval superiority over Italy." "Disappointment and rancor" over the London parley grew in Rome, where it was claimed that the United States had been "rolled."[71] No doubt the Fascist press was preparing the people for the resumption of conversations. A more tangible reaction was the announcement, six days after the London treaty was signed, that during the fiscal year 1930-1931 Italy would lay down 42,900 tons of warships, the approximate equivalent of the French program for that year.[72]

The signing of the treaty was something of an anticlimax in Japan, where the battle had been waged earlier over government acceptance of the Japanese-American compromise. The conflict was to be resumed when the issue of ratification was joined.

VIII

The delegates representing the United States, Great Britain, and Japan were doubtless relieved that the job was done. They could now look forward to the problem of ratification. For three months the delegates had argued, bargained, maneuvered, and, at times, conspired, in an effort to reach an agreement that would be acceptable to their government and their nation. During the negotiations, in the midst of outraged feelings and petty jealousies, an atmosphere of friendliness and co-operation had been maintained. Suspicion and animosity were absent, at least on the surface. The mere fact that senior statesmen from five major powers could remain in such close contact under such potentially volatile conditions was in itself remarkable.

107

The pressures on the delegates were inordinate—from their government, from their experts, and from the public opinion of their nation and of the world. The conflict between national interest and international harmony was considerable, and on several occasions it nearly brought the conference to an early end.

Frank Simonds deplored the absence of any outstanding personalities among the delegates. In contrast to the peace conference at Paris and the Washington conference of 1921-1922, he contended, the London conference lacked a brilliant visionary like Wilson or a "central figure" like Hughes.[73] This appraisal is pertinent, although many of the delegates were distinguished and outstanding statesmen who could scarcely be dismissed as merely competent. But throughout the conference one man was always in view—tired and harassed, pleading with one delegate and cajoling another, denounced by a large segment of the press and the opposition parties, and trying to satisfy the opposing demands of four other nations and the conflicting sentiments of his own. Ramsay MacDonald's performance may not have been brilliant, and his efforts were not completely successful, but scarcely any significant result was achieved without his help. He, more than anyone else, held the conference together. The London Naval Conference was probably his finest hour.

Chapter X

Ratification

What is needed is a form of parity that will insure each
Power combat superiority over every other.
—Norfolk *Virginian-Pilot*, May, 1930.

I

Hoover began active and energetic preparations for ratification immediately upon hearing that the delegates had reached an agreement. He was worried about the hostile comments that had appeared in the American press, and he was anxious that every effort be made to obtain public support for the treaty. Stimson was ordered to ensure that news releases reflected "a clear note of exultation in your success," and each delegate was enjoined to express himself as "satisfied with the result and proud of it." The time between agreement and the signing of the treaty was considered by Hoover and Cotton to be a "critical period," during which newsmen should not be allowed to interpret the treaty or its implications without proper guidance.[1]

The President's next exhortation was made in an effort to "head off sporadic naval outbursts" in Washington. Secretary Adams, he suggested, should deliver a radio address pointing out the advantages of the treaty to the Navy and indicating that he had the support of Admiral Pratt and the naval advisers.[2] The urgency and fervor of Hoover's advice apparently alarmed the delegates. They feared that an excess of boastful claims might give the impression that "we do protest too much." Moreover, self-praise could have an adverse effect on ratification in Japan and prove embarrassing to MacDonald.[3] None the less, the delegates were scarcely dilatory in complying with the President's wishes. Radio addresses to the United States were made by Stimson, Ambassador Gibson, Senator Robinson, and Senator Reed, who attempted to explain the treaty and its benefits to America without claiming an advantage over the other nations.[4]

A dispute arose over the most suitable time for submitting the treaty to the Senate for approval. In Reed's opinion, if the President delayed until December he would encounter little opposition, but if the treaty were sent immediately it would meet objections for "political reasons."[5] From Washington, Cotton reported that Senator James E. Watson, Senate majority leader, wanted to go ahead, Swanson was ready, and Borah seemed favorable. The opposition of Senator Hale, chairman of the Committee on Naval Affairs, was "not as bitter" as the administration had been led to expect. The President, Cotton concluded, would try to delay his decision until Reed and Stimson returned from London, but he was afraid that it might not be possible.[6]

The President's dilemma was probably not serious. Certainly Reed's opinion was important, and he would be expected to bear the brunt of the battle in the Senate. But he had been in London for three months and could not be as familiar with the current attitude of the Senate as were Watson, Swanson, and Borah. The latter, who was chairman of the key Committee on Foreign Relations, could exert a great deal of influence on ratification, and if, as Hoover believed, he was in a favorable mood a delay might prove costly. Hoover was also aware of the hostility toward the treaty in segments of the press, in Congress, and among various private pressure groups. If the submission were delayed until December the treaty would be exploited as a political issue in the November elections, and feelings would be aroused against Japan and Great Britain. Time, it seemed, was on the side of the treaty's opponents.

A minor complication was provided by Senator Hale's announcement that he intended to conduct hearings before the Committee on Naval Affairs. The treaty, under normal procedure, was to be referred to the Committee on Foreign Relations for appropriate action, but Hale gave assurances that he would cause no interference. Senator Borah consented to the arrangement and both committees prepared for the ordeal.[7]

Criticism of the treaty came, paradoxically, from both the pacifists and the militarists. The former complained about the failure to reduce existing armaments, and the latter objected to the strictures imposed on naval construction. During the deliberations at London the Navy League maintained a discreet silence because of the Shearer disclosures and the government's warning against the activities of certain interests. When the conference ended, the League resumed its activities but concentrated on a relatively straightforward clarification of the issues. After the hearings closed and it appeared that the Foreign Relations Committee was going to recommend approval of the treaty, the League appealed to the American people for a delay in ratification until the next regular session of Congress. The Senators, it argued, should have more time to become better informed about the treaty and discover the attitude of their constituents.[8] The semiofficial *Army and Navy Journal* declared that "the history of America's past is the history of victories won by the larger gun,"[9] and the Daughters of the American Revolution adopted a resolution opposing the treaty and pledging support for a strong navy.[10] The Hearst papers denounced Hoover for having sacrificed American security in a way that Coolidge had refused to do at Geneva in 1927, and emphasized the contrast in the actions of the two Presidents.[11]

A judicious but powerful blast was leveled against the treaty by the National Council for the Prevention of War, which denounced the London agreement as the work of naval experts, designed to encourage rather than discourage the expansion of fleets.[12] The announcement that it would cost the United States approximately $1,000,000,000 to reach naval parity with Britain caused a mild furore in Congress. Representative Fred A. Britten, chairman of the House Naval Affairs Committee, defended the expenditure, and he was supported by a Democratic colleague who insisted that naval construction would be even more costly if there had been no treaty. This position was attacked by Congressman Burton L. French, chairman of the House Naval Appropriations Subcommittee, who pointed out that the annual building program over the preceding eight years had not exceeded $50,000,000. He considered it "indefensible" that ratification of the treaty should increase expenditures to $125,000,000 or $150,000,000 a year.[13]

II

Hoover, meanwhile, deciding that action was imperative, sent the treaty to the Senate on May 1. His accompanying message was merely a letter of transmittal that requested nothing more than the advice and consent of the Senate.[14] The Committee on Foreign Relations met on May 12 under its chairman, Senator Borah, and began to conduct hearings on the treaty. Two days later the Committee on Naval Affairs began its own hearings, and, except for Secretary Stimson, the witnesses and the testimony were nearly identical.

Stimson made his only appearance as the first witness before the Committee on Foreign Relations, and his testimony lasted three days. Confident and in good humor, he displayed a thorough knowledge of the treaty and a keen understanding of the issues involved. His attitude was friendly and co-operative, and he evidently tried to anticipate and refute every argument that the opposition might advance. The President, Stimson revealed, gave the delegates no explicit instructions and did not at any time tell them what they could or could not do. He assured the committee that the delegation had agreed unanimously on every "major question" that came before it. The treaty was "fair" to all participants, Stimson asserted, and none had gained an advantage over the others. Disarmament was a "process" that must be gradual, but it would improve with each successive conference.[15]

The Secretary of State then moved from the more general to the more specific areas of contention. It was not practicable, he explained, to consider Britain's bases and her merchant marine in determining parity, for, in rebuttal, she could cite her insular position, her lack of food, and her proximity to numerous potential enemies. Combat strength among the fleets was the only satisfactory method of comparing navies, because commerce protection, while important, was impossible to evaluate satisfactorily. The delegation, Stimson said, chose to accept fewer 8-inch–gun cruisers and more

111

6-inch because the former were untried in battle. He than contradicted his previous denial of advantage by claiming that America's ratio in 6-inch–gun ships came closer to the British strength in these ships than the latter's ratio in 8-inch–gun ships came to America's strength in that type of vessel.[16]

Stimson was subjected to a stiff cross-examination by Senator Hiram Johnson, who was to continue in a similar vein throughout the hearings. Senator Reed then usually examined the witness in a manner calculated to discredit Johnson's point, or a point made by a hostile witness, in an effort to put the treaty in a favorable light. The exchanges occasionally became heated, and in one instance Senator Johnson admonished Reed for being unfair to a witness. Reed apparently took the rebuke in good humor, although there may have been sarcasm in the tone of his reply that is not evident in the printed record.[17]

Severe criticism of the treaty was voiced by Navy witnesses, who usually confined their remarks to technical, tactical, and strategic matters, and thus avoided political considerations. Much of the professional opinion was summed up by Rear Admiral Henry H. Hough when he stated:

"We gave up the right to build the type of ship we need. We abandoned the 5:5:3 ratio. We accepted subdivision of the cruiser category. We surrendered the principle of no replacements until 1936. We should have gotten one more capital ship. We did not press as hard as we might for actual parity. We gave up our superiority in destroyers. We granted parity in submarines for Japan. We did not insist on modification of the base and fortification clause of the Washington Treaty when granting an increase of ratio to Japan."

Senator Reed countered by asking Admiral Hough if he thought that Japan and Great Britain had won a diplomatic victory. When the Admiral replied in the affirmative, Reed cited the agitation against the treaty in those two countries. The Admiral refused to be swayed by this approach.[18]

Reed had special techniques for handling some of the more routine objections expressed by the naval experts. When a witness found fault with the new ratio, the Senator, by adroit questioning, brought out that Japan already possessed considerably more 8-inch– and 6-inch–gun cruisers than the United States, and that the treaty committed Japan virtually to "stand still" for over six years while America built past her. Reed was also successful in obtaining assent to his contention that the only difference between the General Board's requirements and the fleet authorized by the treaty was whether three or four ships should be armed with 8-inch or 6-inch guns.[19]

The conflicting testimony before the two committees fills approximately nine hundred pages, much of it merely repetition. The opinion of the twenty-five witnesses appearing before the Committee on Naval Affairs was tabulated in an abstract prepared by the Committee. On the question of the basis to be used in determining parity, Adams, Pratt, and Jones believed that parity should be based on combat naval strength. Ten admirals declared that factors other than combat strength should be included. When asked if the treaty gave the United States parity with Great Britain by the end of 1936, Adams, Pratt, and two admirals held that it did. Nine admirals claimed that it did not. As to the relative value of the 6-inch– and 8-inch–gun cruisers to the United States, Pratt and two admirals favored the former, and nineteen naval officers favored the latter. On the question of whether a 10,000-ton ship armed with 6-inch guns was the equal of a 10,000-ton ship mounting 8-inch guns, two admirals thought that the two vessels would be even, and seven admirals thought that the more heavily armed ship would be superior. Adams, Pratt, and two admirals considered the ratio with Japan satisfactory. Nineteen naval officers expressed dissatisfaction with the ratio.[20]

In general, the testimony of the naval experts reflected an almost exclusive concern with the fighting effectiveness of the fleet. Other ramifications of the treaty were outside their jurisdiction, and, evidently, often beyond their comprehension.[21] Each naval officer was presenting his conception of the type and number of ships that would be needed in order to win a victory over any conceivable antagonist. The battle, in his opinion, should be decided at sea and not at a conference table. This point of view reflected the narrow mold of the alleged military mind, but the nature of the naval expert's responsibilities made any other attitude unlikely and, probably, undesirable.

The deliberations of the Committee on Foreign Affairs were further complicated by Stimson's refusal, at Hoover's direction, to furnish the Committee with the correspondence bearing on the treaty. The Secretary of State reminded the Senate that ratification should "be determined from the language of the document itself and not from extraneous matter."[22] The Committee adopted a resolution dissenting from this opinion and asserting the right of the Committee, as the agent of the Senate, to have access to all material relating to the treaty.[23] Stimson made no effort to comply with the resolution, but the controversy was to be resumed when the treaty reached the floor of the Senate.

The Committee on Foreign Relations returned the treaty to the Senate on June 23, and recommended that advice and consent be given to its ratification. Senator Henrik Shipstead of Minnesota opposed the Committee's recommendation because of the administration's refusal to furnish the documents necessary to a proper evaluation of the treaty.[24] A minority report objecting to the treaty was filed by Senators Hiram Johnson of California, George H. Moses of New Hampshire, and Arthur H. Robinson of Indiana. They shared the opinions of the majority of the naval experts and concluded that the treaty was "unfair and unjust to the United States."[25] The lines were drawn and the stage was set for a rousing battle in the Senate.

III

As the hearings progressed, the administration became less moderate in its attempts to influence opinion. General Dawes submitted some proposed comments on the treaty to the President in which he used fairly forceful language. Hoover suggested a stronger opening sentence, and Stimson added, "For myself I should welcome a Dawes' indiscretion from you. Tear off your dress suit and say Hell and Maria. The situation is almost ludicrous and yet there is danger of people losing their perspective."[26] The Secretary of State, in an effort to minimize the implications of the modified ratio, was busy assembling data to demonstrate that Japan would be deterred from war with the United States because of her economic ties. Stimson also hinted that it might be well to look on Japan as a "buffer state" between the United States and China in view of the unsettled state of affairs prevailing in the latter country.[27]

The President, determined that the treaty should be ratified, displayed a firmness that probably surprised and dismayed his critics.[28] When Senator Moses and a few of his colleagues clamored for delay and the Senate adjourned without acting on the treaty, Hoover responded by calling a special session of that body for July 7. The real issue, he pointed out, was not whether the United States could have a treaty with more advantages or a greater reduction in armament. It was the question of "whether we shall have this treaty or no treaty." Hoover warned that "the only alternative to this treaty is the competitive building of navies with all its flow of suspicion, hate, ill will, and ultimate disaster." A mass of evidence for and against ratification was available, he reminded the Senators, and they could no longer avoid meeting their responsibility.[29]

The hostile press launched an attack on the treaty to coincide with the opening of the special session. Hearst's New York *American* carried an article by Senator Tasker L. Oddie of Nevada, entitled "Pact Leaves United States Merchant Marine Defenseless." Oddie claimed that "our delegates failed to heed naval experts," and he stressed the need for 8-inch–gun cruisers to protect American commerce against the threat of Japanese and British cruisers, and against the merchant ships of these nations that were armed with 6-inch guns.[30] The Chicago *Tribune* complained that the treaty was "a State Department treaty and not a Navy agreement seeking the best interests of the American naval protections [sic]." America, it added, received no battleship to offset Britain's advantage of the modern *Nelson* and *Rodney,* and the British imposed their own cruiser plan on the United States. The Washington Treaty ratio, which had been based on a non-fortification agreement, was "reversed," the *Tribune* concluded, and Japan obtained greater naval power without offering other compensation.[31]

The debate in the Senate found both sides using most of the conventional tactics and a few new ones as well. The Senate had scarcely convened before Senator McKellar introduced a resolution asking the President to furnish the Senate with "all letters, cablegrams, minutes, memoranda, instructions, and dispatches and all records, files, and other information touching the negotiations of said London naval treaty," in order that the members could decide on the merits of the documents.[32] "If we are going to yield this," McKellar predicted, "why in the future we will be called on to yield other powers."[33] Borah called on the Senate to "rise in its majesty and its might and demand" the material.[34] The resolution was approved on July 10 by a vote of 53 to 4, but administration friends had been able to insert a reservation that qualified the request by making it applicable only "if not incompatible with the public interest."[35]

This effort to uphold the dignity and rights of the Senate was of no avail, for Hoover announced that it "would be incompatible with the public interest" to furnish the papers. Senators were permitted to see the material, however, if they promised not to divulge the contents.[36] Hiram Johnson denounced the President's action in strong language, and concluded that "we are back again, under this administration, with secret diplomacy."[37] Senator MeKellar analyzed Hoover's letter sentence by sentence and disputed every point.[38] All of the sound and fury, which came primarily from opponents of the treaty, did not make the President modify his stand, and none of the Senators took advantage of his invitation to consult the documents.

Hoover's refusal to furnish the material was a sound, if not popular, decision. Part of his reluctance was reportedly due to the outspoken and occasionally unflattering appraisals of foreign statesmen that were contained in Dawes' dispatches, although Stimson was often quite candid in his estimates of MacDonald.[39] Negotiations between the representatives of sovereign nations are at best of a delicate nature, and normal and understandable comments of a critical turn can often be magnified and distorted to the point where they become derogatory and insulting. No doubt the President was motivated by a desire to avoid the disclosure of information that could prove offensive to another nation and jeopardize friendly relations. Nor was he anxious to provide additional ammunition for those who were striving to embarrass the administration and prevent a ratification of the treaty. Then, too, he probably wanted to preserve the integrity and confidential nature of negotiations that were his exclusive responsibility. Hoover did not take lightly his duties and his constitutional obligations, and he was not willing to allow the Senate to usurp his powers.

Not to be eclipsed by the controversy over executive privilege, the debate on the merits of the treaty had continued. Senator Swanson opened on July 8 with a lengthy and detailed speech, in which he concluded that "the best interests of the United States demand the ratification of this treaty."[40] "Rejection would be a tragedy," Senator Alben Barkley of Kentucky contended; it would lead to unrestricted naval competition.[41] Senator Reed defended the treaty with great vigor and skill. He was exposed to a great deal of sharp questioning by other Senators on matters of detail and policy, and hostile journalistic comments and assertions were flung at him by critical colleagues in an effort to discredit the treaty.[42]

Senator Reed made his formal speech in support of the treaty on July 15. After a brief review of previous attempts at disarmament, he compared the navies of Japan and Great Britain with the American fleet. The characteristics of every type of ship were analyzed, and he indicated the way in which the treaty would affect each navy during the subsequent six years. Ratification, Reed declared, was in the best interests of Japan, Great Britain, and the United States, and the security of neither of the nations would be threatened.[43] The speech was clear, unimpassioned, and logical. It contained nothing that had not been said many times during the previous three months, but it was a masterly summation of the evidence in favor of the treaty.

The obstructionists were no less vocal than the ratificationists. Senator McKellar was the more outspoken of the treaty foes and he went far afield in his search for criticism. The Senator claimed that the treaty divided the world into three parts. "It gives about four-fifths of it to Great Britain, it gives a very small strip of it to America, and the remainder of the eastern seas and of the eastern countries is put under the control of Japan."[44] McKellar also read and endorsed an editorial which objected to the treaty because it allegedly constituted an entanglement with Europe.[45]

"It seems," the Norfolk *Virginian-Pilot* observed, "that every time our diplomats bring home a peace treaty, war breaks out in the Senate."[46] The conflict over the London agreement involved personalities as well as issues. In the course of a lengthy speech against the treaty, Senator Frederick Hale of Maine asserted that the American delegates had "surrendered bag and baggage to the British point of view."[47] Senator Reed, taking offense at this and other accusations made by Hale, indignantly insisted that the delegates were "patriotic Americans" who "did their best." They were better qualified to make an agreement on naval limitation, Reed added, than were "a little group of admirals . . . a little group of bureaucrats here in Washington."[48]

In the midst of the name-calling and insinuations, Senator Royal S. Copeland of New York announced that a minority of the Senators was "convinced that the treaty is unwise and improper, that it fails to protect our interests, that we have been 'outsmarted' by the other men in the conference at London."[49] It so happened that the Senator was expressing the

116

sentiments of foes of ratification in England and, as will be revealed later, Japan. A compilation of remarks by critics of the treaty in the Senate and in the House of Commons was released by the State Department, which portrayed in parallel columns the similarity between the hostile observations in the two legislative bodies.[50]

In an effort to circumvent the delaying tactics of the opposition, Senator Reed gave notice on July 17 that he would ask for morning and evening sessions unless an agreement was reached on the time when the Senate would vote on the treaty. Senator Watson promised co-operation in carrying out this program.[51] Two days later the clerk read the treaty and Reed answered most of the questions that arose.[52] The vote was taken on July 21. Fifty-eight Senators voted for the treaty and nine against it. In advising and consenting to the ratification of the treaty the Senate added a reservation to the effect that no documents existed which modified the articles of the treaty, and that no agreements had been made that specified how the provisions of the treaty were to be interpreted.[53] The following day Hoover signed the instrument of ratification.

The President had his treaty. The Senate had preserved some of its self-respect and had asserted its prerogative. Senator Reed had more than justified his selection as a delegate, for he had performed brilliantly in the hearings before the Foreign Relations Committee and on the floor of the Senate. The actions of some Senators were not calculated to enhance the relationship between the Executive and the Senate. It was impossible to determine where opposition to the President stopped and opposition to the treaty began, but the two were often synonymous. In this particular case a small group of recalcitrants was not able to impose its will on the government or on the nation. The victory went to Hoover, and it showed the world that the United States was not averse to all forms of international co-operation.

Most of the American press welcomed ratification. Overtly critical comment was largely confined to the Hearst papers, which insisted that Britain and Japan had "put something over" on the United States. A segment of the press applauded the pact for what it accomplished, but complained that it had not accomplished enough.[54] Thus the three categories of press opinion were clearly drawn, with outright hostility in a minority. Neither party lines nor geography appeared to affect the response. The technicalities of the treaty, the various arguments that were used to support and condemn the pact, and the drawn-out quarrel over ratification, combined to make the American people somewhat apathetic.[55] On the whole, Hoover could be pleased with the reception accorded the treaty, which probably afforded the public a respite from the problems of the tariff, prohibition, and unemployment.

Surprisingly unexploited by the critics of the treaty and unexplained by the supporters, was the significance of aircraft in a war with Japan.[56] American war plans envisioned an engagement of the fleets at some point in the western Pacific—because of the aggressive strategy of the United States, probably at a place chosen by the Japanese. No doubt they would select a location that would enable them to utilize land-based planes in conjunction with their fleet, and thereby secure an incalculable advantage over their enemy. One must recall the atmosphere and attitude of the times in order to understand how such a decisive military factor could have been overlooked. The failure to comprehend the role of air power, the faith in unenforceable agreements, the lack of co-ordination between the civil and military branches of government, the fervent dedication to peace, and the political desire for a treaty, combined to create an unstable and illusory equilibrium of armaments.

IV

The struggle over ratification in Japan was extremely bitter. Basically, it was a conflict between the military and civil branches of the government over the questions of authority and responsibility. The navy held that its administration was delegated by the Emperor directly to the chief of the naval general staff, and that naval authorities alone, under the Emperor, could determine the strength of the fleet. The civilian statesmen, navy spokesmen contended, had exceeded their powers in executing a treaty that applied restrictions which those responsible could not accept. The issue was eagerly embraced by the opposition party, which hoped that it could be used to overthrow the Cabinet. But Premier Hamaguchi, who refused to be intimidated, announced that he was determined to secure the treaty's ratification in spite of political or military opposition.[57]

Agitation against the pact began with the government's approval of the so-called Reed-Matsudaira compromise. Public demonstrations against the ratio were organized by the Black Dragon Society and other nationalistic organizations, which used retired army and naval officers as the principal speakers.[58] Newspapers claimed that the Japanese delegates had failed to obtain all the advantages within reach, and the American ambassador in Tokyo asked Reed and Stimson to explain in the Senate hearings that they had made every possible concession.[59] The *Gaikō Jihō*, a foreign affairs journal, urged that ratification be delayed until Japan was assured that the United States would not commence construction of the three cruisers which it was authorized to lay down during the life of the treaty.[60] Admiral Takarabe, Minister of Marine and delegate to the conference, was presented with a dagger on his return from London and denounced as a traitor for having given in to the demands of "tyrannous" America and Britain.[61] Yet most of the Japanese press accepted the treaty with only minor misgivings, and the enthusiastic welcome accorded Wakatsuki on his return was interpreted by the newspapers as evidence that the public approved the pact.[62]

The Japanese Constitution provided no specific method for the ratification of foreign agreements, but practice and an imperial ordinance had designated the Privy Council as the agency responsible for advising the Emperor on treaties. The debate waxed heavy in the Diet and in the Supreme War Council, with the opposition party and the military faction waging a strenuous battle against the government. On their return from London, Baron Wakatsuki and the delegates had been given a message from the Emperor congratulating them on their work at the conference. This action angered the opposition groups, for it placed them in the position of criticizing the Emperor when they criticized the treaty.[63] Premier Hamaguchi and Foreign Minister Shidehara fought the treaty opponents, including the powerful military faction, in a manner that evoked the admiration of American diplomatic observers and carried the treaty to the Privy Council.[64]

The final act of the drama was staged on October 1, when Hamaguchi, with the Emperor present, argued his case before the Privy Council. The Premier pointed out that the treaty had been submitted to the Council on July 24. This body referred it to an Investigation Committee that first convened on August 18. The Committee had met twelve times during the following month and had interviewed delegates and naval experts. Because these deliberations were secret, the newspapers had indulged in speculation and conjecture in a way calculated to confuse and distort the real issues. The agitation of private organizations had contributed to the controversy, and the public was dismayed and uneasy. Uncertainty over the outcome of the treaty, Hamaguchi concluded, had increased financial unrest and international political instability. The Council, persuaded to take action, voted unanimously to accept the treaty, which then received the Emperor's approval.[65]

On the occasion of the deposit of ratification at London, Premier Hamaguchi announced that the treaty marked a "momentous step forward on the road of international peace and friendship," and halted the "dangerous possibility" of expensive competition in naval weapons.[66] The following month he was fatally shot by a young military fanatic, who was partially motivated by the hatred he shared with many of his colleagues for the London Naval Treaty. The government had prevailed over the military faction and had asserted the right of the Cabinet to determine foreign policy, but it was a pyrrhic victory. The challenge of naval limitation and the assertions of civilian control that reached a climax in 1930 served to consolidate the efforts of a ruthless and determined opposition that later was to dominate the foreign affairs of the nation.

V

The debate over ratification in Great Britain was little more than a continuation or a culmination of the controversy that had been waged in England while the conference was in session. The public paid slight attention to the proceedings because of a more acute interest in budget discussions, the Anglo-Egyptian treaty negotiations, and the situation in India.[67] In all probability both the public and the press had become satiated with the topic of naval limitation during the preceding eight months.

Formal action on the treaty began in the House of Lords on May 8. Lord Bridgeman, former First Lord of the Admiralty and leader of the British delegation to the Geneva Conference in 1927, moved for the papers in an effort to provoke debate and delay ratification. The treaty, he maintained, failed to reduce the size of battleships, it did not give Britain the seventy cruisers that she needed, and it did not establish parity with the United States. Moreover, the only nation obliged to disarm was Great Britain.[68] Lord Carson, also a former First Lord of the Admiralty, claimed that the treaty did not provide for a fleet large enough to protect commerce or defend the Empire.[69] Earl Beatty and Earl Jellico, two of England's most distinguished naval leaders, added their prestige to the agitation against the pact. But the motion for the papers was finally withdrawn and formal opposition in the House of Lords ended.[70]

The treaty received similar treatment in the House of Commons, where the formidable Winston Churchill led the attack. The London agreement, he contended, was not the "natural successor" to the Washington Treaty. The latter had established parity with the United States in capital ships, which were employed in battle fleets, and Britain's ability to protect her trade had not been restricted. Under the terms of the London pact Great Britain had accepted "a permanent secondary position in seapower," for so-called mathematical parity in ships did not constitute equality in battle when one nation was forced to use so many vessels for commerce protection. The reduction of Britain's cruiser needs from seventy to fifty, he argued, was unwarranted and inexcusable.[71]

Churchill's position was based on emotion as well as logic. Steeped in England's past, he was passionately devoted to her greatness, which, he believed, was due in large part to her mastery of the sea. To Churchill, the treaty marked Britain's abdication of her role as mistress of the ocean highways of the world. The empire that had been created by the blood and sweat of countless Englishmen was being destroyed by the stroke of a pen.

Ramsay MacDonald, in supporting the treaty, was careful to point out its imperfections. Disarmament was a "gigantic task," and the conference "simply made a little nibble at the cherry." Nevertheless, he claimed, the pact was a significant advance along a difficult road toward peace. The results achieved at London were to be followed up in conversations with Italy and France and in the Preparatory Commission at Geneva, where the complexities of land and air armaments would be faced.[72] The Prime Minister denied that there was anything sacrosanct about the figure of seventy cruisers. The treaty was to last for a relatively brief period, and changing conditions modified existing needs. If political agreements, such as the Kellogg-Briand Pact, were to have no effect on international attitudes and armament, then there was little point in making them. Military strength alone, MacDonald declared, would never provide security for any nation.[73]

In an attempt to delay ratification, Stanley Baldwin introduced a motion to appoint a committee to examine the treaty.[74] The House divided and the motion was defeated.[75] On July 24 Commons approved the treaty. [76]

The ratifications were deposited in London on October 27, 1930.[77] The occasion was celebrated by world-wide radio addresses from President Hoover, Premier Hamaguchi, and Prime Minister MacDonald. They hailed the treaty as evidence of the friendship that existed among the nations and as an indication of the ability of diplomats to work out problems over the conference table.[78]

The struggles over ratification followed a similar pattern in each nation, with the opposition being centered in the "big navy" groups. Only in Japan did the controversy lead to long-lasting internal dissension that was to change the complexion of the government. In every case ratification was a victory of the internationalists over the nationalists. The advocates of international good will prevailed over the champions of isolation, and the civil authorities triumphed over the military.

Chapter XI

Conclusion

> The most important single judgment that a political or military leader can make is to forecast correctly the nature of the war upon which the nation is to embark.—Clausewitz.

The London Naval Conference of 1930 marked the culmination of a movement for security through disarmament largely inspired by the disillusionment following the First World War. The Washington Treaty imposed limitations on capital ships and aircraft carriers, and established ratios which placed a portion of the nation's naval strength on a relative basis. The inadequacies of this agreement were revealed by a new outburst of competition in auxiliary vessels, which was halted at London by the three great naval powers.

The imperialistic spirit that prevailed at the turn of the century in the United States, Great Britain, and Japan, was formally renounced, and the maintenance of the status quo was acknowledged as an objective of foreign policy. In this respect the aims of the Kellogg-Briand Pact were partially achieved, for each nation abandoned the right to build and maintain sufficient naval forces to sustain a successful offensive war against the other. Repeatedly, the delegates asserted that their sole motive in establishing minimum naval demands was to provide for the security of their country, and force as an instrument of national policy appeared to be obsolescent if not obsolete.

The strategic implications of home defense were not so clearly revealed in the negotiations. Great Britain was dedicated to the protection of the British Isles and the life lines of communication with her empire. Japan was intent on consolidating her position in the Far East. The United States was committed to the defense of the Western Hemisphere and its possessions in the Pacific. In addition, it was imperative that the respective governments be capable of promoting the national interest in other parts of the world. The civil authorities were satisfied that the treaty provided the means to attain these objectives. The naval authorities were sure that it did not.

The treaty temporarily stabilized conditions in the Pacific, but it failed to alleviate the problem of competitive armament in Europe. The reason for this shortcoming lay in the manner in which the security of the various nations could be threatened. An attack on Britain, America, and Japan had to come from the sea. An invasion of France or Italy could be launched by land as well as by sea, and their safety could be jeopardized by a hostile fleet capable of cutting off trade and overwhelming their colonies. This multiple vulnerability of the continental European nations was the basis for their contention that restrictions should be applied to all weapons or to none.

The agreement of the three major naval powers was facilitated by the fact that each was the "potential enemy" of the other two. Great Britain possessed the only navy that offered a threat to the Monroe Doctrine, and she and Japan were America's only probable antagonists in the Far East. Neither of the three nations maintained a large army, and neither was vulnerable to attack by land. Except by their own aggressive actions or through participation in a mutual security pact, their chances of being drawn into a conflict with another nation were slight. Consequently, each nation's naval program was predicated on that of the other two. Great Britain was confronted with the added task of upholding the two-power naval standard in respect to the Continent. But she faced no visible threat in Europe, and her participation in the three-power agreement is an indication that her primary concern was the United States and Japan.

The London Naval Conference demonstrated that agreement on armament limitation was possible only when there were no outstanding political controversies between the nations. Except for the war debt, no critical unresolved problems troubled Japanese, American, or British relations, and a naval settlement was concluded because neither country posed an immediate threat to the interests of the other.

The same was not true of France and Italy. In the first place, the former controlled colonies which the latter coveted. In the second place, France was still suffering from the impact of the German invasion that had laid waste her lands, destroyed many of her people, and financially exhausted the populace and the government. Limitation of armaments, she felt, must await further provisions for her safety. In the third place, France was suspicious of Mussolini's intentions, and she resented the Italian claim to parity. Moreover, Great Britain, America, and Japan enjoyed a measure of security from their geographical isolation, which afforded protection, placed the burden of defense on the navy, and promised invaluable time for military preparation. France and Italy possessed no such advantage. Thus isolation and the absence of major controversies made a three-power pact possible. Proximity and quarrels prevented a five-power agreement.

The French contention that security must precede disarmament was actually accepted by all the participants at London, for each nation was determined to retain sufficient naval strength to ensure its own safety. France was unique in demanding a mutual assistance pact to compensate for a limitation of her fleet. The only nations capable of providing France with adequate guarantees were the United States and Great Britain, and neither was willing or able to do so. Stimson and the French authorities be-

123

lieved that America's participation in a consultative treaty might induce Britain to guarantee the French frontiers, but it is unlikely that such a modest concession by the United States would have enabled MacDonald to offer Tardieu and Briand more satisfactory assurances than he did. Neither the public nor the politicians would allow the authorities in London and Washington to make further commitments.

The press and public opinion played significant roles in determining the positions and the inflexibility of the governments in London, Paris, and Washington. The French reaction to the experiences of the World War led to an almost fanatical quest for security through armaments and mutual security pacts, and the least suspicion of compromise on these vital issues provoked an immediate and violent outburst of indignation in the newspapers and from the legislators. In the United States and Great Britain, the recent war was regarded as an eloquent argument for the avoidance of responsibilities not immediately and directly related to the nation's welfare and interest. This compulsion to remain isolated from embroilments in other parts of the world was so intense that Hoover and MacDonald were practically prisoners of the mood.

Not only did the press and the elected political officials in the United States and Great Britain reveal a virtual unanimity of opinion in opposition to so-called entangling alliances, but they expressed a clear preference for the limitation of armaments. In France there was no such obsession with economy and disarmament, for the danger of war and the price of defeat were too real and immediate. But in either case, the statesmen were restricted to activities which the public and the press were willing to sanction. Whenever either leader attempted to move beyond the prevalent domestic attitude he was brought up short. MacDonald's last-minute effort to satisfy France by a reinterpretation of existing treaties was stifled in the Cabinet after being denounced by the newspapers and the opposition parties. Stimson's midnight announcement on consultation was condemned by a large segment of the press and the Senate. The fact that none of the national leaders made a serious attempt to modify public opinion testifies to the depth of feeling on the subject, although Hoover and the French statesmen evidently shared the views of their constituents.

Disarmament also posed a semantic problem. Meaning, literally, the elimination of arms, in the parlance of the 1920's it came to signify both the reduction and the limitation of weapons. In practice, as at London, it occasionally provided for an increase in the type of armament that it was intended to restrict, or, ideally, to eliminate. Some skeptics exploited this apparent anomaly by arguing that such an outcome demonstrated the ineffectiveness and impracticability of efforts to control the machines of war. Proponents of disarmament, on the other hand, insisted that control of the production of arms was the first step toward their eventual extinction, and that any tangible efforts at international restriction were all to the good.

During the 1920's disarmament caught the popular imagination. The term and the idea became a part of the vocabulary and the conversation of the era. Its universal appeal derived from numerous sources, and it was espoused as a cure-all for many of the problems that beset the civilized world. The revulsion against the recent conflict gave rise in many quarters to the belief that armaments were responsible for war, either because they heightened tensions by their very existence or because the manufacturers encouraged hostilities in order to increase profits. Disarmament, it was believed, would remove one, if not both, of the basic reasons for war. Then, too, the financial cost of the last struggle and the huge sums being spent to maintain an adequate defense program furnished an argument that appealed both to the public and the politicians. Peace and economy made sense to people who gave little thought to the relative merits of 8-inch- and 6-inch–gun cruisers.

The three-power agreement represented a victory of the civil authorities over the naval experts. During the negotiations, the statesmen had to compete with the delegates of other nations and the professional advisers of their own, who believed that the nation's defenses were being jeopardized by the size and type of navy that the delegates were willing to accept. The disparity between naval and political opinion was clearly revealed by the agitation in each country that attended the process of acceptance and ratification of the treaty. In the United States, the elaborate and much publicized Senate hearings bared the conflict and exposed the opposing viewpoints. Basically the issue was one of responsibility and authority. The admirals contended that if they were to be held accountable for America's defense they should determine its composition and its relative strength in respect to the forces of other nations. The civilian authorities, acting in accordance with the Constitution, asserted their legal, political, and moral prerogatives. The naval experts were confined to their professional role of giving technical advice and making recommendations. The statesmen, presumably aware of the complex realities of international relations, exercised their authority and assumed responsibility for the final outcome of the conference.

In part, the dispute can be attributed to the fact that the role of the Navy in foreign policy was neither well understood nor well defined. The Navy was an important instrument in the administration of foreign affairs, and a vital element in the spectrum of national security. Often regarded as a peacetime extravagance that justified its existence in time of crisis or war, it was a decisive, but not always a determinant factor in the establishment and maintenance of relations with other countries. Naval policy had been conceived by the admirals, based on their estimate of the nation's needs and commitments. Following the Navy Bill of 1916, the violation of American neutrality that was encouraged by her weak military position, and the nation's participation in a war that forcibly demonstrated the value of sea power, the Navy contemplated a larger share in the formulation and implementation of foreign policy.

But disappointment began with the Senate's rejection of the League of Nations. Deprived of the role envisaged by Wilson for the enforcement of a world peace, and rebuffed by the tactics of Hughes at Washington in 1921, the Navy finally prevailed at Geneva in 1927. This abortive conference convinced the civilian authorities that negotiations at London should be taken out of the hands of the professionals, and the results testified to the success of their efforts. The American delegates were willing to make the compromises necessary to reach agreement, and in so doing they were defining the national interest as a balance between unilateral military power and multilateral understanding.

Much of the difficulty between the military and civil branches of the government stemmed from the lack of a satisfactory working arrangement between the two. No body existed that was charged with the task of defining national objectives, clarifying political commitments, and correlating the whole with the capabilities of the armed forces. Under the circumstances, the naval experts had to plan for all possible contingencies, basing their conclusions on their own appraisal of present and future policies and their own estimate of existing and prospective conditions. Though their premises, their findings, and their foresight may have differed from that of the civil authorities, the naval planners had no alternative in the light of their own professional responsibilities.

At the heart of the controversy over the treaty was the question of whether it provided America with a navy sufficient to meet her commitments and enforce her foreign policies. Under no obligation to furnish military aid to any nation outside the Western Hemisphere, she had no ties that would draw her into a European struggle. Her fleet, as limited by the pact, was capable of defending the Monroe Doctrine, and, in all probability, deterring a Japanese advance against American possessions in the Pacific. Less certain was the deterrent effect of the Navy in respect to a violation of the traditional Open Door policy. The most rewarding and convenient spot for Japanese expansion was not the Philippines but mainland China. Moreover, such a move would be less likely to provoke American military intervention, and if it should Japan would be in a more favorable strategic position.

One of the crucial defects of the treaty was the arrangement whereby the ratios prescribed were not to be attained until 1936. During the intervening period Japan enjoyed a decided advantage, for the United States was in the position of having to build a great deal more than the other powers in order to reach its allotted figure. Hoover and his colleagues, in effect, took the calculated risk that Japan would behave herself for the life of the treaty. A pact limiting armaments establishes a military equilibrium, an equilibrium designed to prohibit any single nation from becoming sufficiently powerful to launch an attack on one of the signatories with a reasonable expectation of success. In the event one member does not build to treaty strength, or fails to maintain its forces at the established ratio, it becomes too weak to prevent aggression. While a nation may never be prepared for war when it comes, a strong fleet in being, in contrast to a blueprint navy that takes several years to materialize, constitutes an impressive deterrent. Thus it would appear that if military force exists for the purpose of preventing war by discouraging others from interfering with a nation's interests, the agreement at London, from the American point of view, was a miscalculation.

On the other hand, a failure to agree on limitation might have resulted in an outburst of competition that could have increased world tensions immeasurably, and the treaty did help sublimate the suspicion and hostility that had developed from the naval rivalry of Great Britain, Japan, and the United States. It did nothing, however, to temper the motives behind this rivalry; so it alleviated the symptom but accomplished no cure.

Some have maintained that the London agreement was actually of benefit to the American Navy, in that it was responsible for the formulation of an orderly and comprehensive building program. Without the treaty, it is alleged, Congress may have been even more reluctant to authorize the construction of new vessels. The acceptance and ratification of the treaty virtually committed the government and the people to the type and number of ships specified by the terms of the pact. And while this mandate did not authorize a new fleet, it provided a tangible goal at which the sights of the Navy Department and the government could be directed. Public and legislative sanction for a bigger navy was a more powerful argument than the occasionally suspect theories of the professionals.

Unfortunately, the validity of this argument cannot be tested, for until the passage of the Vinson-Trammel Act in 1934 no effective attempt was made to build up the Navy to treaty strength. The depression led Hoover to curtail federal expenditures, and naval appropriations were deeply cut. Whether failure at London and continued competition would have stimulated American building is questionable. Hoover had endorsed the cruiser bill before his inauguration, but his subsequent actions indicate that he considered domestic economic recovery to be a more immediate problem than military preparedness. This priority, however, may have reflected the sense of security into which many had been lulled by the successful control of armaments.

Of primary importance in reaching a three-power agreement was the fact that the authorities in Washington, London, and Tokyo wanted a treaty. Paris was opposed to a settlement confined to naval limitation, and Rome seemed sympathetic but not enthusiastic. Those nations that were sufficiently anxious for a pact made the compromises necessary to obtain one. The less zealous nations—and their lack of ardor stemmed from their circumstances and the prevailing concept of the national interest—refused to make the required concessions and remained outside of the more restrictive provisions of the treaty. Success at London was also a matter of prestige to MacDonald, Hamaguchi, and Hoover. A failure might have brought about a change of government in England and Japan. Hoover was not subject to such immediate repercussions, but he had spoken so hopefully, acted so resolutely, and banked so heavily on a naval limitation treaty that failure would have been a severe personal and political blow. Wishing may not have brought the treaty into being, but it did make one possible and it furnished a powerful motive for compromise.

The complexities of the negotiations were overwhelming. Each ship category affected the other categories, and the delegates were constantly striving to correlate the changing figures. The requirements of one nation were meaningless if not evaluated in the context of the demands of other nations. Technology and tactics were enmeshed with strategy and politics, and there was no clear indication of where the one ended and the other began. Domestic considerations competed with foreign affairs, propaganda contended with public opinion, naval expert quarreled with civilian statesman, and the man in the street groped in vain for a simple answer that did not exist.

The London Naval Treaty of 1930 was important because, for the first time, all of the naval weapons of three great nations were limited and a relative position of naval power was established. The treaty was significant because the United States, Great Britain, and Japan relinquished their freedom of action to provide for their own safety in order to reach an international agreement. But this sacrifice of national autonomy was misplaced, for it put the control of weapons in the wrong sequence on the road to security. The issue which confronted the statesmen was whether disarmament and world order were to be based on the moral force of the Kellogg-Briand Pact or the military implications of the League Covenant. The equilibrium of naval power created at London was not only deceptive, but it was erected on an illusory foundation.

Appendix

Text of the Treaty*

ARTICLE 1

The High Contracting Parties agree not to exercise their rights to lay down the keels of capital ship replacement tonage during the years 1931-1936 inclusive as provided in Chapter II, Part 3 of the Treaty for the Limitation of Naval Armament signed between them at Washington on the 6th February, 1922, and referred to in the present Treaty as the Washington Treaty.

This provision is without prejudice to the disposition relating to the replacement of ships accidentally lost or destroyed contained in Chapter II, Part 3, Section I, paragraph *(c)* of the said Treaty.

France and Italy may, however, build the replacement tonnage which they were entitled to lay down in 1927 and 1929 in accordance with the provisions of the said Treaty.

ARTICLE 2

1. The United States, the United Kingdom of Great Britain and Northern Ireland and Japan shall dispose of the following capital ships as provided in this Article:

United States:
   "Florida".
   "Utah".
   "Arkansas" or "Wyoming".
United Kingdom:
   "Benbow".
   "Iron Duke".
   "Marlborough".
   "Emperor of India".
   "Tiger".
Japan:
   "Hiyei".

(a) Subject to the provisions of sub-paragraph *(b)*, the above ships, unless converted to target use exclusively in accordance with Chapter II, Part 2, paragraph II*(c)* of the Washington Treaty, shall be scrapped in the following manner:

One of the ships to be scrapped by the United States, and two of those to be scrapped by the United Kingdom shall be rendered unfit for warlike service, in accordance with Chapter II, Part 2, paragraph III*(b)* of the Washington Treaty, within twelve months from the coming into force of the present Treaty. These ships shall be finally scrapped, in accordance with paragraph II*(a)* or *(b)* of the said Part 2, within twenty-four months from the said coming into force. In the

---

* Names of delegates and signatories to the treaty are omitted.

129

case of the second of the ships to be scrapped by the United States, and of the third and fourth of the ships to be scrapped by the United Kingdom, the said periods shall be eighteen and thirty months respectively from the coming into force of the present Treaty.

(b) Of the ships to be disposed of under this Article, the following may be retained for training purposes:

by the United States: "Arkansas" or "Wyoming".

by the United Kingdom: "Iron Duke".

by Japan: "Hiyei".

These ships shall be reduced to the condition prescribed in Section V of Annex II to Part II of the present Treaty. The work of reducing these vessels to the required condition shall begin, in the case of the United States and the United Kingdom, within twelve months, and in the case of Japan within eighteen months from the coming into force of the present Treaty; the work shall be completed within six months of the expiration of the above-mentioned periods.

Any of these ships which are not retained for training purposes shall be rendered unfit for warlike service within eighteen months, and finally scrapped within thirty months, of the coming into force of the present Treaty.

2. Subject to any disposal of capital ships which might be necessitated, in accordance with the Washington Treaty, by the building by France or Italy of the replacement tonnage referred to in Article 1 of the present Treaty, all existing capital ships mentioned in Chapter II, Part 3, Section II of the Washington Treaty and not designated above to be disposed of may be retained during the term of the present Treaty.

3. The right of replacement is not lost by delay in laying down replacement tonnage, and the old vessel may be retained until replaced even though due for scrapping under Chapter II, Part 3, Section II of the Washington Treaty.

ARTICLE 3

1. For the purposes of the Washington Treaty, the definition of an aircraft carrier given in Chapter II, Part 4 of the said Treaty is hereby replaced by the following definition:

The expression "aircraft carrier" includes any surface vessel of war, whatever its displacement, designed for the specific and exclusive purpose of carrying aircraft and so constructed that aircraft can be launched therefrom and landed thereon.

2. The fitting of a landing-on or flying-off platform or deck on a capital ship, cruiser or destroyer, provided such vessel was not designed or adapted exclusively as an aircraft carrier, shall not cause any vessel so fitted to be charged against or classified in the category of aircraft carriers.

3. No capital ship in existence on the 1st April, 1930, shall be fitted with a landing-on platform or deck.

ARTICLE 4

1. No aircraft carrier of 10,000 tons (10,160 metric tons) or less standard displacement mounting a gun above 6.1-inch (155 mm.) calibre shall be acquired by or constructed by or for any of the High Contracting Parties.

2. As from the coming into force of the present Treaty in respect of all the High Contracting Parties, no aircraft carrier of 10,000 tons (10,160 metric tons) or less standard displacement mounting a gun above 6.1-inch (155 mm.) calibre shall be constructed within the jurisdiction of any of the High Contracting Parties.

ARTICLE 5

An aircraft carrier must not be designed and constructed for carrying a more powerful armament than that authorized by Article IX or Article X of the Washington Treaty, or by Article 4 of the present Treaty, as the case may be.

Wherever in the said Articles IX and X the calibre of 6 inches (152 mm.) is mentioned, the calibre of 6.1 inches (155 mm.) is substituted therefor.

PART II

ARTICLE 6

1. The rules for determining standard displacement prescribed in Chapter II, Part 4 of the Washington Treaty shall apply to all surface vessels of war of each of the High Contracting Parties.

2. The standard displacement of a submarine is the surface displacement of the vessel complete (exclusive of the water in non-watertight structure) fully manned, engined, and equipped ready for sea, including all armament and ammunition, equipment, outfit, provisions for crew, miscellaneous stores, and implements of every description that are intended to be carried in war, but without fuel, lubricating oil, fresh water or ballast water of any kind on board.

3. Each naval combatant vessel shall be rated at its displacement tonnage when in the standard condition. The word "ton", except in the expression "metric tons", shall be understood to be the ton of 2,240 pounds (1,016 kilos.).

ARTICLE 7

1. No submarine the standard displacement of which exceeds 2,000 tons (2,032 metric tons) or with a gun above 5.1-inch (130 mm.) calibre shall be acquired by or constructed by or for any of the High Contracting Parties.

2. Each of the High Contracting Parties may, however, retain, build or acquire a maximum number of three submarines of a standard displacement not exceeding 2,800 tons (2,845 metric tons); these submarines may carry guns not above 6.1-inch (155 mm.) calibre. Within this number, France may retain one unit, already launched, of 2,880 tons (2,926 metric tons), with guns the calibre of which is 8 inches (203 mm.).

3. The High Contracting Parties may retain the submarines which they possessed on the 1st April, 1930, having a standard displacement not in excess of 2,000 tons (2,032 metric tons) and armed with guns above 5.1-inch (130 mm.) calibre.

4. As from the coming into force of the present Treaty in respect of all the High Contracting Parties, no submarine the standard displacement of which exceeds 2,000 tons (2,032 metric tons) or with a gun above 5.1-inch (130 mm.) calibre shall be constructed within the jurisdiction of any of the High Contracting Parties, except as provided in paragraph 2 of this Article.

ARTICLE 8

Subject to any special agreements which may submit them to limitation, the following vessels are exempt from limitation:

(a) naval surface combatant vessels of 600 tons (610 metric tons) standard displacement and under;

(b) naval surface combatant vessels exceeding 600 tons (610 metric tons), but not exceeding 2,000 tons (2,032 metric tons) standard displacement, provided they have none of the following characteristics:

(1) mount a gun above 6.1-inch (155 mm.) calibre;

(2) mount more than four guns above 3-inch (76 mm.) calibre;

(3) are designed or fitted to launch torpedoes;

(4) are designed for a speed greater than twenty knots.

(c) naval surface vessels not specifically built as fighting ships which are employed on fleet duties or as troop transports or in some other way than as fighting ships, provided they have none of the following characteristics:

(1) mount a gun above 6.1-inch (155 mm.) calibre;

(2) mount more than four guns above 3-inch (76 mm.) calibre;

(3) are designed or fitted to launch torpedoes;

(4) are designed for a speed greater than twenty knots;

(5) are protected by armour plate;

(6) are designed or fitted to launch mines;

(7) are fitted to receive aircraft on board from the air;

(8) mount more than one aircraft-launching apparatus on the centre line; or two, one on each broadside;

(9) if fitted with any means of launching aircraft into the air, are designed or adapted to operate at sea more than three aircraft.

ARTICLE 9

The rules as to replacement contained in Annex I to this Part II are applicable to vessels of war not exceeding 10,000 tons (10,160 metric tons) standard displacement, with the exception of aircraft carriers, whose replacement is governed by the provisions of the Washington Treaty.

ARTICLE 10

Within one month after the date of laying down and the date of completion respectively of each vessel of war, other than capital ships, aircraft carriers and the vessels exempt from limitation under Article 8, laid down or completed by or for them after the coming into force of the present Treaty, the High Contracting Parties shall communicate to each of the other High Contracting Parties the information detailed below:

(*a*) the date of laying the keel and the following particulars:
   classification of the vessel;
   standard displacement in tons and metric tons;
   principal dimensions, namely: length at water-line, extreme beam at or below water-line;
   mean draft at standard displacement;
   calibre of the largest gun.

(*b*) the date of completion together with the foregoing particulars relating to the vessel at that date.

The information to be given in the case of capital ships and aircraft carriers is governed by the Washington Treaty.

ARTICLE 11

Subject to the provisions of Article 2 of the present Treaty, the rules for disposal contained in Annex II to this Part II shall be applied to all vessels of war to be disposed of under the said Treaty, and to aircraft carriers as defined in Article 3.

ARTICLE 12

1. Subject to any supplementary agreements which may modify, as between the High Contracting Parties concerned, the lists in Annex III to this Part II, the special vessels shown therein may be retained and their tonnage shall not be included in the tonnage subject to limitation.

2. Any other vessel constructed, adapted or acquired to serve the purposes for which these special vessels are retained shall be charged against the tonnage of the appropriate combatant category, according to the characteristics of the vessel, unless such vessel conforms to the characteristics of vessels exempt from limitation under Article 8.

3. Japan may, however, replace the minelayers "Aso" and "Tokiwa" by two new minelayers before the 31st December, 1936. The standard displacement of each of the new vessels shall not exceed 5,000 tons (5,080 metric tons); their speed shall not exceed twenty knots, and their other characteristics shall conform to the provisions of paragraph (*b*) of Article 8. The new vessels shall be regarded as special vessels and their tonnage shall not be chargeable to the tonnage of any combatant category. The "Aso" and "Tokiwa" shall be disposed of in accordance with Section I or II of Annex II to this Part II, on completion of the replacement vessels.

4. The "Asama", "Yakumo", Izumo", "Iwate" and "Kasuga" shall be disposed of in accordance with Section I or II of Annex II to this Part II when the first three vessels of the "Kuma" class have been replaced by new vessels. These three vessels of the "Kuma" class shall be reduced to the condition prescribed in Section V, sub-paragraph (*b*) 2 of Annex II to this Part II, and are

to be used for training ships, and their tonnage shall not thereafter be included in the tonnage subject to limitation.

ARTICLE 13

Existing ships of various types, which, prior to the 1st April, 1930, have been used as stationary training establishments or hulks, may be retained in a non-seagoing condition.

ANNEX I

Rules for replacement

SECTION I.—Except as provided in Section III of this Annex and Part III of the present Treaty, a vessel shall not be replaced before it becomes "over-age". A vessel shall be deemed to be "over-age" when the following number of years have elapsed since the date of its completion:

(*a*) For a surface vessel exceeding 3,000 tons (3,048 metric tons) but not exceeding 10,000 tons (10,160 metric tons) standard displacement:

    (i) if laid down before the 1st January, 1920: 16 years;

    (ii) if laid down after the 31st December, 1919: 20 years.

(*b*) For a surface vessel not exceeding 3,000 tons (3,048 metric tons) standard displacement:

    (i) if laid down before the 1st January, 1921: 12 years;

    (ii) if laid down after the 31st December, 1920: 16 years.

(*c*) For a submarine: 13 years.

The keels of replacement tonnage shall not be laid down more than three years before the year in which the vessel to be replaced becomes "over-age"; but this period is reduced to two years in the case of any replacement surface vessel not exceeding 3,000 tons (3,048 metric tons) standard displacement.

The right of replacement is not lost by delay in laying down replacement tonnage.

SECTION II.—Except as otherwise provided in the present Treaty, the vessel or vessels, whose retention would cause the maximum tonnage permitted in the category to be exceeded, shall, on the completion or acquisition of replacement tonnage, be disposed of in accordance with Annex II to this Part II.

SECTION III.—In the event of loss or accidental destruction a vessel may be immediately replaced.

ANNEX II

Rules for disposal of Vessels of War

The present Treaty provides for the disposal of vessels of war in the following ways:

    (i) by scrapping (sinking or breaking up);

    (ii) by converting the vessel to a hulk;

(iii) by converting the vessel to target use exclusively;

(iv) by retaining the vessel exclusively for experimental purposes;

(v) by retaining the vessel exclusively for training purposes.

Any vessel of war to be disposed of, other than a capital ship, may either be scrapped or converted to a hulk at the option of the High Contracting Party concerned.

Vessels, other than capital ships, which have been retained for target, experimental or training purposes, shall finally be scrapped or converted to hulks.

Section I.—*Vessels to be scrapped*

(a) A vessel to be disposed of by scrapping, by reason of its replacement, must be rendered incapable of warlike service within six months of the date of the completion of its successor, or of the first of its successors if there are more than one. If, however, the completion of the new vessel or vessels be delayed, the work of rendering the old vessel incapable of warlike service shall, nevertheless, be completed within four and a half years from the date of laying the keel of the new vessel, or of the first of the new vessels; but should the new vessel, or any of the new vessels, be a surface vessel not exceeding 3,000 tons (3,048 metric tons) standard displacement, this period is reduced to three and a half years.

(b) A vessel to be scrapped shall be considered incapable of warlike service when there shall have been removed and landed or else destroyed in the ship:

(1) all guns and essential parts of guns, fire control tops and revolving parts of all barbettes and turrets;

(2) all hydraulic or electric machinery for operating turrets;

(3) all fire control instruments and rangefinders;

(4) all ammunition, explosives, mines and mine rails;

(5) all torpedoes, war heads, torpedo tubes and training racks;

(6) all wireless telegraphy installations;

(7) all main propelling machinery, or alternatively the armoured conning tower and all side armour plate;

(8) all aircraft cranes, derricks, lifts and launching apparatus. All landing-on or flying-off platforms and decks, or alternatively all main propelling machinery;

(9) in addition, in the case of submarines, all main storage batteries, air compressor plants and ballast pumps.

(c) Scrapping shall be finally effected in either of the following ways within twelve months of the date on which the work of rendering the vessel incapable of warlike service is due for completion:

(1) permanent sinking of the vessel;

(2) breaking the vessel up; this shall always include the destruction or removal of all machinery, boilers and armour, and all deck, side and bottom plating.

Section II.—*Vessels to be converted to hulks*

A vessel to be disposed of by conversion to a hulk shall be considered finally disposed of when the conditions prescribed in Section I, paragraph (b), have been complied with, omitting sub-paragraphs (6), (7) and (8), and when the following have been effected:

(1) mutilation beyond repair of all propeller shafts, thrust blocks, turbine gearing or main propelling motors, and turbines or cylinders of main engines;

(2) removal of propeller brackets;

(3) removal and breaking up of all aircraft lifts, and the removal of all aircraft cranes, derricks and launching apparatus.

The vessel must be put in the above condition within the same limits of time as provided in Section I for rendering a vessel incapable of warlike service.

SECTION III.—*Vessels to be converted to target use*

(*a*) A vessel to be disposed of by conversion to target use exclusively shall be considered incapable of warlike service when there have been removed and landed, or rendered unserviceable on board, the following:

(1) all guns;

(2) all fire control tops and instruments and main fire control communication wiring;

(3) all machinery for operating gun mountings or turrets;

(4) all ammunition, explosives, mines, torpedoes and torpedo tubes;

(5) all aviation facilities and accessories.

The vessel must be put into the above condition within the same limits of time as provided in Section I for rendering a vessel incapable of warlike service.

(*b*) In addition to the rights already possessed by each High Contracting Party under the Washington Treaty, each High Contracting Party is permitted to retain, for target use exclusively, at any one time:

(1) not more than three vessels (cruisers or destroyers), but of these three vessels only one may exceed 3,000 tons (3,048 metric tons) standard displacement;

(2) one submarine.

(*c*) On retaining a vessel for target use, the High Contracting Party concerned undertakes not to recondition it for warlike service.

SECTION IV.—*Vessels retained for experimental purposes*

(*a*) A vessel to be disposed of by conversion to experimental purposes exclusively shall be dealt with in accordance with the provisions of Section III(*a*) of this Annex.

(*b*) Without prejudice to the general rules, and provided that due notice be given to the other High Contracting Parties, reasonable variation from the conditions prescribed in Section III(*a*) of this Annex, in so far as may be necessary for the purposes of a special experiment, may be permitted as a temporary measure.

Any High Contracting Party taking advantage of this provision is required to furnish full details of any such variations and the period for which they will be required.

(*c*) Each High Contracting Party is permitted to retain for experimental purposes exclusively at any one time:

(1) not more than two vessels (cruisers or destroyers), but of these two vessels only one may exceed 3,000 tons (3,048 metric tons) standard displacement;

(2) one submarine.

(*d*) The United Kingdom is allowed to retain, in their present conditions, the monitor "Roberts", the main armament guns and mountings of which have been mutilated, and the seaplane carrier "Ark Royal", until no longer required for experimental purposes. The retention of these two vessels is without prejudice to the retention of vessels permitted under (*c*) above.

(*e*) On retaining a vessel for experimental purposes the High Contracting Party concerned undertakes not to recondition it for warlike service.

SECTION V.—*Vessels retained for training purposes*

(*a*) In addition to the rights already possessed by any High Contracting Party under the Washington Treaty, each High Contracting Party is permitted to retain for training purposes exclusively the following vessels:

United States: 1 capital ship ("Arkansas" or "Wyoming");

France: 2 surface vessels, one of which may exceed 3,000 tons (3,048 metric tons) standard displacement;

United Kingdom: 1 capital ship ("Iron Duke");

Italy: 2 surface vessels, one of which may exceed 3,000 tons (3,048 metric tons) standard displacement;

Japan: 1 capital ship ("Hiyei"), 3 cruisers ("Kuma" class).

(*b*) Vessels retained for training purposes under the provisions of paragraph (*a*) shall, within six months of the date on which they are required to be disposed of, be dealt with as follows:

1. *Capital Ships.*

The following is to be carried out:

(1) removal of main armament guns, revolving parts of all barbettes and turrets; machinery for operating turrets; but three turrets with their armament may be retained in each ship;

(2) removal of all ammunition and explosives in excess of the quantity required for target practice training for the guns remaining on board;

(3) removal of conning tower and the side armour belt between the foremost and aftermost barbettes;

(4) removal or mutilation of all torpedo tubes;

(5) removal or mutilation on board of all boilers in excess of the number required for a maximum speed of eighteen knots.

2. *Other surface vessels retained by France, Italy and Japan.*

The following is to be carried out:

(1) removal of one half of the guns, but four guns of main calibre may be retained on each vessel;

(2) removal of all torpedo tubes;

(3) removal of all aviation facilities and accessories;

(4) removal of one half of the boilers.

(c) The High Contracting Party concerned undertakes that vessels retained in accordance with the provisions of this Section shall not be used for any combatant purpose.

ANNEX III

Special vessels

UNITED STATES

Name and type of vessel	Displacement tons
Aroostoook—Minelayer	4,950
Oglala—Minelayer	4,950
Baltimore—Minelayer	4,413
San Francisco—Minelayer	4,083
Cheyenne—Monitor	2,800
Helena—Gunboat	1,392
Isabel—Yacht	938
Niagara—Yacht	2,600
Bridgeport—Destroyer tender	11,750
Dobbin—Destroyer tender	12,450
Melville—Destroyer tender	7,150
Whitney—Destroyer tender	12,450
Holland—Submarine tender	11,570
Henderson—Naval transport	10,000
	91,496

FRANCE

Name and type of vessel	Displacement tons
Castor—Minelayer	3,150
Pollux—Minelayer	2,461
Commandant-Teste—Seaplane carrier	10,000
Aisne—Despatch vessel	600
Marne—Despatch vessel	600
Ancre—Despatch vessel	604
Scarpe—Despatch vessel	604
Suippe—Despatch vessel	604
Dunkerque—Despatch vessel	644
Laffaux—Despatch vessel	644
Bapaume—Despatch vessel	644
Nancy—Despatch vessel	644
Calais—Despatch vessel	644
Lassigny—Despatch vessel	644
Les Eparges—Despatch vessel	644
Remiremont—Despatch vessel	644

Tahure—Despatch vessel 644
Toul—Despatch vessel 644
Épinal—Despatch vessel 644
Liévin—Despatch vessel 644
(—)—Netlayer 2,293

28,644

BRITISH COMMONWEALTH OF NATIONS

Name and type of vessel	Displacement tons
Adventure—Minelayer (United Kingdom)	6,740
Albatross—Seaplane carrier (Australia)	5,000
Erebus—Monitor (United Kingdom)	7,200
Terror—Monitor (United Kingdom)	7,200
Marshal Soult—Monitor (United Kingdom)	6,400
Clive—Sloop (India)	2,021
Medway—Submarine depot ship (United Kingdom)	15,000
	49,561

ITALY

Name and type of vessel	Displacement tons
Miraglia—Seaplane carrier	4,880
Faà di Bruno—Monitor	2,800
Monte Grappa—Monitor	605
Montello—Monitor	605
Monte Cengio—Ex-monitor	500
Monte Novegno—Ex-monitor	500
Campania—Sloop	2,070
	11,960

JAPAN

Name and type of vessel	Displacement tons
Aso—Minelayer	7,180
Tokiwa—Minelayer	9,240
Asama—Old cruiser	9,240
Yakumo—Old cruiser	9,010
Izumo—Old cruiser	9,180
Iwate—Old cruiser	9,180
Kasuga—Old cruiser	7,080
Yodo—Gunboat	1,320
	61,430

PART III

The President of the United States of America, His Majesty the King of Great Britain, Ireland and the British Dominions beyond the Seas, Emperor of India, and His Majesty the Emperor of Japan, have agreed as between themselves to the provisions of this Part III:

ARTICLE 14

The naval combatant vessels of the United States, the British Commonwealth of Nations and Japan, other than capital ships, aircraft carriers and all vessels exempt from limitation under Article 8, shall be limited during the term of the present Treaty as provided in this Part III, and, in the case of special vessels, as provided in Article 12.

ARTICLE 15

For the purpose of this Part III the definition of the cruiser and destroyer categories shall be as follows:

Cruisers.

Surface vessels of war, other than capital ships or aircraft carriers, the standard displacement of which exceeds 1,850 tons (1,880 metric tons), or with a gun above 5.1-inch (130 mm.) calibre.

The cruiser category is divided into two sub-categories, as follows:

(a) cruisers carrying a gun above 6.1-inch (155 mm.) calibre;

(b) cruisers carrying a gun not above 6.1-inch (155 mm.) calibre.

Destroyers.

Surface vessels of war the standard displacement of which does not exceed 1,850 tons (1,880 metric tons), and with a gun not above 5.1-inch (130 mm.) calibre.

ARTICLE 16

1. The completed tonnage in the cruiser, destroyer and submarine categories which is not to be exceeded on the 31st December, 1936, is given in the following table:

CRUISERS

High Contracting Parties	tons	Metric tons
(a) with guns of more than 6.1-inch (155 mm.) calibre		
United States	180,000	182,880
British Commonwealth of Nations	146,800	149,149
Japan	108,400	110,450
(b) with guns of 6.1-inch (155 mm.) calibre or less		
United States	143,500	145,796
British Commonwealth of Nations	192,200	195,275
Japan	100,450	102,057

DESTROYERS

United States	150,000	152,400
British Commonwealth of Nations	150,000	152,400
Japan	105,500	107,188

SUBMARINES

United States	52,700	53,543
British Commonwealth of Nations	52,700	53,543
Japan	52,700	53,543

2. Vessels which cause the total tonnage in any category to exceed the figures given in the foregoing table shall be disposed of gradually during the period ending on the 31st December, 1936.

3. The maximum number of cruisers of sub-category (a) shall be as follows: for the United States, eighteen; for the British Commonwealth of Nations, fifteen; for Japan, twelve.

4. In the destroyer category not more than sixteen per cent of the allowed total tonnage shall be employed in vessels of over 1,500 tons (1,524 metric tons) standard displacement. Destroyers completed or under construction on the 1st April, 1930, in excess of this percentage may be retained, but no other destroyers exceeding 1,500 tons (1,524 metric tons) standard displacement shall be constructed or acquired until a reduction to such sixteen per cent has been effected.

5. Not more than twenty-five per cent of the allowed total tonnage in the cruiser category may be fitted with a landing-on platform or deck for aircraft.

6. It is understood that the submarines referred to in paragraphs 2 and 3 of Article 7 will be counted as part of the total submarine tonnage of the High Contracting Party concerned.

7. The tonnage of any vessels retained under Article 13 or disposed of in accordance with Annex II to Part II of the present Treaty shall not be included in the tonnage subject to limitation.

ARTICLE 17

A transfer not exceeding ten per cent of the allowed total tonnage of the category or sub-category into which the transfer is to be made shall be permitted between cruisers of sub-category (b) and destroyers.

ARTICLE 18

The United States contemplates the completion by 1935 of fifteen cruisers of sub-category (a) of an aggregate tonnage of 150,000 tons (152,400 metric tons). For each of the three remaining cruisers of sub-category (a) which it is entitled to construct the United States may elect to substitute 15,166 tons (15,409 metric tons) of cruisers of sub-category (b). In case the United States shall construct one or more of such three remaining cruisers of sub-category (a), the sixteenth unit will not be laid down before 1933 and will not be completed before 1936;

the seventeenth will not be laid down before 1934 and will not be completed before 1937; the eighteenth will not be laid down before 1935 and will not be completed before 1938.

ARTICLE 19

Except as provided in Article 20, the tonnage laid down in any category subject to limitation in accordance with Article 16 shall not exceed the amount necessary to reach the maximum allowed tonnage of the category, or to replace vessels that become "over-age" before the 31st December, 1936. Nevertheless, replacement tonnage may be laid down for cruisers and submarines that become "over-age" in 1937, 1938 and 1939, and for destroyers that become "over-age" in 1937 and 1938.

ARTICLE 20

Notwithstanding the rules for replacement contained in Annex I to Part II:

(a) The "Frobisher" and "Effingham" (United Kingdom) may be disposed of during the year 1936. Apart from the cruisers under construction on the 1st April, 1930, the total replacement tonnage of cruisers to be completed, in the case of the British Commonwealth of Nations, prior to the 31st December, 1936, shall not exceed 91,000 tons (92,456 metric tons).

(b) Japan may replace the "Tama" by new construction to be completed during the year 1936.

(c) In addition to replacing destroyers becoming "over-age" before the 31st December, 1936, Japan may lay down, in each of the years 1935 and 1936, not more than 5,200 tons (5,283 metric tons) to replace part of the vessels that become "over-age" in 1938 and 1939.

(d) Japan may anticipate replacement during the term of the present Treaty by laying down not more than 19,200 tons (19,507 metric tons) of submarine tonnage, of which not more than 12,000 tons (12,192 metric tons) shall be completed by the 31st December, 1936.

ARTICLE 21

If, during the term of the present Treaty, the requirements of the national security of any High Contracting Party in respect of vessels of war limited by Part III of the present Treaty are in the opinion of that Party materially affected by new construction of any Power other than those who have joined in Part III of this Treaty, that High Contracting Party will notify the other Parties to Part III as to the increase required to be made in its own tonnages within one or more of the categories of such vessels of war, specifying particularly the proposed increases and the reasons therefor, and shall be entitled to make such increase. Thereupon the other Parties to Part III of this Treaty shall be entitled to make a proportionate increase in the category or categories specified; and the said other Parties shall promptly advise with each other through diplomatic channels as to the situation thus presented.

PART IV

ARTICLE 22

The following are accepted as established rules of International Law:

(1) In their action with regard to merchant ships, submarines must conform to the rules of International Law to which surface vessels are subject.

(2) In particular, except in the case of persistent refusal to stop on being duly summoned, or of active resistance to visit or search, a warship, whether surface vessel or submarine, may not sink or render incapable of navigation a merchant vessel without having first placed passengers, crew and ship's papers in a place of safety. For this purpose the ship's boats are not regarded as a place of safety unless the safety of the passengers and crew is assured, in the existing sea and weather condition, by the proximity of land, or the presence of another vessel which is in a position to take them on board.

The High Contracting Parties invite all other Powers to express their assent to the above rules.

PART V

ARTICLE 23

The present Treaty shall remain in force until the 31st December, 1936, subject to the following exceptions:

(1) Part IV shall remain in force without limit of time;

(2) The provisions of Articles 3, 4 and 5, and of Article 11 and Annex II to Part II so far as they relate to aircraft carriers, shall remain in force for the same period as the Washington Treaty.

Unless the High Contracting Parties should agree otherwise by reason of a more general agreement limiting naval armaments, to which they all become parties, they shall meet in conference in 1935 to frame a new treaty to replace and to carry out the purposes of the present Treaty, it being understood that none of the provisions of the present Treaty shall prejudice the attitude of any of the High Contracting Parties at the conference agreed to.

ARTICLE 24

1. The present Treaty shall be ratified by the High Contracting Parties in accordance with their respective constitutional methods and the ratifications shall be deposited at London as soon as possible. Certified copies of all the *procès-verbaux* of the deposit of ratifications will be transmitted to the Governments of all the High Contracting Parties.

2. As soon as the ratifications of the United States of America, of His Majesty the King of Great Britain, Ireland and the British Dominions beyond the Seas, Emperor of India, in respect of each and all of the Members of the British Commonwealth of Nations as enumerated in the preamble of the present Treaty, and of His Majesty the Emperor of Japan have been deposited, the Treaty shall come into force in respect of the said High Contracting Parties.

3. On the date of the coming into force referred to in the preceding paragraph, Parts I, II, IV and V of the present Treaty will come into force in respect of the French Republic and the Kingdom of Italy if their ratifications have been deposited at that date; otherwise these Parts will come into force in respect of each of those powers on the deposit of its ratification.

4. The rights and obligations resulting from Part III of the present Treaty are limited to the High Contracting Parties mentioned in paragraph 2 of this Article. The High Contracting Parties will agree as to the date on which, and the conditions under which, the obligations assumed under the said Part III by the High Contracting Parties mentioned in paragraph 2 of this Article will bind them in relation to France and Italy; such agreement will determine at the same time the corresponding obligations of France and Italy in relation to the other High Contracting Parties.

Article 25

After the deposit of the ratifications of all the High Contracting Parties, His Majesty's Government in the United Kingdom of Great Britain and Northern Ireland will communicate the provisions inserted in Part IV of the present Treaty to all Powers which are not signatories of the said Treaty, inviting them to accede thereto definitely and without limit of time.

Such accession shall be effected by a declaration addressed to His Majesty's Government in the United Kingdom of Great Britain and Northern Ireland.

Article 26

The present Treaty, of which the French and English texts are both authentic, shall remain deposited in the archives of His Majesty's Government in the United Kingdom of Great Britain and Northern Ireland. Duly certified copies thereof shall be transmitted to the Governments of all the High Contracting Parties.

In faith whereof the above-named Plenipotentiaries have signed the present Treaty and have affixed thereto their seals.

Done at London, the twenty-second day of April, nineteen hundred and thirty.

Notes

I

1. Proceedings of the General Board, I, 112-113, 237, 325, General Board Files, Navy Department, Washington, D.C.; Admiral George Dewey, Senior Member, Joint Army and Navy Board, to Secretary of the Navy, June 24, 1904, General Board File 425.

2. William Reynolds Braisted, *The United States Navy in the Pacific, 1897-1909*, Austin, Texas, 1958, p. 242; Howard K. Beale, *Theodore Roosevelt and the Rise of America to World Power*, Baltimore, 1956, pp. 154-155.

3. General Board No. 420-1 of April 25, 1907, Letterpress, V, 19-28, General Board Files. See Louis Morton, "Military and Naval Preparations for the Defense of the Philippines during the War Scare of 1907," *Military Affairs*, XIII, 1949, 95-104.

4. Thomas A. Bailey, *Theodore Roosevelt and the Japanese-American Crises*, Stanford, 1934, pp. 261-303; Beale, *Theodore Roosevelt and the Rise of America to World Power*, pp. 328-329.

5. E. L. Woodward, *Great Britain and the German Navy*, Oxford, 1935, p. 15.

6. Arthur J. Marder, *The Anatomy of British Sea Power: A History of British Naval Policy in the Pre-Dreadnought Era, 1880-1905*, New York, 1940, p. 545. Mahan viewed the German build-up as a deterrent to Britain, since the former "needs a navy of such strength that the greatest naval power will not lightly incur hostilities." Thus, if Germany wished to pursue a "point of foreign policy to which Great Britain objects," the latter would be especially cautious in determining the extent to which this policy should be opposed. Alfred Thayer Mahan, *Armaments and Arbitration*, New York, 1912, p. 63.

7. Charles S. Campbell, Jr., *Anglo-American Understanding, 1898-1903*, Baltimore, 1957, p. 41.

8. Tatsuji Takeuchi, *War and Diplomacy in the Japanese Empire*, Garden City, N.Y., 1935, p. 128.

9. Woodrow Wilson to Josephus Daniels, Washington, July 21, 1915, Franklin D. Roosevelt Papers, Hyde Park, N.Y., Group 10, Box 156; Report of the General Board, November 9, 1915, *Annual Reports of the Navy Department for the Fiscal Year 1915*, Washington, 1916, p. 74.

10. Memorandum Adopted by the Executive Committee, clipped to copy of General Board No. 420-2 of July 30, 1915, General Board File 420-2.

11. Statement of Woodrow Wilson to his associates in 1919, quoted in Herbert Hoover, *The Ordeal of Woodrow Wilson*, New York, 1958, pp. 194-195; Josephus Daniels, *The Wilson Era—Years of War and After, 1917-1923*, Chapel Hill, 1946, pp. 367-388.

12. Harold and Margaret Sprout, *Toward a New Order of Sea Power: American Naval Policy and the World Scene, 1918-1922*, 2nd ed., Princeton, 1943, p. 59; General Board report of Nov. 11, 1918, subject: "A Plan for League of Nations Navy," fastened to General Board No. 438-2 Serial 1521-0 of April 6, 1932, General Board Files.

13. Naval expenditures in Japan increased from $85,000,000 in 1917 to $245,000,000 in 1921. Raymond Leslie Buell, *The Washington Conference*, New York, 1922, p. 139. Naval appropriations for the fiscal year 1921-1922 amounted to 32 percent of Japan's total budget as compared with 12 percent and 9 percent for the United States and Great Britain respectively. General Board No. 438 Serial 1088 of Sept. 27, 1921, General Board Files.

14. Charles Nelson Spinks, "The Termination of the Anglo-Japanese Alliance," *Pacific Historical Review*, VI, 1937, 326-328; *Documents on British Foreign Policy, 1919-1939*, ed. Ernest L. Woodward and Rohan Butler, 1st Series, VI, London, 1956, 1049-1055.

15. For correspondence concerning the preliminaries of the conference, see *Papers Relating to the Foreign Relations of the United States, 1921*, I, 18-87, hereafter cited as *Foreign Relations*.

16. General Board No. 438 Serial 1088 of Sept. 12, 1921, Washington Conference Files, Box 14, State Department Records, National Archives. The Board concluded that "no interpretative declarations by either government, or by both, can be as satisfactory to the United States as the non-continuance of the alliance." The United States quietly discouraged a renewal of the

pact. See Memorandum of a Conversation between the Secretary of State (Hughes) and the British Ambassador (Geddes), June 23, 1921, *Foreign Relations, 1921,* I, 314-315.

17. General Board No. 438 Serial 1088-A of Sept. 17, 1921, Washington Conference Files, Box 14, State Department Records, National Archives.

18. General Board No. 438 Serial 1088-A of Sept. 17, 1921, Washington Conference Files, Box 14, State Department Records, National Archives; Raymond G. O'Connor, "The 'Yardstick' and Naval Disarmament in the 1920's," *Mississippi Valley Historical Review,* XLV, 1958, 442.

19. Memorandum of a Conversation held in Mr. Hughes' Room at the State Department, Washington, D.C., on Monday, Dec. 12, 1921, Charles Evans Hughes Papers, Box 169, folder 9c, Manuscript Division, Library of Congress.

20. Quoted in Sprout and Sprout, *Toward a New Order of Sea Power,* p. 256.

21. Conference on the Limitation of Armament, *Senate Document,* 67th Cong., 2 sess., No. 126, p. 812.

22. Merlo J. Pusey, *Charles Evans Hughes,* New York, 1951, II, 508. For a comprehensive survey, see Charles Leonard Hoag, *Preface to Preparedness: The Washington Disarmament Conference and Public Opinion,* Washington, 1941.

23. Captain Dudley W. Knox, *The Eclipse of American Sea Power,* New York, 1922, p. vii.

24. General Board No. 420-2 Serial 1108, March 29, 1922, General Board Files.

25. Quoted in Philip C. Jessup, *Elihu Root,* New York, 1938, II, 452.

26. Roland A. Chaput, *Disarmament in British Foreign Policy,* London, 1935, p. 125.

27. Admiral of the Fleet Lord Wester-Wemyss, "Washington and After," *Nineteenth Century and After,* XCI, 1922, 409. Chaput claims that this article represented British opinion on the negative aspects of the treaties. *Op. cit.,* p. 126.

28. Takeuchi, *War and Diplomacy in the Japanese Empire,* p. 236; Pusey, *Charles Evans Hughes,* II, 508; *Japan Times and Mail Weekly Edition,* Jan. 14, 1922, p. 8; Roy Hidemichi Akagi, *Japan's Foreign Relations, 1542-1936, A Short History,* Tokyo, 1936, p. 392.

29. Sprout and Sprout, *Toward a New Order of Sea Power,* p. 262.

30. Apparently the government intended that the ratio should apply to all classes of ships, whereas the Admiralty thought that it was to apply only to battleships and aircraft carriers. Chaput, *Disarmament in British Foreign Policy,* p. 95.

31. Samuel Flagg Bemis has approvingly observed that "Secretary Hughes had the sanest conception of America's real interests in Asia, when, in the Washington treaties of 1922, he shaped American policy towards a face-saving retreat from Asia." "Main Trends of American Foreign Policy," in *Before America Decides: Foresight in Foreign Affairs,* ed. Frank B. Davidson and George S. Viereck, Jr., Cambridge, Mass., 1938, p. 87. Actually, the treaties constituted a further involvement in Asia, for they committed the United States to a concerted effort to maintain the territorial integrity of China which was formalized by a duly ratified agreement. Previously, America's responsibility had been confined to a unilateral declaration of policy that had never received Constitutional sanction.

II

1. Denby to General Board, No. 11158-85 of Jan. 9, 1922, General Board Files.

2. General Board No. 420-2 Serial No. 1108 of March 29, 1922, with blueprint enclosure; General Board No. 420-2 of Sept. 24, 1920. *Ibid.*

3. "Annual Report of the Secretary of the Navy, Dec. 1, 1922," *Annual Reports of the Navy Department for the Fiscal Year 1922,* Washington, 1923, p. 1. In late 1922 the separate Atlantic and Pacific fleets were reorganized into one United States fleet, which was divided between the two oceans and rendezvoused annually for strategic and tactical training.

4. General Board No. 438 Serial 1347-7(c) of April 25, 1927, Naval Record Group 80, National Archives.

5. General Board No. 420-2 Serial 1162 of April 7, 1923, General Board Files. The Board continued to emphasize the need for modern ships, especially cruisers, which the United States lacked. General Board No. 420-2 Serial 1206 of April 18, 1924; No. 420-2 Serial 1271 of

April 3, 1925; No. 420-2 Serial 1338 of Dec. 11, 1926; *ibid.* War plans for a conflict with Japan still envisioned the establishment of a large base in the western Pacific, capable of supporting the entire fleet. See Joint Army and Navy Board to Secretary of War, No. 325 Serial 228 of Aug. 15, 1924, Papers of the Joint Board, War Records Division, National Archives.

6. Admiral Hilary P. Jones to Vice Admiral John D. McDonald, New York, March 10, 1922, Hilary P. Jones Papers, Manuscript Division, Library of Congress.

7. Weeks and Denby to Hughes, Joint Board No. 301 Serial No. 147, Dec. 7, 1921, Records of the Joint Army and Navy Board, War Records Division, National Archives; Hughes to Weeks and Denby, Jan. 17, 1922, and Hughes to Weeks and Denby, March 14, 1922, *ibid.*, file 301.

8. General Board No. 438 Serial 1239 of June 3, 1925, General Board Files. By endorsement dated June 29, 1925, Secretary of the Navy Curtis D. Wilbur returned the report, saying, "Please reconsider this recommendation." The writer was unable to locate a response to this request, but it indicates the unwillingness of the administration to accept a point of view contrary to its own.

9. Rear Admiral William W. Phelps, "America's Naval Limitation Problem," unpublished manuscript dated July 15, 1925, p. 97, General Board File 438.

10. Naval Attaché, London, to Director of Naval Intelligence, Serial 264 of March 2, 1926, General Board Files.

11. Naval Attaché, Paris, to Director of Naval Intelligence, ONI-15 (105-1) of March 8, 1926, *ibid.*

12. Acting Naval Attaché, Tokyo, to Director of Naval Intelligence, ONI-22-26 of March 12, 1926, *ibid.*

13. *Foreign Relations, 1927,* Washington, 1942, I, 1-5. Coolidge says that he acted "with what I understood was the desire of the British Government" in calling the conference. Calvin Coolidge, "Promoting Peace through Limitations of Armaments," *Ladies' Home Journal,* May, 1929, p. 4. Coolidge has been accused of wanting to accomplish something "spectacular" in order to enhance his own and Republican prestige. Merze Tate, *The United States and Armaments,* Cambridge, Mass., 1948, p. 142.

14. Memorandum of a conversation with the Italian Ambassador, William R. Castle to the Secretary of State, Washington, Feb. 22, 1927, *Foreign Relations, 1927,* I, 17-18.

15. General Board No. 438 Serial 1347-7(c) of April 25, 1927, Naval Record Group 80, National Archives. The studies were mimeographed and gathered in a loose-leaf binder labeled "Three-Power Conference for Further Limitation of Naval Armament, General Board Report, 1927, Confidential." Copies were furnished to high-ranking officers and other officials on the policy level concerned with the conference.

16. 203 *House of Commons Debates,* 5th Sess., cols. 1683-1684.

17. "Geneva 1927, Diary of Frank H. Schofield," entry of June 28, p. 20. Rear Admiral Schofield was a naval adviser to the American delegation and he kept a diary of events as they occurred. The original typescript diary is in the General Board Files.

18. Japanese Memorandum of July 6, 1927, quoted in telegram, Gibson to Secretary of State, Geneva, July 6, 1927, *Foreign Relations, 1927,* I, 76.

19. Viscount Cecil (Lord Robert Cecil), *A Great Experiment: An Autobiography,* London, 1941, pp. 185-186. Cecil wanted to grant parity to the United States, but the Cabinet called the delegation home for consultation and sided with Bridgeman. "They, or some of them," Cecil claims, "were determined to maintain our Naval superiority and almost openly regretted the Washington Treaty." *Ibid.,* p. 186.

20. Schofield Diary, entry of July 16, 1927, pp. 84-85.

21. Jessup, *Elihu Root,* II, 452.

22. Quoted in Memorandum, Naval Attaché, London, to Chief of Naval Operations, June 25, 1929, NRG 45, National Archives.

23. Williams, *The United States and Armament,* p. 166.

24. Frank B. Kellogg, Secretary of State, to Rear Admiral Hilary P. Jones, Washington, June 2, 1927, Hilary P. Jones Papers, Manuscript Division, Library of Congress.

25. *Survey of International Affairs, 1927,* London, 1929, pp. 41-42.

III

1. *Foreign Relations, 1927,* I, VIII.

2. Kellogg to Wilbur, Washington, March 12, 1928, Secret and Confidential Files of the Secretary of the Navy and the Chief of Naval Operations, 1928-1930, Naval Record Group 80, National Archives.

3. Telegram, American Chargé (Ray Atherton) to Kellogg, London, Aug. 4, 1928, D/S 500.A15/743, Record Group 43, National Archives.

4. *Foreign Relations, 1928,* I, 265.

5. British Chargé (Chilton) to Kellogg, July 31, 1928, *ibid.,* pp. 264-265; Kellogg to Wilbur, Aug. 16, 1928, General Board Files.

6. General Board No. 438 Serial 1390 of Sept. 11, 1928, *ibid.*

7. Wilbur to Kellogg, Op-13-LMS (SC) A14-7 (L of N), Sept. 11, 1928, *ibid.* Kellogg to the Chargé in France (Armour), Sept. 25, 1928, *Foreign Relations, 1928,* I, 282-286. Armour was told to repeat this mesage to London for delivery to the British government.

8. *Survey of American Foreign Relations, 1930,* ed. Charles P. Howland, New Haven, 1930, pp. 367-369.

9. British Foreign Office Memorandum of June 10, 1929, *Documents on British Foreign Policy, 1919-1939,* ed. Ernest L. Woodward and Rohan Butler, 2d Series, I, London, 1946, 3. Hereafter cited as *British Documents.*

10. New York *Times,* Nov. 12, 1928, p. 2. The address drew "French fire," and the London *Times* was "caustic." New York *Times,* Nov. 13, 1928, pp. 1 and 3.

11. Armin Rappaport, "The Navy League of the United States," unpublished manuscript, 1954, p. 230. Coolidge received a host of critical letters over his espousal of the cruiser bill. See folder 2758, Coolidge Papers.

12. U.S. Statutes, XLV, Pt. I, Public Act No. 726, 70 Cong., 2 sess., 1165.

13. Quoted in the *Literary Digest,* Feb. 23, 1929, p. 16.

14. *Report to the Annual National Convention of the American Legion,* 1929, p. 224, quoted in Baker, *The American Legion and American Foreign Policy,* p. 139.

15. Ray Lyman Wilbur and Arthur Mastick Hyde, *The Hoover Policies,* New York, 1937, p. 479; Herbert Hoover, *The Memoirs of Herbert Hoover: The Cabinet and the Presidency, 1920-1933,* New York, 1952, p. 330.

16. Telegram, Hoover to Coolidge, Ho. Belle Isle, Miami Beach, Florida, Jan. 28, 1929, Calvin Coolidge Papers, Folder 4450.

17. *The State Papers and Other Public Writings of Herbert Hoover,* ed. William S. Myers, New York, 1934, I, 3; William R. Castle Diary, March 21, 1929. This typescript diary is in the possession of Mr. Castle in Washington, D.C.

18. Pearson and Brown, *The American Diplomatic Game,* p. 111; Henry L. Stimson and McGeorge Bundy, *On Active Service in Peace and War,* New York, 1948, pp. 158-159; Henry L. Stimson, Reminiscences, Oral History Project, Columbia University, p. 1; Stimson Diary (typescript), March 1, 1929, to Dec. 31, 1930, p. 2, Yale University Library. This period in the Diary is spotty, and events often are not recorded on the day of their occurrence. In his first talks with the President, Stimson discovered that he was "anxious to get rid of" the Philippines because they were being used by the Navy to justify a larger fleet than would be needed to defend the continental United States, and that Hoover was looking forward to a naval disarmament conference. Stimson believed that he was successful in changing the President's mind. *Ibid.,* p. 4. W. Cameron Forbes has reported two conversations with Hoover, in February and March of 1930, where the President allegedly claimed that Britain's consent to the American disarmament proposals was contingent on the United States retaining possession of the Philippine Islands. W. Cameron Forbes, "Journal," Series 2, III (typescript), 13 and 68. Cited by Gerald E. Wheeler, "Isolated Japan: Anglo-American Diplomatic Co-operation, 1927-1936," *Pacific Historical Review,* XXX (1961), 165-178. It would appear that Stimson used this argument to persuade Hoover to retain the Islands, for there is no evidence in the Anglo-American exchanges to corroborate the President's story.

19. Telegram, Hugh R. Wilson to Kellogg, Geneva, Feb. 9, 1929, *Foreign Relations, 1929,* I, 67.

20. General Board No. 438-1 Serial 1408 of Feb. 28, 1929, Naval Record Group 80, National Archives. This correspondence is marked, "Approved, March 2, 1929," and signed by Secretary of the Navy Wilbur.

21. Kellogg to Gibson, March 23, 1929, *Foreign Relations, 1929,* I, 75-77.

22. Hoover, *The Cabinet and the Presidency,* p. 340.

23. Telegram, Gibson to Stimson, April 16, 1929, *Foreign Relations, 1929,* I, 86.

24. British Foreign Office Memorandum of June 10, 1929, *British Documents,* pp. 3-4.

25. *Foreign Relations, 1929,* I, 91-96.

26. New York *Times,* April 23, 1929, p. 1.

27. Telegram, Gibson to Stimson, April 22, 1929, *Foreign Relations, 1929,* I, 96; British Foreign Office Memorandum of June 10, 1929, *British Documents,* p. 5.

28. The British Ambassador (Sir Esme Howard) to the Secretary of State, April 23, 1929, *Foreign Relations, 1929,* I, 96-97.

29. Telegram, Stimson to Gibson, April 24, 1929, folder, "Instructions, Telegrams, 6th P.C.," General Board Files. The quotations are given in this source at greater length. According to the *Literary Digest,* "scores of American papers approve the Hoover-Gibson declaration of policy without reservations." May 4, 1929, p. 9. New York *Times,* April 24, 1929, p. 1.

30. Telegram, American Embassy, London, to Secretary of State, April 24, 1929, in folder, "Instructions, Telegrams, 6th P.C.," General Board Files; *Review of Reviews* (British), May 15, 1929, clipping in Naval Record Group 45, National Archives.

31. Telegram, American Embassy, Paris, to Secretary of State, April 24, 1929, in folder, "Instructions, Telegrams, 6th P.C.," General Board Files.

32. *Literary Digest,* May 11, 1929, p. 17.

33. Quoted in Tokyo *Trans-Pacific,* May 2, 1929, p. 9.

34. Telegram no. 42, Gibson to Stimson, May 6, 1929, *Foreign Relations, 1929,* I, 104; British Foreign Office Memorandum of June 10, 1929, *British Documents,* p. 5. Members of the French, Japanese, and Italian delegations suspected that these conversations might result in their being presented with a *fait accompli* to accept or reject, but the British and American delegates were apparently successful in convincing them that such a move was not contemplated. *Ibid.,* p. 5, and telegram, no. 43, Gibson to Stimson, May 6, 1929, *Foreign Relations, 1929,* I, 106.

35. Telegram, Stimson to Gibson, May 6, 1929, *ibid.,* p. 101.

36. Charles E. Hughes to Edwin Denby, Sept. 1, 1921, in binder, "The General Board and the Conference on the Limitation of Armament," General Board Files.

37. General Board No. 438, Serial 1088, of Sept. 12, 1921, *ibid.*

38. Hughes to Rear Admiral William L. Rodgers, Feb. 10, 1922, *ibid.*

39. Allen W. Dulles, "The Threat of Anglo-American Naval Rivalry," *Foreign Affairs,* VII, 1929, 180.

40. London *Times,* Jan. 28, 1929, p. 7.

41. Memorandum, the British Embassy to the Department of State, March 28, 1929, *Foreign Relations, 1929,* I, 79-80; Memorandum, the Department of State to the British Embassy, April 4, 1929, *ibid.,* p. 81.

42. Memorandum, the British Embassy to the Department of State, May 3, 1929, *ibid.,* pp. 99-100.

43. Henry L. Stimson, Memorandum of a conversation with the British Ambassador (Sir Esme Howard), May 9, 1929, D/S 500A15A3/1, National Archives.

44. Castle Diary, May 3, 1929.

45. Castle, Memorandum of a conversation with Secretary of the Navy Charles F. Adams, May 4, 1929, *Foreign Relations, 1929,* I, 100.

46. Stimson, Memorandum of conversation with President and General Dawes, June 6, 1929, D/S 500.A15A3/21½, National Archives.

IV

1. Allen, *Great Britain and the United States*, p. 730.

2. Henry R. Winkler, "Arthur Henderson," in *The Diplomats, 1919-1939*, ed. Gordon A. Craig and Felix Gilbert, Princeton, 1953, p. 321. During the London conference, Henderson was often kept in ignorance of developments, and he secured much of his information from George Rublee, one of Morrow's assistants. Rublee Reminiscences, Oral History Project, Columbia University, p. 243.

3. Hugh Dalton, "British Foreign Policy, 1929-1931," *Political Quarterly*, II, 1931, 486.

4. London *Daily Telegraph*, June 14, 1929, clipping in NRG 45, Box 488, National Archives.

5. Charles G. Dawes, *Journal as Ambassador to Great Britain*, New York, 1939, pp. 14-15; Henderson to British Ambassador in Washington (Howard), June 24, 1929, *British Documents*, p. 9.

6. Telegram, Dawes to Stimson, June 17, 1929, *Foreign Relations, 1929*, I, 117-118. Yet not until four days later did the ambassador realize the possible harmful effects of a premature visit to Washington. Dawes manuscript Journal, June 20, 1929, Charles G. Dawes Papers, Northwestern University Library, Evanston, Illinois.

7. Bell, *Why MacDonald Came to America*, pp. 18-19; Bell to Dawes, London, June 17, 1929 [two separate letters, same date], Dawes Papers. Telegram, Atherton to Stimson, May 27, 1929, *Foreign Relations, 1929*, I, 110. Bell, *op. cit.*, p. 24; Pearson and Brown, *The American Diplomatic Game*, pp. 74-75; telegram, Atherton to Stimson, June 11, 1929, *Foreign Relations, 1929*, I, 116-117.

8. Manchester *Guardian*, June 15, 1929, clipping in NRG 45, Box 488, National Archives.

9. *Foreign Relations, 1929*, I, 121-128.

10. London *Daily Herald*, June 20, 1929, clipping in NRG 45, Box 488, National Archives.

11. Manchester *Guardian*, June 20, 1929, *ibid*.

12. Telegram, Fletcher to Stimson, Rome, June 27, 1929, NRG 45, Box 488, National Archives.

13. *Journal*, p. 28.

14. Rappaport, "The Navy League of the United States," manuscript, p. 234. Senator Hale protested against this criticism of the naval experts and defended their position at the two disarmament conferences. Hale to Dawes, Washington, June 25, 1929, Dawes Papers.

15. Adams to General Board, Op-10 Hu (SC) A19, Serial 1427, May 31, 1929, General Board File 438-1.

16. General Board No. 438-1, Serial 1427, of June 10, 1929, *ibid*. An attached note indicates that the Secretary gave the original of this letter to the President.

17. Hoover to Adams, June 14, 1929, Hilary P. Jones Papers, Manuscript Division, Library of Congress. The President specified that he wanted to avoid "troubling the whole of the Navy until we have something more formal to submit," probably a not too subtle effort to by-pass the General Board.

18. Jones to Adams, June 18, 1929, *ibid*.

19. Stimson to Adams, July 9, 1929, General Board File 438-1.

20. General Board No. 438-1, Serial 1437, of July 13, 1929; Adams to Stimson, July 15, 1929, *ibid*.

21. London *Daily Chronicle*, June 18, 1929, clipping in NRG 45, Box 488, National Archives; London *Daily Telegraph*, June 19, 1929, *ibid*.

22. Telegram, Stimson to Dawes, June 21, 1929, *Foreign Relations, 1929*, I, 130.

23. Telegram No. 168, Dawes and Gibson to Stimson, June 25, 1929, *ibid*., pp. 132-135; telegram No. 169, Dawes and Gibson to Stimson, June 25, 1929, *ibid*., pp. 135-136. MacDonald objected to Japan's calling this preliminary conference because of location and possible "suspicion" of Japan's motives. MacDonald, Memorandum of conversation with General Dawes and Mr. Gibson, June 25, 1929, *British Documents*, p. 10.

24. Telegram, Henderson to Howard, June 24, 1929, *British Documents*, p. 9.

25. Gibson to Dawes, Brussels, June 28, 1929, D/S 250/47, RG 43, National Archives.

26. Telegram, Howard to Henderson, Washington, June 28, 1929, *British Documents*, p. 18; telegram, Stimson to Dawes, June 27, 1929, *Foreign Relations, 1929*, I, 137.

27. Telegram, Dawes to Stimson, June 28, 1929, *ibid.*, p. 139.

28. MacDonald to Dawes, July 8, 1929, *ibid.*, pp. 140-141.

29. Telegram, Stimson to Dawes, July 11, 1929, *ibid.*, pp. 141-143.

30. *Op. cit.*, General Board File 438.1.

31. New York *Times*, Aug. 4, 1929, pp. 1, 13.

32. Undersecretary of State Cotton submitted an opinion as to the legality of this action, in which he attempted to draw a line between "postponing" and "suspending" construction. Cotton to Stimson, July 26, 1929, D/S 500.A15A3/435.

33. MacDonald to Dawes, July 18, 1929, *Foreign Relations, 1929*, I, 148-149.

34. Telegram, Stimson to Dawes, July 21, 1929, *ibid.*, pp. 149-152.

35. MacDonald to Dawes, July 25, 1929, *ibid.*, pp. 160-161.

36. Telegram, Dawes to Stimson, July 11, 1929, *Foreign Relations, 1929*, I, 143.

37. *Foreign Relations, 1929*, I, 154. Telegram, Howard to Henderson, July 25, 1929, *British Documents*, p. 30. Also, see telegram, Stimson to Dawes, July 23, 1929, *Foreign Relations, 1929*, I, 156.

38. Paul V. McNutt to Hoover, New York, July 25, 1929, D/S 500.A15A3/89.

39. Telegram, Stimson to Dawes, July 26, 1929, *Foreign Relations, 1929*, I, 162-163.

40. Telegram, Dawes and Gibson to Stimson, July 29, 1929, *ibid.*, pp. 164-165.

41. Memorandum, Division of Western European Affairs, Department of State, July 30, 1929, D/S, 250 Proposals/1, RG 43, National Archives.

42. Telegram No. 195, Stimson to Dawes, July 31, 1929, *Foreign Relations, 1929*, I, 167-168.

43. Telegram No. 196, Stimson to Dawes, July 31, 1929, *ibid.*, pp. 168-170.

44. Telegram, Dawes to Stimson, Aug. 1, 1929, *ibid.*, pp. 170-171; Dawes, *Journal*, p. 46.

45. London *Daily Telegraph*, Aug. 1, 1929, clipping in NRG 45, Box 488, National Archives.

46. New York *Times*, Aug. 2, 1929, pp. 1-2.

47. MacDonald to Dawes, Aug. 1, 1929, *Foreign Relations, 1929*, I, 171-174.

48. Telegram, Stimson to Dawes, Aug. 2, 1929, *ibid.*, pp. 174-176.

49. Telegram, Dawes to Stimson, Aug. 4, 1929, *ibid.*, pp. 176-179.

50. Telegram, Cotton to Dawes, Aug. 5, 1929, *ibid.*, pp. 181-182. Assistant Secretary of State Castle noted that the cables exchanged between the two nations "were delightfully outside the older tradition of diplomacy," and added: "I can imagine the rage of a man like Curzon if he had received such a message as Dawes apparently gave MacDonald in its entirety." Castle Diary, entry of Aug. 5, 1929.

51. According to Dawes, MacDonald began to take the initiative away from the Admiralty, thereby again making progress possible. *Journal*, p. 49.

52. Telegram, Dawes and Gibson to Stimson, Aug. 6, 1929, *Foreign Relations, 1929*, I, 183-185.

53. MacDonald to Dawes, Aug. 8, 1929, *ibid.*, pp. 186-188. Alexander said the reduction to fifty cruisers was agreed to by the Admiralty because of the Kellogg-Briand Pact and "improved world relationships." 238 *House of Commons Debates*, 5th Sess., p. 2196.

54. Telegram, Stimson to Dawes, Aug. 15, 1929, *Foreign Relations, 1929*, I, 190-195.

55. See record of conversation between Stimson and the British ambassador, in telegram, Howard to Henderson, Aug. 21, 1929, *British Documents*, pp. 46-47.

56. New York *Times*, Aug. 20, 1929, p. 3.

57. Dawes, *Journal*, p. 57.

58. MacDonald to Dawes, Aug. 23, 1929, *Foreign Relations, 1929*, I, 196-200. The ambassador termed this offer one of "well-calculated pessimism." It was after receiving a telegram in similar vein from Washington that the Prime Minister had made his ten-ship reduction, and Dawes believed that MacDonald hoped to induce a like concession from Hoover by using the same tactics. Dawes to Gibson, London, Aug. 26, 1929, Dawes Papers.

59. General Board No. 438-1, Serial 1444, of Aug. 23, 1929, General Board Files. An attached note indicates that a copy was given to the President by the Secretary of the Navy, and a copy was sent to the State Department.

60. Telegram, Simson to Dawes, Aug. 28, 1929, *Foreign Relations, 1929*, I, 203-207. Because of a leak to the press of some details concerning the disarmament negotiations, only

Stimson and Cotton were now allowed to see the dispatches. This made it difficult for Assistant Secretary of State William R. Castle to deal effectively with diplomatic representatives of other nations, who assumed that he was abreast of developments. Castle Diary, Aug. 27, 1929. Not until Nov. 6 was he "restored to the mailing list." *Ibid.*, entry of Nov. 6, 1929.

61. Telegram, Stimson to Dawes, Aug. 28, 1929, *Foreign Relations, 1929*, I, 209-210.

62. Telegram, Dawes to Stimson, Aug. 30, 1929, *ibid.*, pp. 211-213.

63. Telegram, Stimson to Dawes, Aug. 28, 1929, *Foreign Relations, 1929*, I, 210.

64. MacDonald to Dawes, Aug. 30, 1929, *ibid.*, pp. 213-214.

65. MacDonald to Dawes, Aug. 31, 1929, *ibid.*, pp. 214-216.

66. Telegram, Stimson to Dawes, Sept. 3, 1929, *ibid.*, pp. 217-218.

67. General Board No. 438-1, Serial 1444-A, of Sept. 11, 1929, General Board Files.

68. Hoover to Stimson, Sept. 11, 1929, D/S 500.A15A3/329.

69. Memorandum, dated Sept. 11, 1929, General Board File 438-1. This account of the meeting, unsigned, was probably prepared by Captain Robert L. Ghormley, who was the secretary of the General Board.

70. Ghormley Memorandum, Sept. 11, 1929, General Board File 438-1.

71. Hoover to Stimson, Sept. 11, 1929, D/S 500.A15A3/329. Dawes gives an account of Stimson's version of the incident in his *Journal*, pp. 95-96, and cites it as evidence of Hoover's "constant struggle to get fair play from the Naval Board." In his manuscript Journal, Nov. 9, 1929, the General more pungently observes: "This impudent assumption by the Naval Board that they possess such power [to frame military policy] is an evidence of a gross indifference to their military and naval duty." Dawes Papers. This probably reflected the feelings of the President and his Secretary of State.

72. Telegram No. 243, Stimson to Dawes, Sept. 11, 1929, *Foreign Relations, 1929*, I, 223. The previous telegram, containing the American figures, is No. 242, Stimson to Dawes, Sept. 11, 1929, *ibid.*, pp. 222-223.

73. MacDonald to Dawes, Sept. 13, 1929, *ibid.*, pp. 226-229.

74. Telegram, Stimson to Dawes, Sept. 14, 1929, *ibid.*, pp. 230-231.

75. London *Times*, Sept. 15, 1929, clipping in NRG 45, Box 489, National Archives.

76. Hoover to Stimson, Sept. 17, 1929, *Foreign Relations, 1929*, I, 241-242. This letter was transmitted to Dawes for delivery to MacDonald. *Ibid.*, p. 240, note 63. The New York *Herald Tribune* of Aug. 30, 1929, announced that since Anglo-American naval conversations had reached the point where it was certain that the United States would have to build up in order to attain parity, work would be resumed on the cruisers ordered delayed by the President. Clipping in NRG 45, Box 488, National Archives.

77. Telegram, Stimson to Dawes, Sept. 19, 1929, *Foreign Relations, 1929*, I, 249-250; Dawes, *Journal*, p. 69.

78. *Ibid.*, pp. 75, 82.

79. Manchester *Guardian*, Sept. 28, 1929, p. 19.

80. *Foreign Relations, 1929*, I, 263-265.

V

1. Quoted in *Literary Digest*, Sept. 28, 1929, pp. 7-9.

2. London *Times*, Sept. 30, 1929, clipping in NRG 45, Box No. 489, National Archives.

3. MacDonald, Memorandum concerning conversations with Hoover, *British Documents*, p. 113; Hoover, *The Cabinet and the Presidency*, p. 342. Official notes and documents on the meeting are contained in *Foreign Relations, 1929*, II, 3-33; and *British Documents*, pp. 106-126.

4. MacDonald, Memorandum, *British Documents*, p. 106.

5. *Ibid.*, pp. 107-108.

6. *Ibid.*, p. 106. MacDonald was careful to explain why he was willing to deal with the issue. *Ibid.*, pp. 106-107.

7. Stimson, Memorandum, Oct. 7, 1929, *Foreign Relations, 1929*, III, 4-5.

8. *Ibid.*, p. 4; MacDonald, Memorandum, *British Documents*, pp. 110-113. Telegram No. 505, Henderson to Howard, Oct. 8, 1929, *ibid.*, pp. 119-120; telegram No. 506, Henderson to

Howard, Oct. 8, 1929, *ibid.,* pp. 120-121; telegram No. 515, Henderson to Howard, Oct. 9, 1929, *ibid.,* p. 124. MacDonald, Memorandum, *ibid.,* p. 112.

9. Stimson, Memorandum, Oct. 7, 1929, *Foreign Relations, 1929,* III, 6.

10. Telegram No. 505, Henderson to Howard, Oct. 8, 1929, *British Documents,* p. 119. The Navy General Board objected to the proposal because the British bases in the Western Hemisphere were in no condition to "menace" the United States. General Board No. 438-1, Serial 1453, of Oct. 8, 1929, General Board Files.

11. MacDonald, Memorandum, *British Documents,* pp. 114-115.

12. Stimson, Memorandum, *Foreign Relations, 1929,* III, Annex VIII, 30.

13. MacDonald, Memorandum, *British Documents,* p. 116. According to MacDonald, Cotton and other Hoover advisers were doubtful that such an amendment would be accepted by the American people. *Ibid.*

14. Department of State, Conference Series, No. 6, *Proceedings of the London Naval Conference of 1930 and Supplementary Documents,* Washington, 1931, pp. 7-8. The draft of a more candid press release prepared by the President but not approved by MacDonald is printed in Hoover, *The Cabinet and the Presidency,* pp. 343-345.

15. *Literary Digest,* Oct. 19, 1929, p. 5.

16. *Ibid.,* p. 5. For American press opinion, generally favorable, see *ibid.,* pp. 5-7.

17. New York *Herald-Tribune,* Oct. 11, 1929, p. 23.

18. Telegram, Atherton to Stimson, Oct. 18, 1929, NRG 45, Box No. 489, National Archives; telegram, Atherton to Stimson, Oct. 26, 1929, D/S 500.A15A3/316, National Archives.

19. *Truth,* Oct. 16, 1929. This article and accompanying comments are in NRG 45, Box 489, National Archives.

20. Hugh Dalton, "British Foreign Policy, 1929-1931," *Political Quarterly,* II, 1931, 499.

21. Armour to Stimson, Paris, Nov. 6, 1929, D/S 500.A15A3/401, National Archives. Telegram, Gordon to Stimson, Paris, Oct. 11, 1929, D/S 500.A15A3/257, National Archives; New York *Times,* Oct. 11, 1929, p. 3. London *Times,* Oct. 11, 1929, clipping in NRG 45, Box No. 489, National Archives.

22. Rome *Tevere,* quoted in New York *Times,* Oct. 9, 1929, p. 2.

23. Stimson to Neville (chargé in Tokyo), June 24, 1929, *Foreign Relations, 1929,* I, 131-132.

24. Henderson to Sir John Tilley (Tokyo), June 18, 1929, *British Documents,* p. 7; telegram, Dawes to Stimson, June 17, 1929, *Foreign Relations, 1929,* I, 118. Matsudaira and Dawes were friends of long standing. Dawes, *Journal,* p. 26.

25. Telegram, Stimson to Dawes, June 24, 1929, *Foreign Relations, 1929,* I, 131.

26. Office of Naval Intelligence, Report, Aug. 6, 1929, NRG 45, Box No. 488, National Archives. A translation of the article is included.

27. Telegram, Neville (chargé in Tokyo) to Stimson, June 20, 1929, *Foreign Relations, 1929,* I, 130.

28. Telegram, Tilley to Henderson, Tokyo, Aug. 12, 1929, *British Documents,* p. 38.

29. Telegram, Dawes to Stimson, July 25, 1929, *Foreign Relations, 1929,* I, 160. William R. Castle, Jr. (Assistant Secretary of State) to Cotton, reporting a conversation with Debuchi, Aug. 12, 1929, *ibid.,* p. 189.

30. Telegram, Dawes to Stimson, Aug. 12, 1929, *ibid.,* p. 189.

31. *British Documents,* p. 60, note 2; Nelson T. Johnson (Assistant Secretary of State), Memorandum of a conversation with Debuchi, Aug. 27, 1929, D/S 500.A15A3/142, National Archives.

32. Nelson T. Johnson, Memorandum of a conversation with Debuchi, Aug. 27, 1929, D/S 500.A15A3/142, National Archives.

33. MacDonald, Memorandum, Sept. 2, 1929, *British Documents,* p. 64. Also see Sir Ronald Lindsay, Memorandum, Sept. 25, 1929, *ibid.,* p. 98. MacDonald, Memorandum, Sept. 2, 1929, *ibid.,* p. 64.

34. Telegram, Dawes to Stimson, Sept. 16, 1929, *Foreign Relations, 1929,* I, 233-234.

35. Stimson, Memorandum of a conversation with Debuchi, Sept. 24, 1929, *ibid.,* pp. 258

259. Leading senators voiced a determined opposition to a change in the cruiser ratio more favorable to Japan. New York *Times*, Sept. 13, 1929, p. 1. Stimson, Memorandum of a conversation with Ronald Ian Campbell (counselor of the British Embassy), Nov. 7, 1929, Record Group 43, National Archives (no file number).

36. Telegram, Atherton to Stimson, Nov. 14, 1929, *Foreign Relations, 1929*, I, 278.

37. Henderson to Campbell, Nov. 16, 1929, *British Documents*, p. 140. Japan had twelve 8-inch–gun cruisers built and building, which displaced only 108,400 tons. *Ibid*.

38. Telegram, Stimson to Dawes, Nov. 20, 1929, *Foreign Relations, 1929*, I, 283.

39. Memorandum, "The Japanese Position," prepared by the Division of Western European Affairs, State Department, Oct. 14, 1929, D/S 500.A15A3/284, National Archives; telegram, Henderson to Tilley, Nov. 18, 1929, *British Documents*, p. 140, note 1.

40. G. C. Allen, *A Short Economic History of Modern Japan, 1867-1937*, London, 1946, pp. 93, 104; Elizabeth B. Schumpter, "The Yen Bloc: Program and Results," *Annals of the American Academy of Political and Social Science*, CCXV, 1941, 29.

41. K. K. Kawakami, "The London Naval Conference as Viewed from Japan," *The Nineteenth Century and After*, CVI, 1929, 741-742.

42. This fact was emphasized by the Tokyo correspondent of the London *Times*. London *Times*, Nov. 4, 1929, quoted in "Press Extracts on London Conference," typescript, NRG 45, Box No. 488, National Archives. The slogan is quoted in the New York *Times*, Dec. 18, 1929, p. 2. Wakatsuki presented Japan's case in terms of the slogan while he was in Washington, and revealed a determination to hold firm on the new ratio. See Draft Minutes of the Informal Conversations between the American and Japanese Delegates to the London Naval Conference, meeting at Woodley, Dec. 17, 1929, in Japanese Foreign Office Documents (Microfilm, Library of Congress), S2.12.0.0-35, no. 81.

43. Takeuchi, *War and Diplomacy in the Japanese Empire*, p. 283.

44. State Department to the Japanese Embassy, Dec. 26, 1929, *Foreign Relations, 1929*, I, 307-313. Copies of this memorandum were sent to the British, French, and Italian embassies. See Minutes of the Informal Meeting between the Japanese and American Delegates, Held in the Secretary's Office in the Department of State, Thursday, Dec. 19, 1929, in Japanese Foreign Office Documents (Microfilm, Library of Congress), S2.12.0.0-35, nos. 55-65.

45. Baron Reijiro Wakatsuki, "The Aims of Japan," *Foreign Affairs*, XIII, 1935, 583.

46. MacDonald, Memorandum, *British Documents*, p. 108.

47. Arthur Cadogan to René Massigli, July 6, 1929, *British Documents*, p. 19. Massigli was chief of the League of Nations Section of the French Foreign Office and France's representative on the Preparatory Commission.

48. London *Daily Telegraph*, July 26, 1929, clipping in NRG 45, Box No. 488, National Archives.

49. London *Times*, July 26, 1929, clipping in *ibid*.

50. Stimson, Memorandum, Sept. 20, 1929, *Foreign Relations, 1929*, I, 250-253.

51. Sir Ronald Lindsay, Memorandum, Sept. 25, 1929, *British Documents*, pp. 97-98.

52. French Embassy to State Department, Sept. 25, 1929, *Foreign Relations, 1929*, I, 59-61.

53. Tyrell to Henderson, Paris, Oct. 14, 1929, *British Documents*, p. 127. Also, see Stimson, Memorandum of conversation with the French ambassador, Oct. 10, 1929, *Foreign Relations, 1929*, I, 61.

54. Stimson, Memorandum of conversation with the French ambassador, Oct. 2, 1929, *ibid.*, pp. 261-262; telegram, Gibson to Stimson, Oct. 29, 1929, *ibid.*, pp. 270-271; London *Times*, Oct. 17, 1929, clipping in NRG 45, Box No. 489, National Archives.

55. Telegram, Campbell to Henderson, Dec. 1, 1929, *British Documents*, p. 154.

56. Telegram, Gibson to Stimson, Oct. 29, 1929, *Foreign Relations, 1929*, I, 271; Henderson to Tyrell, Nov. 15, 1929, reporting a conversation between the French ambassador and the Prime Minister, *British Documents*, p. 137.

57. Telegram, Armour to Stimson, Dec. 11, 1929, *Foreign Relations, 1929*, I, 295-296.

58. French Memorandum of Dec. 20, 1929, *ibid.*, pp. 299-304.

59. New York *Times*, Dec. 20, 1929, p. 26.

60. Manchester *Guardian*, Dec. 23, 1929, and London *Daily Herald*, Dec. 23, 1929,

clippings in NRG 45, Box No. 490, National Archives. London *Daily Telegraph*, Dec. 28, 1929, *ibid.* London *Daily Herald*, Dec. 28, 1929; London *Daily Telegraph*, Dec. 28, 1929; London *Daily News*, Dec. 28, 1929, *ibid.*

61. New York *Times*, Dec. 28, 1929, p. 5. Telegram, Walter E. Edge (American ambassador) to Stimson, Paris, Dec. 31, 1929, *Foreign Relations, 1929*, I, 315.

62. Memorandum, British Foreign Office to French ambassador, Jan. 10, 1930, *British Documents*, pp. 195-198.

63. New York *Times*, Dec. 28, 1929, pp. 1, 5.

64. Telegram, Edge to Stimson, Dec. 21, 1929, *Foreign Relations, 1929*, I, 304-305; telegram, Edge to Stimson, Dec. 26, 1929, *ibid.*, p. 313.

65. Walter Evans Edge, *A Jerseyman's Journal*, Princeton, 1948, pp. 152, 156-157.

66. Telegram, Edge to Stimson, Dec. 31, 1929, *Foreign Relations, 1929*, I, 315.

67. New York *Times*, Jan. 5, 1930, p. 9.

68. H. Stuart Hughes, "The Early Diplomacy of Italian Fascism, 1922-1932," in Craig and Gilbert, eds., *The Diplomats, 1919-1939*, p. 231.

69. Memorandum, "Attitude of Italy on Naval Questions," Oct. 21, 1929, prepared by the State Department, Division of Western European Affairs, D/S 250 Italy/1, RG 43, National Archives.

70. New York *Times*, Dec. 8, 1929, p. 8.

71. Castle, Memorandum of a conversation with the Italian ambassador, Oct. 24, 1929, *Foreign Relations, 1929*, I, 269-270.

72. Sir R. Graham to Henderson, Nov. 11, 1929, *British Documents*, p. 134; Graham to Henderson, Nov. 22, 1929, *ibid.*, p. 148.

73. Telegram, Graham to Henderson, Jan. 10, 1930, *ibid.*, p. 195. Also, see telegram, Tyrrell to Henderson, Paris, Jan. 15, 1930, *ibid.*, pp. 200-201.

74. New York *Times*, Dec. 8, 1929, p. 8; *ibid.*, Jan. 5, 1930, section 3, p. 1.

75. Memorandum, Cotton to Stimson, Oct. 10, 1929, D/S 250/43, RG 43, National Archives.

76. Memorandum of conversation between Cotton, Ingalls, Marriner, and Boal, Oct. 28, 1929, D/S 500.A15A3/575, National Archives. The suspicious Undersecretary of State was even withholding some of the telegrams from the Navy Department. Castle Diary, entry of Nov. 27, 1929.

77. Clifford L. Lord, "History of Naval Aviation" (manuscript, in Office of Naval History), IV, 1200, and *passim*.

78. Memoranda of these conversations, held between Oct. 22 and Nov. 22, are contained in State Department Record Group 43, National Archives, file numbers 250/63, Oct. 22; 250/73, Oct. 22; 250 U.S./6, Oct. 23; 250 U.S./7, Oct. 25; 250 U.S./8, Oct. 26; 250/74, Oct. 28; 252.25/11, November 6; 250/44, Nov. 15; and 250/77, Nov. 22. As a result of this indoctrination, and even before all of the conferences were concluded, one official was reported as declaring that the Secretary of State "knows the technical details of the naval problem from the bottom up." New York *Times*, Nov. 9, 1929, p. 8.

79. Telegram, Henderson to ambassadors in Washington, Paris, Rome, and Tokyo, Nov. 9, 1929, *British Documents*, p. 133; Campbell to Stimson, Nov. 11, 1929, *Foreign Relations, 1929*, I, 272. Stimson to Campbell, Nov. 12, 1929, *ibid.*, p. 273.

80. New York *Times*, Oct. 22, 1929, p. 20; Claudius O. Johnson, *Borah of Idaho*, New York, 1936, p. 272.

81. New York *Times*, Oct. 19, 1929, p. 10.

82. William H. Standley and Arthur A. Ageton, *Admiral Ambassador to Russia*, Chicago, 1955, p. 22.

83. Memorandum of the First Meeting of Delegates to the London Naval Conference, Dec. 11, 1929, D/S 110.001/3, RG 43, National Archives.

84. New York *Times*, Nov. 8, 1929, pp. 1, 3.

85. New York *Times*, Dec. 9, 1929, p. 1.

86. Telegram, Henderson to Campbell, Nov. 26, 1929, *British Documents*, p. 149.

87. Telegram, Campbell to Henderson, Dec. 2, 1929, *ibid.*, p. 155, telegram, Stimson to

Dawes, Dec. 3, 1929, *Foreign Relations, 1929,* I, 290-291. Telegram, Dawes to Stimson, Dec. 4, 1929, *ibid.,* pp. 294-295. Memorandum, British Embassy to State Department, Dec. 12, 1929, *ibid.,* p. 297.

88. London *Daily Telegraph,* Nov. 22, 1929, quoted in "Press Extracts on London Conference," typescript, NRG 45, Box No. 488, National Archives; Hoover, *The Cabinet and the Presidency,* p. 348; William Starr Myers, *The Foreign Policies of Herbert Hoover, 1929-1933,* New York, 1940, pp. 75-79. Hoover told a British diplomat, "I wish you could find a Shearer." Telegram, Howard to Henderson, Sept. 12, 1929, *British Documents,* p. 48.

89. *Shipbuilding and Shipping Record* (England), Oct. 17, 1929, clipping in NRG 45, Box No. 489, National Archives; London *Daily Telegraph,* Dec. 3, 1929, and Dec. 4, 1929, clippings in NRG 45, Box No. 490, National Archives; Memorandum by U.S. Naval Attaché, London, Dec. 10, 1929, *ibid.*

90. Manchester *Guardian,* Dec. 18, 1929, clipping in *ibid.;* London *Daily Telegraph,* Jan. 3, 1930, clipping in NRG 45, Box No. 491, National Archives.

91. London *Observer,* Oct. 13, 1929, clipping in NRG 45, Box No. 489, National Archives.

92. London *Daily Telegraph,* Oct. 28, 1929, *ibid.* Dawes, *Journal,* p. 105.

93. London *Daily Telegraph,* Jan. 3, 1930, and Jan. 11, 1930, clippings in NRG 45, Box No. 491, National Archives. London *Evening Standard,* Jan. 15, 1930, *ibid.* Vice Admiral E. A. Taylor, Royal Navy, publicly denied the truth of Alexander's statement that the Admiralty had agreed to the figure of fifty cruisers. *Ibid.*

94. Telegram, Atherton to Stimson, Jan. 6, 1930, NRG 45, Box No. 491, National Archives.

95. London *Daily Telegraph,* Jan. 6, 1930, clipping in *ibid.* New York *Times,* Jan. 7, 1930, p. 2. This report by Hugh Byas from Tokyo was based on information contained in Japanese newspapers and periodicals.

96. *Poglio d'Ordini,* Jan. 13, 1930, quoted translation in U.S. Military Attaché, Rome, report of Jan. 22, 1930, NRG 45, Box No. 491, National Archives. According to this report, the *Poglio d'Ordini* was the official bulletin of the National Fascist Party.

97. Memorandum communicated by the Spanish ambassador, London, Dec. 30, 1929, *British Documents,* p. 184.

98. New York *Times,* Jan. 10, 1930, p. 4. On Thursday, Oct. 24, 1929, the stock market had collapsed. The following month the President asked the Secretary of the Navy to investigate methods of alleviating the anticipated unemployment, such as repair work and the purchase of supplies, as well as construction for which authorization and appropriations might be secured. Hoover to Adams, Nov. 18, 1929, in Bureau of Aeronautics confidential file A1-3, quoted in Lord, "History of Naval Aviation," IV, 1254.

99. Telegram, State Department to U.S. Embassy, London, Nov. 7, 1929, D/S 500.A15A3P43/30, National Archives. For a complete list of the sixty-eight persons in the delegation and their official position or duties, see the New York *Times,* Dec. 18, 1929, p. 2.

VI

1. Quoted in Pearson and Brown, *The American Diplomatic Game,* p. 118.

2. Stimson, Memorandum of a Conference wtih the Prime Minister of Great Britain, Mr. Ramsay MacDonald, Jan. 17, 1929, D/S 110.001/19, RG 43, National Archives.

3. *Ibid.*

4. *Ibid.*

5. *Ibid.;* telegram, Stimson to Cotton, Jan. 19, 1930, *Foreign Relations, 1930,* I, 4.

6. Stimson Diary, Jan. 19, 1930; telegram, Stimson to Cotton, Jan. 20, 1930, *Foreign Relations, 1930,* I, 5.

7. Memorandum, Conversation between Stimson and Grandi, Jan. 19, 1930, D/S 110.001/20, RG 43, National Archives.

8. Telegram, Stimson to Cotton, Jan. 20, 1930, *Foreign Relations, 1930,* p. 5.

9. *Stimson Diary,* Jan. 12, 1930.

10. Dawes, *Journal,* pp. 125-126.

11. Hugh R. Wilson, *Diplomat between Wars,* New York, 1941, p. 236.

12. Minutes of the Meeting of the American Delegation, Jan. 22, 1930, D/S 110.022/1, RG 43, National Archives.

13. *Proceedings*, pp. 28-31.

14. *Ibid.*, pp. 31-42.

15. *Ibid.*, p. 46.

16. First Report of the First Committee, Feb. 20, 1930, *ibid.*, p. 124.

17. See Annex to First Report of the First Committee, Feb. 20, 1930, *ibid.*, pp. 125-126.

18. Stimson wrote Tardieu that "the whole purpose of the appointment of Committees is to gain time so that the *real issues* may be settled by *informal* discussion *outside*. I just said the same to Briand." Stimson to Tardieu, Jan. 27, 1930, Stimson Papers, #3F-0417. The Secretary of State later acknowledged that the First Committee "made ultimately a number of important recommendations of a procedural or technical character, many of which were embodied in the final treaty after they had been approved at the next to the last Plenary Session in April." Stimson Diary, Jan. 30, 1930.

19. *Proceedings*, pp. 46-47.

20. *Ibid.*, p. 47.

21. *Ibid.*, p. 48.

22. *Ibid.*, pp. 50-52.

23. Telegram, Stimson to Cotton, Jan. 23, 1930, *Foreign Relations, 1930,* I, 7.

24. *Proceedings*, pp. 53-54.

25. *Ibid.*, pp. 55-56.

26. *Ibid.*, pp. 56-57.

27. *Ibid.*, pp. 57-58.

28. Dawes, *Journal*, pp. 126-127, 130. The minutes of the informal meetings of the principal delegates were submitted to each delegation for correction and approval. See N. Sato to Sir Maurice Hankey, Jan. 22, 1930, Japanese Foreign Office Documents, S2.12.0.0-35, No. 225, and transmittal letters following this document.

29. *Proceedings*, pp. 59-60.

30. *Ibid.*, pp. 64-65.

31. *Ibid.*, pp. 66-70.

32. *Ibid.*, p. 70.

33. *Ibid.*, pp. 71-73.

34. Castle Diary, Jan. 21, 1930; telegram, Castle to Cotton, Jan. 23, 1930, D/S 500.A15A3/638, National Archives. U.S. Army, Far East Command, General Headquarters, Military Intelligence Section, General Staff, *The Saionji-Harada Memoirs. Supplement: Prince Saionji and the London Disarmament Treaty,* mimeographed, Tokyo, 1946, pp. 1-5, 7. This portion of the *Memoirs* is concerned almost exclusively with the intrigue that attended the acceptance and ratification of the final treaty. Prince Saionji was a distinguished member of the royal family, and his secretary, Baron Harada, was *persona grata* with many of the party leaders and ranking naval officers.

35. Telegram, Castle to Cotton, Jan. 25, 1930, *Foreign Relations, 1930,* I, 9-10; Castle Diary, Jan. 31, 1930. Castle was appointed American ambassador to Japan for the duration of the conference. He was a fortunate selection, for he was greatly admired and respected by the Japanese. *Saionji-Harada Memoirs,* p. 6.

36. New York *Times,* Feb. 2, 1930, p. E-1.

37. Telegram no. 191, Edge to Stimson, Paris, Feb. 7, 1930, typed excerpt in NRG 45, Box 492, National Archives.

38. U.S. Military Attaché, Rome, to London Delegations, Report No. 6, Jan. 31, 1930, NRG 45, Box 491, National Archives; U.S. Military Attaché, Rome, to London Delegation, Report No. 7, Feb. 1, 1930, NRG 45, Box 492, National Archives; U.S. Military Attaché, Rome, to London Delegation, Report No. 8, Feb. 3, 1930, *ibid.;* U.S. Military Attaché, Rome, to London Delegation, Report No. 10, Feb. 7, 1930, *ibid.*

39. Commander Harold C. Train, "Daily Log," I, entry of Jan. 26, 1930. Train maintained an official log, or journal, throughout the conference. Volume I covers the period Jan. 21-March 10, 1930. Volume II covers the period March 10-April 23, 1930. The "first copy," typed,

is in the General Board Files. Reed had been designated to head the investigation and preparation of the American plan. Stimson Diary, Jan. 24, 1930.

40. Memorandum, D/S, Division of Western European Affairs, May 28, 1930, D/S 500.A15A3/910½, National Archives.

41. Jones, "Résumé of Daily Occurrences," Hilary P. Jones Papers; Dawes, *Journal*, p. 148.

42. Commander Train's Daily Log reveals that the naval experts met formally with the delegates on Jan. 28, Jan. 29, Jan. 30, Feb. 4, and April 1. The Secretary of State claimed that Senator Reed's "cross-examinations of the naval witnesses were very potent in producing final unanimity in our Delegation." Stimson to Hoover, Feb. 17, 1930, copy in Stimson Diary.

43. The General Board Files contain four large looseleaf binders, one labeled "London Naval Conference," three labeled "W. W. Smyth, 1930." Captain Smyth served the delegation as co-ordinating secretary or office manager. Each of these binders is filled with data concerning the conference, from penciled notes, typed suggestions, and memoranda of conversations to mimeographed statements, tables of naval statistics, and printed documents.

44. Dawes, *Journal*, pp. 133-134. See testimony of Rear Admiral J. P. R. Pringle, Senate Committee on Foreign Relations, *Hearings on Treaty on the Limitation of Naval Armaments,* 71 Cong., 2 sess., pp. 200-201, May 21, 1930. Adams and Robinson were the last of the delegates to accept the lower figure. Stimson Diary, Feb. 3, 1930.

45. General Board Memorandum of Jan. 6, 1930, General Board File 438.1.

46. "Tentative Plan of the American Delegation," Jan. 28, 1930 (Revised), mimeographed, looseleaf binder "London Naval Conference," General Board Files.

47. Telegram, Stimson to Cotton, Feb. 4, 1930, *Foreign Relations, 1930,* I, 13-17. Stimson later revealed that the new battleship was included as a bargaining point to be used to induce MacDonald to accept the American figure of eighteen 8-inch–gun cruisers instead of the fifteen that he wanted the United States to have. Stimson testimony, Senate Committee on Naval Affairs, *Hearings on London Naval Treaty of 1930,* 71 Cong., 2 sess., p. 42, May 14, 1930.

48. Telegram, Cotton to Stimson, Feb. 5, 1930, *Foreign Relations, 1930,* I, 18; Dawes, Journal, p. 141.

49. Notes of a meeting of representatives of the delegations of the United States of America, France, and the United Kingdom, Feb. 4, 1930, *British Documents,* p. 219; notes of a meeting of representatives of the delegations of the United States of America, the United Kingdom, and Japan, Feb. 17, 1930, *ibid.,* pp. 227-228.

50. Both messages are contained in telegram, Stimson to Cotton, Feb. 5, 1930, *Foreign Relations, 1930,* I, 18.

51. Takeuchi, *War and Diplomacy in the Japanese Empire,* p. 292. Telegram, Castle to Cotton, Tokyo, Feb. 10, 1930, D/S 500.A15A3/684, National Archives.

52. Telegram, Cotton to Stimson, Feb. 13, 1930, D/S 250 Japan/75, RG 43, National Archives.

53. Telegram, Stimson to Cotton, Feb. 6, 1930, *Foreign Relations, 1930,* I, 19-20. Telegram, Stimson to Cotton, Feb. 7, 1930, *ibid.,* p. 21; telegram, Cotton to Stimson, Feb. 7, 1930, *ibid.,* p. 21. U.S. Military Attaché, Rome, to London Delegation, Report No. 11, Feb. 8, 1930, NRG 45, Box 492, National Archives.

54. Train, "Daily Log," I, entry of Feb. 7, 1930. Stimson later recalled that he "was very unpopular with the press" because he was not aware of what he called the European habit of taking reporters into one's confidence. Henry L. Stimson, Reminiscences, Oral History Project, Columbia University, p. 7.

55. Memorandum, *British Documents,* pp. 205-209.

56. Telegram, Stimson to Cotton, Feb. 12, 1930, *Foreign Relations, 1930,* I, 23-24.

57. Telegram, Stimson to Cotton, Feb. 11, 1930, D/S 252.22 United States/32, RG 43, National Archives. Telegram, Stimson to Castle, Feb. 12, 1930, D/S 391/17, RG 43, National Archives. Senator Reed, *Congressional Record,* 71 Cong., Special Session, p. 66.

58. Telegram, Stimson to Cotton, Feb. 23, 1930, *Foreign Relations, 1930,* I, 28-29.

59. Telegram, Stimson to Cotton, Feb. 28, 1930, *ibid.,* p. 32.

60. Telegram, Stimson to Cotton, Feb. 24, 1930, D/S 500.A15A3/710, National Archives.

61. Telegram, Stimson to Cotton, Feb. 23, 1930, *Foreign Relations, 1930,* I, 29.

62. New York *Times*, Dec. 14, 1929, p. 1.

63. Admiral Beamish, RN, "Admiral's Warning Note," London *Morning Post*, Jan. 30, 1930, quoted in U.S. Naval Attaché, Memorandum, Feb. 3, 1930, NRG 45, Box 492, National Archives.

64. New York *Times*, April 8, 1930, p. 1.

65. *Congressional Record*, 71 Cong., Special Session, p. 111.

VII

1. General Board No. 438-1, Serial 1464, Jan. 3, 1930, General Board Files.

2. Notes of a meeting of representatives of the delegations of the United States, France, and the United Kingdom, Feb. 14, 1930, *British Documents*, p. 220.

3. "Comment by Rear Admiral Moffett on British Naval Proposal in regard to Aircraft Carriers," Feb. 1930, in looseleaf binder labeled "London Naval Conference," General Board Files.

4. Notes of a meeting of representatives of the delegations of the United States, the United Kingdom, and Japan, Feb. 17, 1930, *British Documents*, p. 229.

5. For an admirable exposition of the reception of military air power in the United States, Great Britain, and Italy, see Harry Howe Ransom, "The Politics of Air Power—A Comparative Analysis," in *Public Policy, A Yearbook of the Graduate School of Public Administration, Harvard University, 1958*, ed. Carl J. Friedrich and Seymour E. Harris, Cambridge, Mass., 1958, pp. 88-119.

6. Lord, "History of Naval Aviation," IV, 1176. "To bring the Navy to full acceptance of the airplane was a slow, tortuous, and at times discouraging, process." *Ibid.*, I, 1.

7. *Proceedings of the London Naval Conference*, pp. 148-149. These restrictions were formulated by the First Committee.

8. Stimson to Hoover, Feb. 17, 1930, copy in Stimson Diary.

9. Dawes, *Journal*, p. 146. In noting that he "had fought a single handed battle with the whole delegation" on the "battle ship proposition," Dawes commented, "I rather like being in a minority, even if of one, if I am right." Manuscript Diary, Feb. 13, 1930.

10. Telegram, Stimson to Cotton, Feb. 16, 1930, D/S 250.01 France-Great Britain/4, RG 43, National Archives.

11. Dawes, *Journal*, p. 150.

12. Telegram, Castle to Cotton, Feb. 14, 1930, *Foreign Relations, 1930*, I, 24-25. See *British Documents*, pp. 265-266, note 1.

13. Burnett, Memorandum of a conversation with Ambassador Matsudaira on Jan. 29, 1930 (Memorandum dated January 31, 1930), D/S 250 Japan/68, RG 43, National Archives.

14. Stimson to Hoover, Feb. 17, 1930, copy in Stimson Diary.

15. Notes of a meeting of representatives of the delegations of the United States, the United Kingdom, and Japan, Feb. 17, 1930, *British Documents*, pp. 229-233.

16. Stimson to Hoover, Feb. 17, 1930, copy in Stimson Diary.

17. Louis Morton, "American and Allied Strategy in the Far East," *Military Review*, XXIX, 1949, 25.

18. Telegram, Stimson to Cotton, Feb. 27, 1930, *ibid.*, p. 31; telegram, No. 107, Stimson to Cotton, March 4, 1930, *ibid.*, pp. 43-44. Telegram No. 108, Stimson to Cotton, March 4, 1930, *ibid.*, p. 46.

19. Telegram, Cotton to Stimson, March 5, 1930, *ibid.*, p. 46.

20. Senator Reed, *Congressional Record*, 71 Cong., Special Session, p. 342.

21. Telegram, Castle to Cotton, March 7, 1930, *Foreign Relations, 1930*, I, 49-51.

22. Kikujiro Ishii, *Diplomatic Commentaries*, ed. William R. Langdon, Baltimore, 1936, p. 200. The latter point was stressed in the Japanese press and noted by the foreign office. See the Japan *Times*, Jan. 24, and Feb. 18, 1930, in Japanese Foreign Office Documents, microfilm, Library of Congress, S2.12.0.0-12, Nos. 252 and 529. Numerous newspaper clippings bearing on the conference are in these files, which include a document listing the Washington newspaper correspondents attending the conference and containing a brief analysis of their qualifications and points of view. *Ibid.*, S2.12.0.0-35.

23. San Francisco *Union,* quoted in *Literary Digest,* March 8, 1930, p. 11.

24. Telegram, Stimson to Cotton, March 8, 1930, *Foreign Relations, 1930,* I, 52-54.

25. Telegram, Stimson to Cotton, March 10, 1930, *ibid.,* p. 56.

26. Telegram, Stimson to Cotton, March 12, 1930, *ibid.,* p. 58. Stimson Diary, March 12, 1930.

27. Telegram, Stimson to Cotton, March 13, 1930, *Foreign Relations, 1930,* I, 60.

28. Telegram, Cotton to Stimson, March 13, 1930, *ibid.,* p. 59.

29. Telegram, Stimson to Cotton, March 13, 1930, *ibid.,* p. 61; telegram, Stimson to Cotton, March 14, 1930, *ibid.,* p. 62; telegram, Cotton to Stimson, March 14, 1930, *ibid.,* p. 62.

30. Baron Reijiro Wakatsuki, "The Aims of Japan," *Foreign Affairs,* XIII, 1935, 591.

31. Takeuchi, *War and Diplomacy in the Japanese Empire,* pp. 292-293.

32. Captain W. W. Smyth, memorandum, no date, looseleaf binder labeled "W. W. Smyth," General Board Files.

33. Train, "Daily Log," entries of March 24 and March 31, 1930.

34. Telegram, Tilly to Henderson, Tokyo, March 18, 1930, *British Documents,* pp. 259-260; Takeuchi, *War and Diplomacy in the Japanese Empire,* p. 303. The Japanese foreign minister, Shidehara, observed that there were "streams of public opinion, the topmost stream being the most noisy but not necessarily the most important." He was trying to tap "the deeper streams which run beneath the surface in the hope and belief that he can prove public opinion to be in favor of the agreement reached by the delegations in London." Castle Diary, March 24, 1930.

35. *Saionji-Harada Memoirs,* p. 10.

36. Tokyo *Nichi Nichi,* March 20, 1930, quoted in telegram, Castle to Cotton, March 20, 1930, *Foreign Relations, 1930,* I, 68-69.

37. Telegram, Stimson to Castle, March 19, 1930, D/S 250 Japan/105, RG 43, National Archives; telegram, Castle to Stimson, March 20, 1930, D/S 250 Japan/106, *ibid.;* telegram, Stimson to Cotton, March 21, 1930, *Foreign Relations, 1930,* I, 71.

38. *Saionji-Harada Memoirs,* p. 20.

39. Notes of a meeting of representatives of the delegations of the United States, the United Kingdom, and Japan, April 2, 1930, *British Documents,* pp. 282-289; telegram, Stimson to Cotton, April 2, 1930, *Foreign Relations, 1930,* I, 100. Telegram, Stimson to Cotton, April 10, 1930, *Foreign Relations, 1930,* I, 105. Stimson had advised the American correspondents against claiming any advantage for the United States when the Japanese reply was received because, he said, gloating was not "patriotic" and it would antagonize public opinion in Japan. Telegram, Stimson to Cotton, April 1, 1930, D/S 500.A15A3/813, National Archives.

40. Hoover sent Stimson a letter from Edward Price Bell, in which the journalist had urged a conciliatory policy toward Japan, and had concluded: "I think the Japs are our first line of defense in the Far East; and I am certainly glad they are fairly well armed." The President, in his forwarding letter, observed: ". . . his reflections here are of very considerable importance." Hoover to Stimson, Feb. 25, 1930, #1F-0936; Bell to Hoover, London, Feb. 12, 1930, #1F-0937. Stimson Papers.

VIII

1. *Proceedings of the London Naval Conference of 1930,* pp. 78-82.

2. *Ibid.,* pp. 82-84. Admiral Jones insisted that abolition would be effective only if all nations concurred and "all plans and drawings of submarines throughout the world [were] destroyed." H. C. Train, Memorandum, Oct. 17, 1929, Hilary P. Jones Papers. Rear Admiral George C. Day maintained that the Navy was not consulted regarding the American decision to advocate the abolition of submarines. Testimony, Senate Committee on Foreign Relations, *Hearings on Treaty on the Limitation of Naval Armaments,* 71 Cong., 2 sess., p. 298, May 26, 1930.

3. *Proceedings,* pp. 84-88.

4. *Ibid.,* 89-91.

5. *Ibid.,* pp. 91-92.

6. *Ibid.,* p. 93. The text of the American resolution is printed on p. 93. The French resolution is printed on p. 88.

7. Third Report of the Committee of Experts, March 11, 1930, *ibid.,* p. 169.

8. *Ibid.,* p. 170.

9. Third Report of the First Committee, April 12, 1930, *ibid.,* p. 165.

10. Third Report of the Committee of Experts, March 11, 1930, *ibid.,* pp. 171-174.

11. *Ibid.,* pp. 174-175.

12. Third Report of the First Committee, April 12, 1930, *ibid.,* p. 167. The American naval advisers did not care how high the unit-tonnage figure was so long as it was not below 1,800 tons. Train, "Daily Log," I, entry of March 7, 1930.

13. Third Report of the First Committee, April 12, 1930, *Proceedings,* p. 167.

14. Telegram, Stimson to Cotton, Feb. 28, 1930, *Foreign Relations, 1930,* I, 33-34. Two memoranda, dated Feb. 25 and Feb. 26, concerning meetings relating to this problem are filed in looseleaf binder labeled "W. W. Smyth," General Board Files.

15. Telegram, Stimson to Cotton, Feb. 28, 1930, *Foreign Relations, 1930,* I, 34-35. Root's views are contained in Root to Cotton, New York, March 7, 1930, *ibid.,* pp. 51-52. Moore's comments are in Moore to Cotton, Winter Park, Florida, March 9, 1930, *ibid.,* p. 54.

16. Telegram, Cotton to Stimson, March 13, 1930, *ibid.,* p. 59.

17. Telegram, Stimson to Cotton, March 19, 1930, *ibid.,* pp. 67-68. Root's reaction to this proposal is given in telegram, Cotton to Stimson, March 22, 1930, *ibid.,* p. 74.

18. Report of Committee of Jurists, April 3, 1930, *Proceedings,* pp. 189-190.

19. Second Addendum to First Report of First Committee, April 12, 1930, *ibid.,* p. 143.

20. Annex II to Second Report of the Committee of Experts, March 15, 1930, *ibid.,* pp. 160-161.

21. Annex III to Second Report of the Committee of Experts, March 15, 1930, *ibid.,* pp. 162-163.

22. Second Report of the Committee of Experts, March 15, 1930, *ibid.,* p. 154.

23. Second Report of the First Committee, March 15, 1930, *ibid.,* pp. 146-147.

24. Annex III to Second Report of the Committee of Experts, March 15, 1930, *ibid.,* pp. 162-163.

25. Fourth Report of the First Committee, April 12, 1930, *ibid.,* pp. 191-196.

26. Fifth Report of the First Committee, April 12, 1930, *ibid.,* pp. 197-198.

27. Statement of the French Delegation, Feb. 12, 1930, *ibid.,* pp. 227-230.

28. Statement of the French Delegation to the Press, Feb. 13, 1930, *ibid.,* p. 234.

29. Arnold Wolfers, *Britain and France between Two Wars: Conflicting Strategies of Peace since Versailles,* New York, 1940, pp. 344-346; Winkler, "Arthur Henderson," Craig and Gilbert, eds., *The Diplomats,* pp. 316-317. In all probability, the Labour government would not have ratified the Geneva Protocol even if it had remained in office. *Ibid.,* p. 317, and Richard W. Lyman, *The First Labour Government, 1924,* London, 1957, pp. 176-177. MacDonald seemed to contradict himself on the issue and apparently had reservations on the matter of sanctions.

30. Notes of a meeting of representatives of the delegations of the United States, France, and the United Kingdom, Feb. 13, 1930, *British Documents,* pp. 213, 216-217.

31. Craigie, Note of a conversation with Massigli, Feb. 13, 1930, *ibid.,* pp. 210-211.

32. Notes of a meeting of representatives of the delegations of the United States, France, and the United Kingdom, Feb. 14, 1930, *ibid.,* pp. 218-226.

33. Telegram, Stimson to Cotton, Feb. 16, 1930, *Foreign Relations, 1930,* I, 26.

34. New York *Times,* Feb. 3, 1930, p. 1.

35. *Ibid.,* Feb. 17, 1930, p. 1.

36. *Ibid.,* Feb. 18, 1930, p. 1. *Christian Science Monitor,* Feb. 20, 1930, clipping in RG 43, Box 1, National Archives. Washington *Post,* Feb. 22, 1930, clipping in RG 43, Box 2, National Archives. New York *Times,* Feb. 20, 1930, p. 19.

37. Telegram, Stimson to Cotton, Feb. 23, 1930, *Foreign Relations, 1930,* I, 28-29. MacDonald agreed that British public opinion was incensed at France. Telegram, Stimson to Cotton, Feb. 24, 1930, D/S 500.A15A3/710, National Archives.

38. *Dawes, Journal* pp. 159-160.

39. Note by Craigie of a conversation with Massigli, Feb. 25, 1930, *British Documents*, p. 236. The draft of the proffered pact is printed in *ibid.*, pp. 237-238.

40. Telegram, Cotton to Stimson, Feb. 26, 1930, *Foreign Relations, 1930*, I, 31.

41. New York *Times*, Feb. 28, 1930, p. 4. Report from British ambassador in Paris, quoted in telegram, Stimson to Cotton, March 5, 1930, D/S 500.A15A3/739, National Archives.

42. Dwight W. Morrow, Memorandum of conversation, Feb. 24, 1930, in Stimson Diary. The source of this information was Louis Aubert, a member of the French delegation, who was described by Stimson as "the right-hand man of Tardieu during the interregnum." Telegram, Stimson to Hoover and Cotton, March 4, 1930, *Foreign Relations, 1930*, I, 45.

43. Telegram, Cotton to Stimson, Feb. 28, 1930, *ibid.*, pp. 32-33; Hoover to Stimson, March 3, 1930, *ibid.*, p. 39.

44. New York *Times*, March 10, 1930, p. 2.

45. Myers, *The Foreign Policies of Herbert Hoover*, pp. 89-90. Myers prints two telegrams originated by the organization. See New York *Times*, March 3, 1930, pp. 1, 28.

46. Telegram, Hoover to Stimson, March 3, 1930, *Foreign Relations, 1930*, I, 40-41.

47. Telegram, Stimson to Cotton, March 3, 1930, *ibid.*, pp. 36-39.

48. Telegram, Cotton to Stimson, March 4, 1930, *ibid.*, pp. 41-42.

49. Telegram, Stimson to Cotton, March 5, 1930, *ibid.*, p. 47.

50. Confidential memorandum of a conversation between Prime Minister MacDonald and H. L. S., March 5, 1930, Stimson Diary.

51. Telegram, Cotton to Stimson, March 5, 1930, *Foreign Relations, 1930*, I, 46; telegram, Cotton to Stimson, March 6, 1930, *ibid.*, pp. 48-49.

52. New York *Times*, March 10, 1930, p. 3.

53. Telegram, Stimson to Cotton, March 8, 1930, *Foreign Relations, 1930*, I, 53.

54. Record of a conversation between MacDonald, Henderson, and Briand, March 9, 1930, *British Documents*, pp. 238-240.

IX

1. Stimson to Hoover, March 11, 1930, D/S 500.A15A3/767A, National Archives. Stimson noted, "By that time I had finally cleared in my mind the dangers to be avoided in the consultative pact question, namely, that under the existing circumstances even a consultative pact would carry an implication of material assistance if we persuaded France to reduce her fleet." Stimson Diary, March 8, 1930.

2. Telegram, Stimson to Cotton, March 12, 1930, *Foreign Relations, 1930*, I, 57-58; Stimson Diary, March 11, 1930.

3. See Sidney B. Fay, *The Origins of the World War*, New York, 1938, 2nd ed., I, 318-324.

4. Quoted in "Summary of British Press Items Regarding the London Naval Conference, Evening of March 12, 1930, and morning of March 13," NRG 45, Box 492, National Archives.

5. New York *Times*, March 13, 1930, p. 2.

6. *Ibid.*

7. Raymond Leslie Buell, "News Bulletin," Foreign Policy Association, XI, No. 1, March 19, 1930.

8. Telegram, Stimson to Cotton, March 12, 1930, D/S 391/33, RG 43, National Archives. "In refusing a 'Mediterranean Locarno,' Mr. MacDonald is correctly interpreting the prevalent current of British public opinion." *Economist*, March 15, 1930, p. 571.

9. U.S. Military Attaché, Rome, to American Delegation, London, Report No. 23, March 17, 1930, NRG 45, Box 492, National Archives.

10. Notes of a meeting of representatives of the delegations of the United States, France, and the United Kingdom, March 12, 1930, *British Documents*, pp. 245, 247. For comment on the dull and deadly atmosphere at the conference from the point of view of newsmen, see *Literary Digest*, March 8, 1930, p. 12.

11. Train, "Daily Log," entry of March 12, 1930.

12. Record of a conversation between MacDonald, Alexander, Briand, and Tardieu, March 16, 1930, *British Documents*, p. 253.

13. Dwight W. Morrow, Memorandum of Conversation, March 16, 1930; Morrow, Memorandum of Conversation, March 19, 1930; Morrow, Memorandum of Conversation, March 22, 1930. Copies in Stimson Diary. And Stimson Diary, entry of March 21, 1930.

14. *Time and Tide*, March 21, 1930; *Nation and Athenaeum*, March 22, 1930; London *Daily Herald*, March 26, 1930. Clippings in NRG 45, Box 492, National Archives.

15. *New Statesman*, March 22, 1930, *ibid*.

16. New York *Times*, March 21, 1930, p. 10.

17. Dawes, *Journal*, p. 162.

18. Telegram, Stimson to Cotton, March 17, 1930, *Foreign Relations, 1930*, I, 65.

19. Stimson, Memorandum of Conversation on March 20, 1930, in Stimson Diary.

20. Stimson Diary, March 22, 1930.

21. *Ibid*.

22. Telegram, Stimson to Cotton, March 23, 1930, *Foreign Relations, 1930*, I, 79.

23. Notes of a meeting between representatives of the delegations of the United States and the United Kingdom, March 24, 1930, *British Documents*, p. 267; telegram, Stimson to Cotton, March 25, 1930, *Foreign Relations, 1930*, I, 80-81; Stimson Diary, March 22, 1930.

24. Telegram No. 259, Cotton to Stimson, March 25, 1930, *Foreign Relations, 1930*, I, 81-82. Cotton sent two other telegrams on March 25 complaining about the rumors of a consultative agreement. *Ibid*., pp. 81-83.

25. Telegram, Stimson to Cotton, March 26, 1930, *ibid*., pp. 84-85.

26. Telegram, Cotton to Stimson, March 26, 1930, *ibid*., pp. 85-86.

27. *Proceedings of the London Naval Conference, 1930*, pp. 273-274; Stimson Diary, March 25, 1930.

28. New York *Times*, March 27, 1930, p. 1.

29. *Ibid*., March 28, 1930, p. 1; New York *World*, March 28, 1930, p. 1.

30. New York *Times*, March 27, 1930, pp. 1 and 26.

31. *Ibid*., p. 2; telegram, Edward R. Murrow to Ray Lyman Wilbur, Pullman, Washington, March 27, 1930, D/S 500.A15A3/807½, National Archives.

32. "Summary of British Press Editorials Regarding the London Naval Conference, Evening of March 26 and Morning of March 27, 1930," mimeographed, NRG 45, Box 492, National Archives.

33. London *Daily Telegraph*, March 27, 1930, clipping in NRG 45, Box 492, National Archives.

34. "Summary of British Press News Items Regarding the London Naval Conference, Evening of March 28 and Morning of March 29, 1930," NRG 45, Box 492, National Archives. *Time and Tide*, March 28, 1930; *Saturday Review*, March 29, 1930; *Nation and Athenaeum*, March 29, 1930; *Week End Review*, March 29, 1930. Clippings in NRG 45, Box 492, National Archives. "Summary of British Press Editorials Regarding the London Naval Conference, Evening of March 26 and Morning of March 27, 1930," NRG 45, Box 492, National Archives. New York *Times*, March 27, 1930, p. 2.

35. London *Times*, March 27, 1930, "Summary of British Press Editorials Regarding the London Naval Conference, Evening of March 26 and Morning of March 27, 1930," NRG 45, Box 492, National Archives. New York *Times*, March 28, 1930, pp. 1-2. Morton D. Hull, MC, to Cotton, Washington, March 27, 1930, D/S 500.A15A3/800, National Archives. The New York *Times* claimed that Hoover could conclude a consultative pact on his own authority. New York *Times*, March 24, 1930, editorial, p. 20.

36. Telegram, Cotton to Stimson, March 28, 1930, *Foreign Relations, 1930*, I, 89-90. In his memoirs, Hoover claims that he was "compelled to instruct [Stimson] that we could not agree" to a consultative pact. *The Cabinet and the Presidency*, p. 348.

37. Telegram to Cotton, March 29, 1930, *Foreign Relations, 1930*, I, 92-95.

38. Stimson Diary, March 25, 1930.

39. Dawes, *Journal*, pp. 174-175; telegram, Stimson to Cotton, March 27, 1930, *Foreign Relations, 1930*, I, 88; telegram, Stimson to Cotton, March 29, 1930, *ibid*., p. 92.

40. Cotton, Memorandum of a conversation with the Japanese Ambassador, March 27,

1930, D/S 500.A15A3/797, National Archives; Cotton, Memorandum of a conversation with the French Ambassador, March 28, 1930, D/S 500.A15A3/808, National Archives.

41. The message is contained in telegram, Cotton to Stimson, March 31, 1930, *Foreign Relations, 1930*, I, 96-97.

42. Telegram, Stimson to Cotton, April 3, 1930, *ibid.*, p. 101.

43. David D. Burks, "The United States and the Geneva Protocol of 1924: 'A New Holy Alliance'?," *American Historical Review*, LXIV, 1959, 891-905. France had ample reason to be skeptical of British intentions. The agreement to include trained reserves in the strength of armies when considering a reduction of armaments, which had been reached in 1928, was repudiated by Lord Cecil. At the Hague Conference in the summer of 1929, the Labour government rejected certain provisions of the Young Plan which had been previously accepted by Britain, and exerted pressure on France for the complete evacuation of occupied territory in Germany. Harold G. Moulton and Leo Pasvolsky, *War Debts and World Prosperity*, Washington, 1932, pp. 204-207; Elaine Windrich, *British Labour's Foreign Policy*, Stanford, 1952, pp. 74-76.

44. Telegram, Stimson to Cotton, Feb. 16, 1930, *Foreign Relations, 1930*, I, 26; telegram, Stimson to Cotton, March 10, 1930, *ibid.*, p. 56.

45. Extract from a conversation between Sir R. Vansittart and Signor Grandi and Signor Bordonaro, March 11, 1930, *British Documents*, p. 241.

46. Telegram, Henderson to Graham, March 15, 1930, *British Documents*, pp. 251-252; Record of a conversation between MacDonald, Alexander, Briand, and Tardieu, March 16, 1930, *ibid.*, p. 257.

47. Telegram, Graham to Henderson, March 16, 1930, *ibid.*, p. 237; telegram, Graham to Henderson, March 18, 1930, *ibid.*, p. 258; telegram, Graham to Henderson, March 20, 1930, *ibid.*, p. 263. *Ibid.*, p. 263, note 2. Dwight W. Morrow, Memorandum of Conversation, March 17, 1930, in Stimson Diary.

48. Grandi to MacDonald, London, April 9, 1930, *British Documents*, pp. 308-309. The Dallas *News* perceptively remarked, "Italy demands the right to wish for as many battleships as France wishes for." Quoted in *Literary Digest*, April 12, 1930, p. 15.

49. Cotton, Memorandum of conversation with the Spanish Ambassador, Jan. 13, 1930, D/S, 500.A15A3/618, National Archives.

50. Notes of a Private Conversation between the Heads of the U.S. Delegation and United Kingdom Delegation held on March 24, 1930, dated March 31, 1930. D/S 110.02/17, RG 43, National Archives. For the Spanish reaction to the London Naval Conference and a statement of the Spanish attitude toward disarmament, a Mediterranean pact, and bases, see Pedro Maria Cardona y Prieto, *La Conferencia y el Tratado Maritimo-Naval de Londres (1930), desde el Punto de Vista Español*, Madrid, 1931.

51. 237 *House of Commons Debates*, 5 s. 29.

52. *Foreign Relations, 1930*, I, 98, note 13.

53. Telegram, Stimson to Cotton, April 9, 1930, *ibid.*, p. 104; Stimson Diary, March 25, 1930.

54. Notes of a meeting of representatives of the delegations of France and the United Kingdom, April 8, 1930, *British Documents*, pp. 293-300. The British draft declaration, with the modifications indicated, is printed in *ibid.*, pp. 300-301.

55. Notes of a meeting of representatives of the delegations of France and the United Kingdom, April 9, 1930, *ibid.*, p. 302.

56. Notes of a meeting of representatives of the delegations of France, the United Kingdom, and Italy, April 10, 1930, *ibid.*, pp. 309-311.

57. Stimson believed that the United States should have entered into a consultative pact. See Henry L. Stimson, *The Far Eastern Crisis: Recollections and Observations*, New York, 1936, p. 203; and Henry L. Stimson, Reminiscences, Oral History Project, Columbia University, p. 8. Stimson later recalled that he was "sad" when he had to tell Briand that it was impossible. *Ibid.*

58. Telegram No. 211, Stimson to Cotton, April 10, 1930, *Foreign Relations, 1930*, I, 105; telegram No. 212, Stimson to Cotton, April 10, 1930, *ibid.*, pp. 106-107; telegram, Cotton to Stimson, April 11, 1930, *ibid.*, p. 107.

59. Train, "Daily Log," II, entry "Sunday, 13 April 1930 until Monday, 21 April 1930,

inclusive." See Nicolson, *Dwight Morrow*, pp. 374-375, and New York *Times*, April 19, 1930, p. 4.

60. *Proceedings of the London Naval Conference*, p. 96. This approval was, of course, merely a formality, for the delegates had agreed to the reports in private sessions.

61. *Ibid.*, pp. 102-103.

62. *Ibid.*, pp. 109, 115. For Wakatsuki, signing the treaty was "an ungrateful task." Wakatsuki, "The Aims of Japan," p. 591.

63. *Proceedings of the London Naval Conference*, pp. 203-220. For the text of the treaty, see Appendix I.

64. "Summary of British Press News Regarding the London Naval Conference, evening of April 10 and morning of April 11, 1930," NRG 45, Box 493, National Archives; New York *Times*, April 12, 1930, p. 2; "Disarmament, The London Naval Conference, etc., As Discussed in the Daily Press, London, Week of April 21-27, 1930," Office of U.S. Naval Attaché, London, NRG 45, Box 493, National Archives; Raymond Bouy, *Le Désarmement Naval. La Conférence de Londres*, Paris, 1931, pp. 266-267; André Geraud, "The London Naval Conference: A French View," *Foreign Affairs*, VIII, 1930, 521. New York *Times*, April 23, 1930, p. 18. France was indignant over Italy's presumption in demanding equality, and cynical about the article restricting submarine warfare. J. Docteur, Vice Admiral, French Navy, "How the Result [of the London Treaty] Is Viewed in Each Nation: France," *Current History*, XXXII, 1930, 451, 453.

65. Tupper and McReynolds, *Japan in American Public Opinion*, pp. 254, 255, 263.

66. *Literary Digest*, May 3, 1930, p. 10. Tupper and McReynolds concur with this assessment. *Op. cit.*, p. 262. For examples of praise and criticism in the American press, see *Literary Digest*, April 26, 1930, pp. 8-9.

67. New York *Times*, April 13, 1930, p. E4.

68. London *Morning Post*, April 12, 1930; *Sunday Graphic*, April 13, 1930; *Saturday Review* (British), April 12, 1930; London *Daily Telegraph*, April 23, 1930. Clippings in NRG 45, Box 493, National Archives.

69. London *Post*, April 23, 1930; Manchester *Guardian*, April 23, 1930; London *Daily Herald*, April 23, 1930; London *Times*, April 23, 1930; *Week End Review*, April 19, 1930; *Time and Tide*, April 26, 1930; *Saturday Review* (British), April 26, 1930; *Economist*, April 26, 1930, p. 932; *Spectator*, April 26, 1930, p. 692. Clippings in NRG 45, Box 493, National Archives. According to H. Wickham Steed, "The people of Great Britain regard the London naval treaty with relief rather than with satisfaction." "How the Result [of the London Treaty] is Viewed in Each Nation: Great Britain," *Current History*, XXXII, 1930, 449. Stimson reported press comment as generally favorable. Telegram, Stimson to Cotton, April 14, 1930, D/S 391/52, RG 43, National Archives.

70. Telegram, John W. Garrett to Cotton, Rome, April 22, 1930, NRG 45, Box 493, National Archives.

71. New York *Times*, April 20, 1930, p. E3; Carlo Shanzer, "How the Result [of the London Treaty] is Viewed in Each Nation: Italy," *Current History*, XXXII, 1930, 454; Chicago *Tribune* (Paris edition), April 22, 1930, clipping in NRG 45, Box 493, National Archives.

72. Maxwell H. H. Macartney and Paul Cremona, *Italy's Foreign and Colonial Policy, 1914-1937*, London, 1938, p. 265. For Italian accounts of the conference, see Giovanni Engely, *The Politics of Naval Disarmament*, London, 1932, translated from the Italian by II. V. Rhodes. Also, Rudolfo Mosca, *Il Disarmo Navale e la Conferenza di Londra*, Pavia, 1931. Both of these works are intensely partisan, but they contain some useful information.

73. Washington *Star*, Feb. 23, 1930, part 2, p. 1.

X

1. Telegram, Cotton to Stimson, April 11, 1930, D/S 500.A15A3/838A, National Archives.

2. Telegram, Cotton to Stimson, April 14, 1930, D/S 500.A15A3/840b, National Archives.

3. Telegram, Stimson to Cotton, April 15, 1930, D/S 500.A15A3/841, National Archives.

4. These speeches are printed in *Proceedings of the London Naval Conference*, pp. 274-283, 284-296.

5. Telegram, Stimson and Reed to Cotton, April 14, 1930, D/S 110.1215/3, RG 43, National Archives.

6. Telegram, Cotton to Stimson, April 17, 1930, D/S 110.1215/10, RG 43, National Archives.

7. New York *Times*, April 19, 1930, p. 1.

8. Rappaport, "The Navy League of the United States," manuscript, pp. 239-241.

9. Quoted in *Literary Digest*, May 31, 1930, p. 11.

10. New York *Times*, April 17, 1930, pp. 1, 5.

11. Boston *American*, May 31, 1930; New York *American*, June 2, 1930; Washington *Herald*, June 3, 1930. Clippings enclosed in letter, Stimson to Morrow, June 4, 1930, Morrow Papers. Stimson was anxious to know whether Coolidge would have accepted a British figure of fifty cruisers.

12. Laura Puffer Morgan, *An Observer's Estimate of the London Naval Conference*, Washington, National Council for the Prevention of War, n.d.

13. *Literary Digest*, May 24, 1930, p. 14. The Congressman need not have been over-concerned, for the President was soon to direct the Navy Department to practice economy and reduce the budget. Hoover to Adams, July 29, 1930, cited in Lord, "History of Naval Aviation," IV, 1258-1259.

14. *Senate Document*, 71 Cong., 2 sess., No. 141.

15. Senate Committee on Foreign Relations, *Hearings on Treaty on the Limitation of Naval Armaments*, 71 Cong., 2 sess., p. 1.

16. *Ibid.*, p. 10.

17. *Ibid.*, p. 194.

18. *Ibid.*, p. 291. A more analytical but less comprehensive summation is presented in the testimony of Captain Dudley W. Knox, *ibid.*, pp. 355-356.

19. *Ibid.*, pp. 121-122, 179-180.

20. *Senate Document*, 71 Cong., 2 sess., No. 197, pp. 4, 8, 11, 27, 31.

21. Admiral Pratt acknowledged that international good will and building costs should be considered along with naval effectiveness in determining the soundness of the treaty. *Hearings*, Committee on Foreign Relations, p. 63. Senator Reed conceded that "Pratt was a trump throughout" the hearings. Reed to Morrow, Kennebunkport, Maine, Aug. 14, 1930, Morrow Papers, London Naval Conference file. Admiral Pratt became Chief of Naval Operations in September, succeeding Admiral Hughes, who held views contrary to his own. Fleet Admiral William D. Leahy, Diary, I, 314, Library of Congress, Manuscript Division.

22. Stimson to Borah, June 6, 1930, *Congressional Record*, 71 Cong., Special Session, p. 27.

23. *Senate Report*, 71 Cong., 2 sess., No. 1880, p. 1.

24. *Ibid.*, p. 16.

25. *Ibid.*, Part 2, pp. 1-20.

26. Telegram, Dawes to Stimson, June 4, 1930, D/S 500.A15A3/938, National Archives; telegram, Stimson to Dawes, June 4, 1930, D/S 500.A15A3/939, National Archives.

27. Memorandum, prepared by the Division of Far Eastern Affairs, June 13, 1930, D/S 500.A15A3/965, National Archives.

28. Hoover's new firmness and leadership were noted by the *Wall Street Journal*, and columnist David Lawrence contrasted it with the President's previous failure to assert himself. See *Literary Digest*, June 14, 1930, p. 5.

29. *Congressional Record*, 71 Cong., Special Session, pp. 4-5.

30. New York *American*, July 6, 1930, printed in *ibid.*, pp. 109-110.

31. Chicago *Tribune*, July 7, 1930, quoted in *ibid.*, pp. 37-38.

32. *Ibid.*, pp. 5-6.

33. *Ibid.*, p. 35.

34. *Ibid.* (Daily Edition), p. 64.

35. *Congressional Record*, 71 Cong., Special Session, p. 89. The resolution is printed on pp. 88-89.

36. Hoover to the Senate, July 11, 1930, *ibid.*, p. 108.

37. *Ibid.*, p. 110.

38. *Ibid.*, pp. 124-127.

39. Howland, ed., *American Foreign Relations,* 1931, p. 408, note 146. Charles P. Howland, director of research for the Council on Foreign Relations, was a friend of, and on a first-name basis with, both Stimson and Cotton.

40. *Congressional Record,* 71 Cong., Special Session, pp. 12-22.

41. *Ibid.,* p. 33.

42. *Ibid.,* p. 29 and *passim.*

43. *Ibid.,* pp. 156-163.

44. *Ibid.,* p. 310.

45. *Ibid.,* p. 37.

46. Quoted in *Literary Digest,* July 19, 1930, p. 13.

47. *Congressional Record,* 71 Cong., Special Session, p. 99.

48. *Ibid.,* pp. 102-103.

49. *Ibid.,* p. 69.

50. New York *Times,* July 13, 1930, p. 2.

51. *Congressional Record,* 71 Cong., Special Session, p. 239.

52. *Ibid.,* pp. 327-348.

53. *Ibid.,* p. 378.

54. *Literary Digest,* Aug. 2, 1930, p. 6. For numerous press quotations on the occasion of ratification, see *ibid.,* pp. 5-6; and New York *Times,* July 22, 1930, p. 2, which quotes approving views from nineteen newspapers throughout the nation.

55. Tupper and McReynolds, *Japan in American Public Opinion,* p. 262.

56. Senator Oddie did point out the advantage Japan possessed in this respect by virtue of her bases, although he did not apply it to fleet action, and he did not develop the topic. The treaty defenders did not reply to the Senator on this subject. *Congressional Record,* 71 Cong., Special Session, p. 151.

57. Telegram, Castle to Stimson, Tokyo, May 5, 1930, D/S 500.A15A3/909, National Archives; *Saionji-Harada Memoirs,* p. 30; London *Daily Herald,* May 1, 1930, clipping in NRG 45, Box 493, National Archives.

58. New York *Times,* April 4, 1930, p. 6. Hugh Byas, the *Times* correspondent in Tokyo, furnished admirable detailed accounts of the developments.

59. Telegram, Castle to Stimson, Tokyo, May 15, 1930, D/S 500.A15A3/898, National Archives.

60. "On the Ratification of the London Pact," *Gaiko Jiho,* May 15, 1930. Translation by Office of Naval Intelligence, NRG 45, Box 493, National Archives. An accompanying note says, "The magazine has for over 33 years maintained an impartial attitude in party conflicts."

61. New York *Times,* May 19, 1930, p. 1.

62. Tokyo *Trans-Pacific,* April 10, 1930, p. 8; Takeuchi, *War and Diplomacy in the Japanese Empire,* p. 305; telegram, Neville to Stimson, Tokyo, June 19, 1930, D/S 500.A15-A3/968, National Archives.

63. *Saionji-Harada Memoirs,* pp. 98-99. These memoirs reveal a fantastic amount of behind-the-scenes maneuvering by the pro-treaty forces.

64. Telegram, Neville to Stimson, Tokyo, June 17, 1930, D/S 500.A15A3/992, National Archives.

65. "Record of the Privy Council Regarding the Imperial Ratification of the London Naval Treaty of 1930, 1st October 1930," *Tokyo War Crimes Documents,* No. 891-A.

66. *Proceedings of the London Naval Conference,* pp. 299-300.

67. Telegram, Atherton to Stimson, London, May 9, 1930, D/S 500.A15A3/903, National Archives.

68. 77 *House of Lords Debates,* 5 s., 436-444.

69. *Ibid.,* 444-451.

70. For some of the drama that attended the efforts of the two admirals and the anticlimactic withdrawal of the motion for the papers, see Gladys Murphy Graham, "The House of Lords Debates the London Naval Treaty," *Quarterly Journal of Speech,* XVI, 1930, 414-420.

71. 238 *House of Commons Debates,* 5 s., 2098-2110.

72. *Ibid.*, pp. 2095-2096.
73. 239 *House of Commons Debates*, 5 s., 1806-1808. Detailed replies to Churchill's arguments were made by Philip Noel-Baker, parliamentary private secretary in the Foreign Office. *Ibid.*, pp. 1827-1836.
74. *Ibid.*, p. 1791.
75. *Ibid.*, pp. 1919-1920. The vote was 201 for the motion and 282 against.
76. 241 *House of Commons Debates*, 5 s., 2557.
77. Except for that of the Irish Free State, which was deposited on Dec. 31, 1930.
78. The speeches are printed in *Proceedings of the London Naval Conference*, pp. 299-303.

Bibliography

1. BIBLIOGRAPHIES

Albion, Robert Greenhalgh, *Maritime and Naval History: An Annotated Bibliography,* Revised. Mystic, Connecticut, 1955.

Carnegie Endowment for International Peace. Library. *Disarmament and Security: Select List of Recent Books, Pamphlets and Periodical Articles.* Compiled by Mary Alice Matthews. Washington, D.C., 1931.

League of Nations. *Annotated Bibliography on Disarmament and Military Questions.* Geneva, 1931.

Library of Congress, Division of Bibliography. *Disarmament, with Special Reference to Naval Limitation: A Bibliographical List.* Compiled by Florence S. Hellman. Washington, D.C., 1929.

————. *Disarmament, with Special Reference to Naval Limitation: A List of Recent References.* Compiled by Florence S. Hellman. Washington, D.C., 1934.

————. *London Naval Conference, 1930: A Bibliographical List.* Washington, D.C., 1930.

Read, Conyers, "Recent United States and British Government Publications on the London Naval Conference of 1930." *American Historical Review,* LIV, 1949, 307-314.

2. MANUSCRIPTS

A. *Personal Manuscripts*

William R. Castle Diary. Washington, D.C.

Calvin Coolidge Papers. Library of Congress.

Charles G. Dawes Papers and Diary. Northwestern University Library.

Rear Admiral William F. Fullam Papers. Navy Historical Foundation Collection, Library of Congress.

Charles Evans Hughes Papers. Library of Congress.

Rear Admiral Hilary P. Jones Papers. Navy Historical Foundation Collection, Library of Congress.

Commodore Dudley W. Knox Papers. Navy Historical Foundation Collection, Library of Congress.

Fleet Admiral William D. Leahy Diary. Library of Congress.

Franklin D. Roosevelt Papers. Hyde Park, N.Y.

Dwight W. Morrow Papers. Amherst College Memorabilia, Amherst, Mass.

Henry L. Stimson Papers and Diary. Yale University Library.

J. Mayhew Wainwright Papers. World War I Branch, War Records Division, National Archives.

Admiral Harry E. Yarnell Papers. Navy Historical Foundation Collection, Library of Congress.

B. *Government Manuscripts*

U.S., Department of the Army. Records of the Adjutant General's Office (Disarmament). National Archives.

U.S., Joint Board of the Army and Navy. Records of the Joint Board of the Army and Navy, 1919-1931. National Archives.

U.S., Department of State. Series 500.A15A3. 1929-1930. National Archives.

———. London Naval Conference of 1930, Files of the American Delegation. National Archives.

———. Washington Conference on the Limitation of Armaments, Files of the American Delegation. National Archives.

U.S., Navy Department. Correspondence of the Office of the Secretary of the Navy and the Office of the Chief of Naval Operations, 1927-1930. National Archives.

———. Files of the Navy General Board, 1900-1930. U.S. Navy Service Center, Arlington, Virginia, under the jurisdiction of the Director of Naval History.

Japan, Archives in the Japanese Ministry of Foreign Affairs, microfilm. Library of Congress.

3. GOVERNMENT DOCUMENTS

A. *United States Documents*

Congressional Record, 71st Congress. Washington, 1929-1930.

Department of State Conference Series No. 3, *London Naval Conference, Speeches and Press Statements by Members of the American Delegation, January 20-April 29, 1930.* Washington, 1930.

Department of State Conference Series No. 4, *London Naval Conference: Digest of the London Naval Treaty of 1930, with Fleet-Tonnage Tables.* Washington, 1930.

Department of State Conference Series No. 6, *Proceedings of the London Conference of 1930 and Supplementary Documents.* Washington, 1931.

Hearings Before the Committee on Naval Affairs, U.S. Senate, 71 Cong., 2 sess., sess., on Treaty on the Limitation of Naval Armaments, Washington, 1930.

Hearings before the Committee on Naval Affairs, U.S. Senate, 71 Cong., 2 sess., on the London Naval Treaty of 1930, Washington, 1930.

Navy Department. *Annual Reports of the Navy Department, 1913-1930.* Washington, 1914-1931.

Papers Relating to the Foreign Relations of the United States, 1921-1930. Washington, 1936-1945.

Records of the International Military Tribunal for the Far East, *Record of the Privy Council Regarding the Imperial Ratification of the London Naval Treaty of 1930, 1st October 1930.* Document No. 891-A.

Senate Documents, 67 Cong., 2 sess., No. 126, Washington, 1922.

———, 70 Cong., 1 sess., No. 55, Washington, 1928.

———, 71 Cong., 2 sess., No. 141, Washington, 1930.

———, 71 Cong., 2 sess., No. 197, Washington, 1930.

Senate Reports, 71 Cong., 2 sess., No. 1080, Washington, 1930.
Statutes at Large, XLV, Part I, 70 Cong., 2 sess., Washington, 1929.

B. *Foreign Documents*

Great Britain, Foreign Office. *Documents on British Foreign Policy, 1919-1939,* Ernest L. Woodward and Rohan Butler, ed. 1st Series, Vol. VI. London, 1956.

Great Britain, Foreign Office. *Documents on British Foreign Policy, 1919-1939,* Ernest L. Woodward and Rohan Butler, ed. 2nd series, Vol. I. London, 1946.

Great Britain, *Parliamentary Debates, House of Commons, 1927-1930.* London, 1927-1930.

Great Britain, *Parliamentary Debates, House of Lords, 1930.* London, 1930.

League of Nations, *Records of the Conference for the Limitation of Naval Armament, Held at Geneva from June 20th to August 7th, 1927.* Genève, 1927.

4. ALMANACS, HANDBOOKS, AND ENCYCLOPEDIAS

Jane, Thomas F. *Jane's Fighting Ships, 1916-1930.* London.

League of Nations. *Armaments Year Book: General and Statistical Information, 1924-1930.* Geneva, 1924-1930.

Mallory, Walter H., ed. *Political Handbook of the World: Parliaments, Parties and Press, as of January 1, 1930.* New Haven, 1930.

Parkes, Oscar. *The World's Warships.* London, 1929.

5. NEWSPAPERS

Japan Times and Mail Weekly Edition. Tokyo.
London *Times.* London.
New York *Herald-Tribune.* New York.
New York *Times.* New York.
Tokyo *Trans-Pacific.* Tokyo.

Numerous newspaper clippings and reports of press opinion pertaining to the London Naval Conference of 1930 are contained in six file boxes in Navy Record Group 45, National Archives, boxes No. 488-493; and in the Archives, Japanese Ministry of Foreign Affairs, microfilm, Library of Congress.

6. PERIODICALS AND MAGAZINES

Literary Digest, 1921-1930. New York.
United States Naval Institute *Proceedings,* 1900-1930. Annapolis, Md.

7. COLLECTED WORKS

Myers, William S., ed. *The State Papers and Other Public Writings of Herbert Hoover.* 2 vols. New York, 1934.

8. DIARIES

Dawes, Charles G. *Journal as Ambassador to Great Britain.* New York, 1939.
U.S. Army, Far East Command, General Headquarters, Military Intelligence

Section, General Staff. *The Saionji-Harada Memoirs: Supplement. Prince Saionji and the London Disarmament Treaty.* Tokyo, 1946.

9. REMINISCENCES AND AUTOBIOGRAPHIES

Cecil, Viscount (Lord Robert Cecil). *A Great Experiment: An Autobiography.* Oxford, 1941.

Coontz, Robert E. *From the Mississippi to the Sea.* Philadelphia, 1930.

Daniels, Josephus. *The Wilson Era: Years of War and After, 1917-1923.* Chapel Hill, 1946.

Hoover, Herbert. *The Memoirs of Herbert Hoover: The Cabinet and the Presidency, 1920-1933.* New York, 1952.

Ishii, Kikujiro. *Diplomatic Commentaries.* William R. Langdon, ed. Baltimore, 1936.

Rublee, George. *Reminiscences of.* Oral History Project, Columbia University.

Standley, William H., and Arthur A. Ageton. *Admiral Ambassador to Russia.* Chicago, 1955.

Stimson, Henry L., and McGeorge Bundy. *On Active Service in Peace and War.* New York, 1947.

Stimson, Henry L., *Reminiscences of.* Oral History Project, Columbia University.

Watson, James E. *As I Knew Them: Memoirs of James E. Watson.* Indianapolis, 1936.

Wilson, Hugh R. *Diplomat between Wars.* New York, 1941.

10. BIOGRAPHIES

Bryn-Jones, David. *Frank B. Kellogg.* New York, 1937.

Current, Richard N. *Secretary Stimson: A Study in Statecraft.* New Brunswick, N.J., 1954.

Hamilton, Mary Agnes. *Arthur Henderson.* London, 1938.

Jessup, Phillip C. *Elihu Root.* 2 vols. New York, 1938.

Johnson, Claudius O. *Borah of Idaho.* New York, 1936.

McKenna, Marian C. *Borah.* Ann Arbor, 1961.

Morison, Elting E. *Admiral Sims and the Modern American Navy.* Boston, 1942.

———. *Turmoil and Tradition: A Study of the Life and Times of Henry L. Stimson.* Boston, 1960.

Nicolson, Harold. *Dwight Morrow.* New York, 1935.

Pusey, Merlo J. *Charles Evans Hughes.* 2 vols. New York, 1951.

Sacks, Benjamin. *J. Ramsay MacDonald in Thought and Action.* Albuquerque, N.M., 1952.

11. MONOGRAPHS AND SPECIAL STUDIES

Abbott, A. H. "The League's Disarmament Activities and the Washington Conference." *Political Science Quarterly,* XXXVII, 1922, 1-24.

Adler, Selig. *The Isolationist Impulse: Its Twentieth Century Reaction.* London and New York, 1957.

172

Albion, Robert G. "The Naval Affairs Committees, 1816-1947." U.S. Naval Institute *Proceedings,* LXXVIII, 1952, 1227-1237.

Allen, G. C. *A Short Economic History of Modern Japan, 1867-1937.* London, 1946.

Archimbaud, L. *La Conférence de Washington.* Paris, 1923.

Arnold-Forster, William. *The Disarmament Conference.* London, 1931.

Atkinson, J. D. "The London Naval Conference of 1930." Unpublished doctoral dissertation, Georgetown University, 1949.

Bailey, Thomas A. *The Man in the Street: The Impact of American Public Opinion on Foreign Policy.* New York, 1948.

———. *Theodore Roosevelt and the Japanese-American Crises.* Stanford, 1934.

———. *Woodrow Wilson and the Lost Peace.* New York, 1944.

Baker, Roscoe. *The American Legion and American Foreign Policy.* New York, 1954.

Baldwin, Hanson W. *The Price of Power.* New York, 1948.

Bardoux, Jacques. *L'Ile et L'Europe: la Politique Anglaise, 1930-1932.* Paris, 1933.

Beale, Howard K. *Theodore Roosevelt and the Rise of America to World Power.* Baltimore, 1956.

Beard, Charles A. *The Navy: Defense or Portent?* New York, 1932.

Bell, Edward P. *Why MacDonald Came to America.* Chicago, 1929.

Bellairs, Carlyon W. *The Naval Conference and After.* London, 1930.

Beloff, Max. *The Foreign Policy of Soviet Russia, 1929-1941.* Vol. I. London, 1947.

Bemis, Samuel Flagg. "Main Trends of American Foreign Policy," in Frank B. Davidson and George S. Viereck, Jr., ed., *Before America Decides: Foresight in Foreign Affairs.* Cambridge, Mass., 1938.

———. "The Shifting Strategy of American Defense and Diplomacy," in Dwight E. Lee and George E. McReynolds, ed., *Essays in History and International Relations in Honor of George Hubbard Blakeslee.* Worcester, Mass., 1949.

Berdahl, Clarence A. "The Policy of the United States with Respect to the League of Nations." *Publications of the Graduate Institute of International Studies* —No. 4 Geneva, 1932.

Bernardo, C. Joseph, and Eugene H. Bacon. *American Military Policy: Its Development since 1775.* Harrisburg, Penna., 1955.

Bernotti, Romeo. "Italian Naval Policy under Fascism." U.S. Naval Institute *Proceedings,* LXXXII, 1956, 722-731.

Bouy, Raymond. *Le Désarmement Naval: La Conférence de Londres.* Paris, 1931.

Bowen, A. D. "The Disarmament Movement, 1918-1935." Unpublished doctoral dissertation, Columbia University, 1956.

Braisted, William Reynolds. *The United States Navy in the Pacific, 1897-1909.* Austin, 1958.

Brebner, J. B. "Canada, the Anglo-Japanese Alliance and the Washington Conference." *Political Science Quarterly,* L, 1935, 45-58.

Brooks, Edward H. "The National Defense Policy of the Wilson Administration, 1913-1917." Unpublished doctoral dissertation, Stanford University, 1950.

Brown, Delmer M. *Nationalism in Japan*. Berkeley and Los Angeles, 1955.

Buell, Raymond L. *The Washington Conference*. New York, 1922.

Burks, David D. "The United States and the Geneva Protocol of 1924: 'A New Holy Alliance?'." *American Historical Review*, LXIV, 1959, 891-905.

Byas, Hugh. *Government by Assassination*. New York, 1942.

Cardona y Prieto, Pedro Maria. *La Conferencia y el Tratado Maritimo-Naval de Londres (1930) desde el Punto de Vista Español*. Madrid, 1931.

Carter, Gwendolen M. *The British Commonwealth and International Security: The Role of the Dominions, 1919-1939*. Toronto, 1947.

Causton, E. E. N. *Militarism and Foreign Policy in Japan*. London, 1936.

Chaput, Roland A. *Disarmament in British Foreign Policy*. London, 1935.

Clinard, Outten Jones. "Japan's Influence on American Naval Power, 1897-1917," *University of California Publications in History, No. 36*. Berkeley and Los Angeles, 1947.

Colegrove, Kenneth. "Militarism in Japan's Foreign Policy." *Annals of the American Academy of Political and Social Science*, CCXV, 1941, 7-16.

———. "The Treaty-Making Power in Japan." *American Journal of International Law*, XXV, 1931, 270-297.

Coolidge, Calvin. "Promoting Peace through Limitation of Armaments." *Ladies' Home Journal*, May 1929, 3-4.

Cooper, Russell M. *American Consultation in World Affairs for the Preservation of Peace*. New York, 1934.

Craig, Gordon A., and Felix Gilbert, ed. *The Diplomats, 1919-1939*. Princeton, 1953.

Crosby, Gerda Richards. *Disarmament and Peace in British Politics, 1914-1919*. Harvard Historical Monographs, Number 32. Cambridge, Mass., 1957.

Currey, Muriel I. *Italian Foreign Policy, 1918-1932*. London, 1932.

Curti, Merle. *Peace or War: The American Struggle, 1636-1936*. New York, 1936.

Custer, Ben Scott. "The Geneva Conference for the Limitation of Naval Armament—1927." Unpublished doctoral dissertation, Georgetown University, 1948.

Dalton, Hugh. "British Foreign Policy, 1929-1931." *Political Quarterly*, II, 1931, 485-505.

Davis, George T. *A Navy Second to None: The Development of Modern American Naval Policy*. New York, 1940.

DeConde, Alexander, ed. *Isolation and Security*. Durham, N.C., 1957.

Dennett, Tyler. "Japan's 'Monroe Doctrine' Appraised." *Annals of the American Academy of Political and Social Science*, CCXV, 1941, 61-65.

Dennis, Alfred L. P. *The Anglo-Japanese Alliance*. Berkeley, 1923.

DeSanti, Louis Aldo. "U.S. Relations with Italy under Mussolini: 1922-1941." Unpublished doctoral dissertation, Columbia University, 1951.

Dewar, Captain Alfred C. "The London Naval Treaty." *Brassey's Naval and Shipping Annual*, 1931, 69-84.

Dorling, Henry F. "The Naval Treaty and After." *The Nineteenth Century and After*, CIX, 1931, 414-428.

Dulles, Allen W. "The Threat of Anglo-American Naval Rivalry." *Foreign Affairs,* VII, 1929, 173-182.

Edge, Walter E. *A Jerseyman's Journal: Fifty Years of American Business and Politics.* Princeton, 1948.

Ekirch, Arthur A., Jr. *The Civilian and the Military.* New York, 1956.

Engely, Giovanni. *The Politics of Naval Disarmament.* Translated from the Italian by H. V. Rhodes. London, 1932.

Estienny, Paul. *Problème de la Limitation et de la Reduction des Armaments Navals, 1921-1931.* Paris, 1931.

Fagan, George Vincent. "Anglo-American Naval Relations, 1927-1937." Unpublished doctoral dissertation, University of Pennsylvania, 1954.

———. "Edward Price Bell: The Journalist as Diplomat." Newberry Library *Bulletin,* IV, Nov. 1955, 24-27.

Fay, Sidney B. *The Origins of the World War.* 2nd ed., 2 vols. in 1. New York, 1938.

Ferrell, Robert H. *American Diplomacy in the Great Depression: Hoover-Stimson Foreign Policy, 1929-1933.* New Haven, 1957.

———. *Peace in Their Time: The Origins of the Kellogg-Briand Pact.* New Haven, 1952.

Fleming, D. F. *The United States and World Organization, 1920-1933.* New York, 1938.

Gardes, André. *Le Désarmement devant la Société des Nations.* Paris, 1930.

Gardiner, William Howard. "National Policy and Naval Power." U.S. Naval Institute *Proceedings,* LII, 1926, 229-248.

Géraud, André. "The London Naval Conference: A French View." *Foreign Affairs,* VIII, 1930, 519-532.

Glinberg, Aron. *Le Problèm du Désarmement devant la Société des Nations et en dehors d'elle.* Paris, 1930.

Godfrey, James L. "Anglo-American Naval Conversations Preliminary to the London Naval Conference of 1930." *South Atlantic Quarterly,* XLIX, 1950, 303-316.

Graham, Gladys Murphy. "The House of Lords Debates the London Naval Treaty." *Quarterly Journal of Speech,* XVI, 1930, 414-420.

Grassmuck, George A. "Sectional Biases in Congress on Foreign Policy." *The Johns Hopkins University Studies in Historical and Political Science,* Series LXVIII:3. Baltimore, 1951.

Griswold, A. Whitney. *The Far Eastern Policy of the United States.* New York, 1938.

Groelling, Dorothy T. "Submarines, Disarmament and Modern Warfare." Unpublished doctoral dissertation, Columbia University, 1935.

Hankey, Lord. *Diplomacy by Conference.* London, 1946.

Harris, Henry W. *Naval Disarmament.* London, 1930.

Hishida, Seiji. *Japan among the Great Powers.* New York, 1940.

Hoag, Charles Leonard. *Preface to Preparedness: The Washington Conference and Public Opinion.* Washington, D.C., 1941.

Hoover, Herbert. *The Ordeal of Woodrow Wilson.* New York, 1958.

Huntington, Samuel P. *The Soldier and the State: The Theory and Politics of Civil-Military Relations.* Cambridge, Mass., 1959.

Ichihashi, Yamato. *The Washington Conference and After.* Stanford, 1928.

Jordan, W. M. *Great Britain, France and the German Problem, 1918-1939.* London, 1943.

Kawakami, K. K. "The London Naval Conference as Viewed from Japan." *The Nineteenth Century and After,* CVI, 1929, 731-742.

———. "The Hidden Conflict at the Three-Power Naval Conference." *Current History,* XXVII, 1927, 106-111.

Kenworthy, J. M. (Lord Strabolgi) and George Young. *Freedom of the Seas.* New York, 1933.

Kerwin, Jerome G., ed. *Civil-Military Relationships in American Life.* Chicago, 1948.

Knox, Captain Dudley W. *The Eclipse of American Sea Power.* New York, 1922.

Langer, William L. *The Diplomacy of Imperialism.* 2 vols. New York, 1935.

Latimer, Hugh. *Naval Disarmament: A Brief Record from the Washington Conference to Date.* London, 1930.

Lippmann, Walter. "The London Naval Conference: An American View." *Foreign Affairs,* VIII, 1930, 499-518.

Livermore, Seward W. "American Strategy Diplomacy in the South Pacific, 1890-1914." *Pacific Historical Review,* XII, 1943, 33-51.

———. "The American Navy as a Factor in World Politics, 1903-1913." *American Historical Review,* LXIII, 1958, 863-879.

Lord, Clifford L. "History of Naval Aviation, 1908-1939," mimeographed. 4 vols. Office of Naval History.

Lyman, Richard D. *The First Labour Government, 1924.* London, 1957.

Macartney, Maxwell H. H., and Paul Cremona. *Italy's Foreign and Colonial Policy, 1914-1937.* Oxford, 1938.

MacDonald, James Ramsay. "The London Naval Conference, 1930." *Journal of the Royal Institute of International Affairs,* IX, 1930, 429-451.

———, and Henry L. Stimson. "The London Naval Conference, 1930." *Encyclopedia Britannica,* XIV, 373-374B. 14th ed.

Maddox, William P. *Foreign Relations in British Labour Politics.* Cambridge, Mass., 1934.

Mahan, Alfred Thayer. *Armaments and Arbitration, or the Place of Force in the International Relations of States.* New York, 1912.

———. *The Interest of America in Sea Power, Present and Future.* Boston, 1897.

———. *The Problem of Asia and its Effect upon International Politics.* Boston, 1900.

Marder, Arthur J. *The Anatomy of British Sea Power: A History of British Naval Policy in the Pre-Dreadnought Era, 1880-1905.* New York, 1940.

Maxon, Yale Candee. "Control of Japanese Foreign Policy: A Study of Civil-Military Rivalry, 1930-1945." *University of California Publications in Political Science,* V. Berkeley, 1957.

May, Ernest R. "The Development of Political-Military Consultation in the United States." *Political Science Quarterly,* LXX, 1955, 161-180.

McCallum, Ronald B. *Public Opinion and the Last Peace*. London, 1944.

Medlicott, W. N. *British Foreign Policy since Vesailles*. London, 1940.

Mitchell, Donald W. *History of the Modern American Navy: From 1883 through Pearl Harbor*. New York, 1946.

Moore, Frederick. *With Japan's Leaders: An Intimate Record of Fourteen Years as Counsellor to the Japanese Government, Ending December 7, 1941*. New York, 1942.

Morgan, Laura Puffer. *The Background of the London Naval Conference*. Washington, D.C., 1930.

———. *An Observer's Estimate of the London Naval Conference*. Washington, D.C., n.d.

Morison, Samuel Eliot. *The Battle of the Atlantic, September 1939–May 1943*. Boston, 1947.

———. *The Rising Sun in the Pacific, 1931–April 1942*. Boston, 1948.

———. *Strategy and Compromise*. Boston, 1958.

Morton, Louis. "Military and Naval Preparations for the Defense of the Philippines during the War Scare of 1907." *Military Affairs*, XIII, 1949, 95-104.

———. "War Plan Orange: Evolution of a Strategy." *World Politics*, XI, 1959, 221-250.

Mosca, Rudolfo. *Il Disarmo Navale e la Conferenza di Londra*. Pavia, 1931.

Moulton, Harold G., and Leo Pasvolsky. *War Debts and World Prosperity*. Washington, D.C., 1932.

Myers, William S. *The Foreign Policies of Herbert Hoover, 1929-1933*. New York, 1940.

———, and Walter H. Newton. *The Hoover Administration: A Documented Narrative*. New York, 1936.

Noel-Baker, Philip J. *Disarmament and the Coolidge Conference*, London, 1927.

———. *The Private Manufacture of Armaments*. New York, 1937.

O'Connor, Raymond G. "The 'Yardstick' and Naval Disarmament in the 1920's." *Mississippi Valley Historical Review*, XLV, 1958, 441-463.

O'Gara, Gordon Carpenter. *Theodore Roosevelt and the Rise of the Modern Navy*. Princeton, 1943.

Pearson, Drew, and Constantine Brown. *The American Diplomatic Game*. New York, 1935.

Perticone, Giacomo. *La Politica italiana nell' ultimo trentennio*. 3 vols. Rome, 1945-1947.

Pomeroy, Earl S. *Pacific Outpost: American Strategy in Guam and Micronesia*. Stanford, 1951.

Puleston, Captain W. D. *The Influence of Force in Foreign Affairs*. New York, 1955.

Ransom, Harry Howe. "The Politics of Air Power—A Comparative Analysis." *Public Policy: A Yearbook of the Graduate School of Public Administration, Harvard University, 1958*. Ed. Carl J. Friedrich and Seymour E. Harris. Cambridge, Mass., 1958.

Rappaport, Armin. "The Navy League of the United States." Unpublished manuscript, 1954.

177

————. "The Navy League of the United States." *South Atlantic Quarterly*, LIII, 1954, 203-212.

Rappard, William E. *The Quest for Peace since the World War.* Cambridge, Mass., 1940.

Read, Conyers. "More Light on the London Naval Treaty of 1930: London Naval Conference." *American Philosophical Society Proceedings*, XCIII, 1949, 290-308.

Reynolds, P. A. *British Foreign Policy in the Inter-War Years.* London, 1954.

Richmond, Sir Herbert William. *Economy and Naval Security.* London, 1931.

Rodgers, Rear Admiral W. L. "The Navy as an Aid in Carrying Out Diplomatic Policies." U.S. Naval Institute *Proceedings*, LV, 1929, 99-104.

Schilling, Warner R. "Civil-Naval Politics in World War I." *World Politics*, VII, 1955, 572-591.

Schmitt, Bernadotte E. "British Foreign Policy, 1919-1939." *Journal of Modern History*, XXI, 1949, 320-326.

Schumpeter, Elizabeth B. "The Yen Bloc: Program and Results." *Annals of the American Academy of Political and Social Science*, CCXV, 1941, 29-35.

Shaw, Roger. "The London Naval Conference of 1930: A Study in Naval and Political Relations among the Western Powers." Unpublished doctoral dissertation, Fordham University, 1946.

Simonds, Frank H. *American Foreign Policy in the Post-War Years.* Baltimore, 1935.

Sipple, Chester E. "British Foreign Policy since the World War." *University of Iowa Studies in the Social Sciences*, X, No. 1. Iowa City, 1932.

Sloutzki, Nokhim M. *The World Armaments Race, 1919-1939.* Geneva, 1941.

Smith, Louis. *American Democracy and Military Power.* Chicago, 1951.

Spinks, C. N. "The Termination of the Anglo-Japanese Alliance." *Pacific Historical Review*, VI, 1937, 321-340.

Sprout, Harold, and Margaret Sprout. "Changing Power Relations in the Pacific," *Annals of the American Academy of Political and Social Science*, CCXV, 1941, 107-114.

————. *The Rise of American Naval Power, 1776-1918.* 2nd ed. Princeton, 1942.

————. *Toward a New Order of Sea Power: American Naval Policy and the World Scene, 1918-1922.* Princeton, 1943.

Steiner, Zara S. "Great Britain and the Creation of the Anglo-Japanese Alliance." *The Journal of Modern History*, XXXI, 1949, 27-36.

Stewart, Robert B. *Treaty Relations of the British Commonwealth of Nations.* New York, 1939.

Stimson, Henry L. "Bases of American Policy during the Past Four Years." *Foreign Affairs*, XI, 1933, 383-396.

————. *The Far Eastern Crisis: Recollections and Observations.* New York, 1936.

Storry, Richard. *The Double Patriots: A Study of Japanese Nationalism.* London, 1957.

Takeuchi, Tatsuji. *War and Diplomacy in the Japanese Empire.* Garden City, N.Y., 1935.

Tate, Merze. *The Disarmament Illusion.* New York, 1942.

————. *The United States and Armaments*. Cambridge, Mass., 1948.

Tiedemann, Arthur E. "The Hamaguchi Cabinet: First Phase, July 1929—February 1930." Unpublished doctoral dissertation, Columbia University, New York, 1959.

Tilley, Sir John. *London to Tokyo*. London, 1942.

Tompkins, Pauline. *American-Russian Relations in the Far East*. New York, 1949.

Treat, Payson J. *Japan and the United States, 1853-1921: Revised and Continued to 1928*. Stanford, 1928.

Tupper, Eleanor, and George E. McReynolds. *Japan in American Public Opinion*. New York, 1937.

Turnbull, A. D., and Clifford L. Lord, *History of United States Naval Aviation*. New Haven, 1949.

Vagts, Alfred. *Defense and Diplomacy: The Soldier and the Conduct of Foreign Relations*. New York, 1956.

Vinson, John Chalmers. *The Parchment Peace: The United States Senate and the Washington Conference, 1921-1922*. Athens, Ga., 1955.

Wallin, Homer N. "Permissible Building Programs under the London Naval Treaty." U.S. Naval Institute *Proceedings*, LVI, 1930, 1074-1979.

Watson, Mark Skinner. *Chief of Staff: Prewar Plans and Preparations*. Washington, D.C., 1950.

Wheeler, Gerald Everett. "Japan's Influence on American Naval Policies, 1922-1931." Unpublished doctoral dissertation, University of California, Berkeley, 1954.

————. "Isolated Japan: Anglo-American Diplomatic Co-operation, 1927-1936." *Pacific Historical Review*, XXX, 1961, 165-178.

————. "The United States Navy and the Japanese 'Enemy': 1919-1931." *Military Affairs*, XXI, 1957, 61-74.

Wheeler-Bennett, John W. *Disarmament and Security since Locarno, 1925-1931*. London, 1932.

————. *Information on the Reduction of Armaments*. London, 1925.

Wester-Wemyss, Admiral of the Fleet, Lord. "Washington and After." *The Nineteenth Century and After*, XCI, 1922, 405-416.

Wilbur, Ray Lyman, and Arthur M. Hyde. *The Hoover Policies*. New York, 1937.

Williams, Benjamin H. *The United States and Disarmament*. New York, 1931.

Windrich, Elaine. *British Labour's Foreign Policy*. Stanford, 1952.

Wolfers, Arnold. *Britain and France between Two Wars: Conflicting Strategies of Peace since Versailles*. New York, 1940.

Woodward, E. L. *Great Britain and the German Navy*. Oxford, 1935.

Wright, Quincy, ed. *Interpretations of American Foreign Policy*. Chicago, 1930.

Yates, Louis A. R. *The United States and French Security, 1917-1921*. New York, 1957.

Young, Eugene J. *Powerful America: Our Place in a Rearming World*. New York, 1936.

12. GENERAL WORKS

Akagi, Roy Hidemichi. *Japan's Foreign Relations, 1542-1936: A Short History.* Tokyo, 1936.

Allen, H. C. *Great Britain and the United States: A History of Anglo-American Relations, 1783-1952.* New York, 1955.

Carr, Edward H. *International Relations since the Peace Treaties.* London, 1937.

Gathorne-Hardy, G. M. *A Short History of International Affairs, 1920-1939.* London, 1952.

Howland, Charles P., ed. *Survey of American Foreign Relations, 1928-1931.* New Haven, 1928-1931.

Mowat, Charles Loch. *Britain between the Wars, 1918-1940.* London, 1955.

Sontag, Raymond J. *European Diplomatic History, 1871-1932.* New York, 1933.

Toynbee, Arnold J. *Survey of International Affairs, 1920-1930.* London, 1924-1931.

Yanaga, Chitoshi. *Japan since Perry.* New York, 1949.

Index

Acton, Admiral Alfredo, 64, 107

Adams, Charles F.: and Japanese concessions, 81, 82; meets with Hoover, 43; and parity, 113; and Stimson yardstick, 34; mentioned, 44, 58, 69

Admiralty, British: adopts new naval policy, 3, 60, 151n53; influences MacDonald, 38, 39, 40, 41, 43, 151n51; position on size of capital ships, 62; reaction to staggered building, 80; rejects American demands, 70; mentioned, 14, 48

Age of vessels, 87-88

Agenda: for London Naval Conference, 67

Aircraft, 76, 77, 118, 159n6

Aircraft carriers: American position on, 76-77; British position on, 73; Hoover-MacDonald conversations concerning, 48; and London Naval Treaty, 105; ratio established at Washington Conference, 6; mentioned, 8, 20, 67, 122

Air Ministry (British), 14

Air power: role of, 118

Alaska, 1

Alexander, Albert V.: on method of limitation, 68; on reduction of cruisers, 151n53; presents British position on submarines, 84; mentioned, 38, 60, 63

Alliance, military, of 1919, 88

American Legion: and Kellogg-Briand Pact, 23; and parity with Great Britain, 38; urges larger fleet, 12

American reaction: to Stimson remarks of March 11, 95

Anglo-American Conversations: account of, Ch. IV, 59; after Geneva Naval Conference, 20; French apprehension of, 54; Japanese inquiry concerning, 51; Japanese protest of, 52; preparation for, 29-30

Anglo-Egyptian Treaty, 120

Anglo-French Naval Compromise of 1928, 21-22, 31

Anglo-French negotiations, 101

Anglo-Italian negotiations, 101-102

Anglo-Japanese Alliance; American attitude toward, 145n16; General Board attitude toward, 6; reaction toward, 5; results of, 3; Theodore Roosevelt and, 2; mentioned, 8, 9, 52

Appropriations, naval: for 1921-1922, 145n13

Armistice: and naval power, 4

Army, U.S., 123; and defense of Philippines, 79; American involvement in, 146n31

Army Air Force, 76

Asia: Japanese position in, 5-6

Asiatic Squadron: role of, 2

Aubert, Louis, 95, 162n42

Australia; presents position, 66; threat to build cruisers, 73; mentioned, 64

Auxiliary vessels: competition in, 122; Japanese demands, 51; mentioned, 6, 71

Balance of power: at end of World War I, 4

Baldwin, Stanley, 23, 32, 39, 47, 121

Barkley, Senator Alben: defends treaty, 116

Bases, Naval: Hoover-MacDonald conversation concerning, 49; mentioned, 111, 147n5

Battleships, 62, 77, 114, 120. See also Capital ships

Beatty, Adm. Earl, 120

Belgium, 5

Bell, Edward Price, 32, 160n40

Belligerents, rights of during wartime. See Freedom of the seas

Benn, William Wedgwood, 63

Big Navy Bloc: U.S., 12, 14, 22, 121; French, 56

Black Dragon Society, 118

Borah, Senator William E.: calls for papers on treaty, 115; on a consultative pact, 98; rejects appointment as delegate, 58; views on British Navy, 39-40; mentioned, 92, 109, 110, 111

Bordonaro, Antonio Chiaramonte, 64

Briand, Aristide: agrees to further conversations with Italy, 103; and amendment to Kellogg-Briand Pact, 92-93; and consultative pact, 96, 164n57; demands larger navy, 89; on security pact, 99-101, 104, 124; protests naval reduction, 95; mentioned, 56, 63

Bridgeman, W. C.: and Geneva Naval Conference, 17; protests cruiser figures, 60; protests treaty, 120

British Commonwealth, 66

British delegation: composition of, 63

British Foreign Office, 90

British naval policy: at Geneva Naval Conference of 1927, 17-18

British position: announced February 7, 72-73; on capital ships, 72; on cruisers, 73; on destroyers, 73; on submarines, 73

Britten, Representative Fred A.: protests treaty, 111; reaction to Gibson Geneva speech, 26

Brown, Constantine, 32

Buell, Raymond Leslie, 95

Buffer state, Japan as, 114

Building program, 127; Great Britain's, 40; Italian, 107; U.S.: factors affecting, 1; post-World War I, 4-5; staggering of, 80

Building programs, cruiser: Japan and Great Britain after Washington treaties, 13

Burnett, Lieutenant Colonel Charles: on amendment to Immigration Act, 77, 78

Bywater, Hector C., 60

Cabinet, British: and cancellation of Anglo-French Naval Compromise, 22; disagrees on disarmament, 35; rejects security pact, 102, 124

Capital ships: British position on, 72; Hoover-MacDonald discussions concerning, 47; General Board position on, 71; and London Naval Treaty, 67, 105, 112; modernization of, 74; not discussed at Geneva Conference, 20; parity in, 74; ratio at Washington Conference on Limitation of Armament, 6, 7, 8, 78, 122; ratio with Japan, 51, 61; replacement of, 38. *See also* Battleships

Caribbean: and American sea power, 78

Carson, Lord, 120

Castle, William R.: appointed ambassador to Japan, 157n35; cautions American delegation, 80, 118; denied access to dispatches, 152n60; on diplomatic notes, 151n50; reports Japanese interest in Conference, 68-69

Categories, limitation by: France protests, 20, 55, 69; Great Britain favors, 20; United States favors, 36, 68; mentioned, 67

Categories, transfer between, 48

Cecil, Viscount (Lord Robert Cecil): at Geneva Naval Conference, 17; and parity, 147n19

Chamber of Deputies: reaction to French note of December 20, 56

Chamberlain, Sir Austen: on a formula to determine parity, 29

China: invited to attend Washington Conference, 5; and Japanese expansion, 126; and Nine-Power Treaty, 7; territorial integrity of, 83

Churchill, Winston: defends British fleet, 2; denounces treaty, 120; protests parity, 32

Civil-military relations, 125

Colonies, 123

Combat strength: factors determining, 36

Communism: containment of, 83

Committees: establishment of, 64-65

Committee of Experts: considers submarines, 85; establishment of, 65; mentioned, 104

Committee of Imperial Defense, 48

Committee on Foreign Relations, Senate: conducts hearings on treaty, 111-113; recommends ratification of treaty, 113; mentioned, 58, 110, 117

Committee of Jurists: establishment of, 65; and restrictions on submarine warfare, 86

Committee on Naval Affairs, House, 111

Committee on Naval Affairs, Senate: decides to conduct hearings, 110; testimony of naval experts before, 112-113; mentioned, 33, 37, 109

Competition, naval, 127

Congress, U.S., 78; and naval construction in 1929, 22

Consultative pact: American "peace groups" favor, 91; *Christian Science Monitor* urges, 90; efforts to agree on, 100; Great Britain advocates, 56, 96; Hoover and, 91, 97, 99, 163n36; influence of on Conference, 103, 124; Raymond Leslie Buell on, 95; Stimson and, 94, 162n1, 164n57

Coolidge, Calvin: and Geneva Naval Conference, 147n13; calls Geneva Conference of 1927, 15-16; reaction to Anglo-French Naval Compromise, 22; mentioned, 20, 110

Copeland, Senator Royal S.: denounces treaty, 116

Cotton, Joseph P.: on consultative pact, 97; on handling of newsmen, 109; and Mediterranean Pact, 102; objects to General Board activities, 58; and suspension of ship construction, 151n32; mentioned, 43, 44

Covenant of the League of Nations: and amendment to the Kellogg-Briand Pact, 49; as a basis for disarmament, 56, 90, 102; and a consultative pact, 92; and a security pact, 56, 90, 102

Cruisers: agreement with Great Britain, 74; American position on, 69-70, 70-72, 111-113; American specifications following Washington treaties, 11; British position on, 73, 120; categories of, 67; delay in construction of, 37, 82; demands for at Geneva Naval Conference, 17; Hoover-MacDonald conversations concerning, 47-48; provided for in Act of 1929, 22; ratio with Japan, 52, 77, 80, 81, 82; scrappable age of, 39; U.S.-British ratio, 27, 34, 37-38, 40-45, 52, 61; and Washington Treaty, 8; mentioned, 125

Cruiser Act of 1929, 22, 148n11

Darlan, Captain Jean Françoise, 57

Daughers of the American Revolution, 110

Dawes, Charles G.: comments on treaty, 114; complains about conference, 67; on consultative pact, 96; conversations with MacDonald, 31-32, 35, 37, 39, 41, 79; dispatches of, 115; on General Board, 152n71; meets with Hoover, 30; protests bargaining, 77, 159n9; reaction to pre-conference conversations, 63; views on disarmament, 33; on yardstick, 42; mentioned, 38, 40, 44, 45, 51, 58

Day, Rear Admiral George C., 160n2

Debuchi, Katsuji, 51, 52

Delegation, U.S.: arrival in London, 62; composition of, 58; formulates American program, 69-71

Denby, Edwin: directs General Board to formulate naval policy based on Washington treaties, 11; invites State Department cooperation, 12

Destroyers: American position on, 71; British position on, 72; displacement of, 87; Hoover-MacDonald conversations concerning, 48; Japanese demands, 79; loss of superiority in, 112; ratio with Japan, 80, 81, 82; scrappable age of, 39; scrapping of, 37; total tonnage of, 74; mentioned, 67

Dewey, John, 91

Diet, Japanese: debates treaty, 119; mentioned, 69

Disarmament: general, 56; Dawes' views on, 33; definition of, 124-125; and naval strength, 5

Disposal of warships, 87

Dominions, British: reaction to staggered building program, 80

Dulles, Allen W.: and the yardstick, 29
Dumesnil, Jacques-Louis, 63

Edge, Walter E., 56, 90
Emperor Hirohito, 83, 118, 119
Empire, American in the Pacific: beginnings, 1
Equality, naval, 39; Franco-Italian, 57. *See also* Ratio
Equilibrium, of naval power, 128
Escalator clause, 40, 90, 105
Exclusion Act of 1924. *See* Immigration Act of 1924
Exempt vessels, 87, 105

Far East: America's interest in, 1, 3; British concern in, 42; Post-World War I situation in, 5
Fess, Senator Simeon D., 92
Field, Vice Admiral Sir F. L., 17
First Committee: considers submarines, 85, 86; establishment of, 65; function of, 68, 157; and "special vessels," 87; mentioned, 104
Five-power conference: preparations for, 46
Five-power treaty: basis for, 102; defeat of, 103, 123; mentioned, 93, 104
Fleet, American: disposition of, 78
Fleet Cruise, the (1907-1909), 2
Fleuriau, Aimé-Joseph de, 63
Flying decks, 77
Food ships: Hoover-MacDonald conversations concerning, 48-49
Forbes, W. Cameron, 148n*18*
Foreign Office, British, 51
Foreign Office, French, 54
Foreign Policy Association, 97, 98
Foreign trade: Japanese after WWI, 53
Formula. *See* yardstick
Fosdick, Raymond B., 91
Four-Power Treaty, 9, 56, 62, 92, 96, 97
France: and Italian demands, 165n*64*; position on naval limitation, 15, 55-56, 88, 103; preliminary conversations with, 54-57; refuses invitation to Geneva Naval Conference, 16; Tardieu presents position of, 66. *See also* Security
Franco-Italian conversations: continued, 103
Freedom of the seas: and Dawes-MacDonald conversations, 31, 32; Hoover-MacDonald conversations concerning, 48; and London Naval Conference, 74; and Naval Act of 1929, 22; opposed in British Empire, 60; Wilson and, 4
French delegation: composition of, 63
French naval requirements: British reaction to, 89
French, Representative Burton L., 111
Furutaka class, 81

General Board: and Anglo-French Naval Compromise, 21; and Anglo-Japanese Alliance, 145n*16*; Anglophobia of, 13-14; assesses American defense needs, 2; and battleships, 24, 71; and British bases, 153n*10*; comment

on British proposal, 41; establishment of, 1; formulates naval policy based on Washington treaties, 11; meeting with Hoover, 43-44; on cruisers, 43, 146n*5*; recommendations for Geneva Naval Conference, 16-17, 19; recommendations of 1915, 3; recommendations of 1921, 5-6; recommendations protested by Cotton, 58; and yardstick, 28-29, 33-34, 43-44; mentioned, 42, 45, 69, 70, 112
Geneva Naval Conference of 1927: account of, 16-19; and armament manufacturers, 59; Dawes' reasons for failure of, 33; effect of, 20; General Board and, 58; Italian refusal to attend, 57; and naval parity, 36; reasons for failure of, 17-19; mentioned, 31, 74, 80, 110, 120, 126
Geneva Protocol, 88, 101, 161n*29*
George V, King, 47, 60, 64
George, Senator Walter: on a consultative pact, 98
German-British naval rivalry, 2-3
German cruisers. *See* Pocket battleships
German naval building: French apprehension of, 55
German Navy: effect on Navy planning, 1; Mahan on, 145n*6*
Germany: imperialism of, 2; miiltary threat of, 4, 91, 103
Ghormley, Captain Robert L., 152n*69*
Gibson, Hugh: addresses Preparatory Commission, 1929, 25; assists Dawes, 34, 38; defends MacDonald, 40; instructions to for meeting of Preparatory Commission, 24; at Geneva Naval Conference of 1927, 17; on methods of limitation, 68; misgivings concerning British program, 35; supports treaty, 109; and yardstick, 27, 28; mentioned, 29, 54, 58
Gibson speech: reaction to, 149n*29*
Global tonnage: on conference agenda, 67; French advocacy of, 20, 55; Italian support of, 21
Grandi, Dino: agrees to continue limitation talks, 103; presents Italian position on armaments, 66, 95, 101; presents Italian position on submarines, 57, 85; on ratios, 68; on the United States, 63; welcome on returning home, 107; mentioned, 64, 69
Great Britain: attitude toward disarmament, 1926, 14; cruiser demands at Geneva Naval Conference, 17; German threat to, 2; MacDonald presents position of, 66; renounces imperialism, 122; threat to United States, 4; mentioned, 51
Grey, Sir Edward, 94
Guam: effect of acquisition on Japan, 2

Hague Conference, 164n*43*
Hale, Senator Frederick: announces hearings on treaty, 110; defends naval experts, 150n*14*; denounces treaty, 116; reaction to

Dawes' Society of Pilgrims speech, 33, mentioned, 72, 109
Hamaguchi, Premier: accepts Japanese-American compromise, 83; effect of treaty on, 128; hails treaty, 121; and treaty ratification, 118, 119; mentioned, 82
Hankey, Sir Maurice, 67
Harada, Baron, 157
Harding, Warren G.: and calling of Washington Conference, 5; defends Washington treaties, 9; welcomes delegates, 6
Hawkins class cruisers, 38, 39
Henderson, Arthur: and French security, 89, 94, 100; and Geneva Protocol, 88; and MacDonald, 31; and United States-Japanese negotiations, 78-79; mentioned, 63, 69, 93, 96
Hepburn, Rear Admiral Arthur J., 82
Hoover, Herbert: asks Admiral Jones for advice, 34; announces delay in cruiser construction, 37; approves American proposal of February 4, 71; calls special session of the Senate, 114; congratulates delegation, 104; and consultative pact, 92, 163n36; and Dawes' Society of Pilgrims speech, 32; and escalator clause, 90; hails treaty, 121; and Japan's role in the Far East, 83, 160n40; and Japanese negotiations, 51, 54, 78, 79-80; and Kellogg-Briand Pact, 99; meeting with General Board, 43-44; and naval spending, 166n28; on parity with Great Britain, 35, 40, 45; and Philippine Islands, 148n18; position on Cruiser Bill of 1929, 23; and ratification of treaty, 109-117; rejects Senate request for papers on treaty, 115; and security pact, 91, 99, 124; and Senator Swanson, 58; sends treaty to Senate, 111; on two-power treaty, 81; and yardstick, 24, 27-28, 29; mentioned, 25, 26
Hoover-MacDonald conversations: conducted, 47-49; joint statement at conclusion of, 49; French reaction to, 55; results of, 50-51; mentioned, 75
Hough, Rear Admiral Henry H.: testimony on treaty, 112
House of Commons: debate over treaty, 117, 120-121; MacDonald criticized in, 35, 38, 39; mentioned, 74, 102
House of Lords: debate over treaty, 120
House of Representatives, 98
Howland, Charles P., 167n39
Hughes, Charles Evans: and Joint Army-Navy Board, 12-13; and yardstick, 28; and Washington Conference, 5, 6-9, 146n31; mentioned, 108, 126

Immigration Act of 1924: amendment to, 77; influence on Japan, 13; mentioned, 53
Imperialism: renunciation of, 122; mentioned, 53
Imperialism, American, 1
Imperialism, Japanese, 5, 7
India, 120

Ingalls, David S.: favors air power, 58
Inspection, 88
Irish Free State, 64
Ishii, Viscount Kikujiro: on Japanese-American ratio, 80; mentioned, 17
Italy: claim for French colonies, 62; French fear of, 89; Grandi presents position of, 66; pre-conference conversations, 57; refuses invitation to Geneva Naval Conference, 16
Italian delegation: composition of, 64
Italian press reaction. *See* Press reaction, Italian

Japan: agreement with, 81; and cruiser ratio, 42; attitude of T. Roosevelt toward, 2; attitude toward disarmament in 1926, 15; demands at Geneva Naval Conference, 17; effect of Washington treaties on, 9-10; election in, 79; imperialism of, 15; role in the Far East, 4, 83; pre-conference negotiations with, 51-54; ratification of treaty in, 118-119; reaction to American proposal of February 4, 72; renounces imperialism, 122; results of Alliance with Great Britain, 3; Wakatsuki explains attitude toward disarmament, 66
Japanese-American Compromise, Ch. VII
Japanese delegation: composition of, 64; dispute over cruiser figure, 77
Japanese proposal: reaction of American delegates to, 77
Jellicoe, Admiral John (Earl), 13, 17, 120
Johnson, Senator Hiram W.: denounces Hoover's action in denying Senate treaty papers, 115; opposes consultative pact, 92; protests treaty, 113-114; questions Stimson, 112
Joint Army and Navy Board, 12
Jones, Admiral Hilary P.: appointed adviser to delegation, 58; conception of parity with Great Britain, 34, 113; deplores press attitude, 12; discusses cruiser demands with American delegates, 70; and Geneva Naval Conference of 1927, 17, 18; on parity in battleships, 74; represents United States at Preparatory Commission, 24; and submarines, 160n2
Jutland, Battle of: effect of upon Japanese demands, 69

Kato, Admiral: reaction to Japanese-American agreement, 82, 83
Kellogg, Frank B., 16, 21
Kellogg-Briand Pact: approval of, 22-23; and disarmament, 25, 30, 32, 36, 57, 60, 71, 99, 121, 122, 151n53; Hoover-MacDonald conversations concerning, 49; and security, 100; shortcomings of, 55, 89-90, 91, 128; mentioned, 27

League of Nations: French demand for disarmament negotiations within, 54-55, 61; and French security, 95; and Preparatory

Commission, 14, 46, 104; Senate rejection of, 126; withdrawal of French demand, 63
League for Independent Political Action, 91
Lexington, 58
Leygues, George, 57, 63
Limited transfer, right of between categories, 36
Locarno treaties, 15, 88, 89, 102
Lodge, Henry Cabot: and modern American Navy, 1; mentioned, 6
London Naval Conference of 1930: invitations issued, 46; procedures for, 64-65
London Naval Treaty of 1930: assessment of, 128; preparation of draft, 104; provisions of, 105; text of, 129-144

MacDonald, Ramsay: accepts United States compromise, 74; adjourns conference, 104; and Admiralty, 38, 43, 151n51; agrees to continue negotiations with France and Italy, 103; attacked on cruiser figures, 73; attitude toward disarmament, 30; chosen chairman, 64; complains about French demands, 95, 96; concept of parity, 39, 69-70; and consultative pact, 92, 93; criticized in House of Commons, 35; disappointment over yardstick, 42; efforts at conference, 108; and French security, 102; and negotiations with Dawes, 31-32, 40-41; and negotiations with Japan, 51-52, 54, 79, 150n23; and Pact for Mediterranean, 102; political position of, 60, 128; pre-conference conversation with Stimson, 62; presents British position, 66; protests naval officers as delegates, 18; and publicity, 65; reaction to two-power pact, 81; rejects use of Singapore as bargaining factor, 59; and a security pact, 89, 97, 99, 100, 124; supports treaty, 120-121; trip to the United States, 47-49; mentioned, 63, 68, 71, 72, 90, 94, 101, 109, 115
Mahan, Alfred Thayer: influence of, 1; on German Navy, 145n6; mentioned, 4
Massigli, René, 63, 90
Manchuria, 3
Manifest destiny, 1
Matsudaira, Tsuneo: confers with Reed, 82; discusses amendment to Immigration Act, 77, 78; and pre-conference negotiations, 51, 52, 53; mentioned, 64
McKellar, Senator Kenneth: calls for papers on treaty, 115; denounces treaty, 116
Mediterranean: Franco-Italian rivalry in, 15
Mediterranean Pact: British attitude toward, 56, 62, 92; Spanish attitude toward, 60-61, 102; and United States, 90, 92
Merchant Marine, British, 111
Merchant Marine, U.S., 114
Middle East, 3
Midway Islands: annexation of, 1
Military equilibrium, 127
Modernization of battleships, 74
Moffett, Rear Admiral W. A.: and aircraft carriers, 76

Monroe Doctrine: and naval policy, 1, 2, 5, 126; threat to, 123
Moore, John Bassett, 86
Morrow, Dwight W.: and negotiations with France, 95-96; prepares final treaty, 104; mentioned, 58, 69
Moses, Senator George H.: advocates delay of approval, 114; favors consultative pact, 92; protests treaty, 113-114
Moysset, Henry, 63
Mussolini, Benito: demands parity with France, 103; explains failure to participate in Geneva Naval Conference, 57; French suspicion of, 89, 123; proposed appeal to, 101

Nagai, Matsuzo, 64
National Council for the Prevention of War, 110
National Student Federation of America, 98
Naval Acts: of 1916, 4, 126; of 1924, 13; of 1928, 20; of 1929, 22, 32, 37
Naval Affairs Committee, Senate, 72
Naval Appropriations Subcommittee, House, 111
Naval bases. *See* Bases, naval
Naval limitation, 30
Naval reduction, 33
Navy: role of in foreign policy, 125-126; modern American, origin of, 1
Navy Department: announces acceleration of construction, 61; prepares for Geneva Naval Conference, 14; reaction to American proposals, 36; reaction to Dawes' Society of Pilgrims speech, 33; mentioned, 41, 127
Navy League: and Dawes' Society of Pilgrims speech, 33; and London Naval Treaty, 110; supports large navy, 12
Navy League, British, 60; Canadian, 60; South African, 60
Negotiations, complexity of, 128
Nelson, 71, 114
Netherlands, the, 5
New Zealand, Dominion of: position explained, 66; threat to build cruisers, 73; mentioned, 64
Niebuhr, Reinhold, 91
Nine-Power Treaty, 7, 9
Noel-Baker, Philip, 168n73
Non-fortification of naval bases, 18, 112, 114
Non-fortification agreement at Washington, 8, 12
Notification of construction, 88

Oddie, Senator Tasker L., 114, 167n56
Omaha class, 43, 44
Open Door in China: and naval policy, 5, 126; mentioned, 7

Page, Arthur W., 62
Panama Canal, 3
Paris Peace Pact. *See* Kellogg-Briand Pact
Parity: American concept of, 19; Anglo-American, 6, 8, 40, 41, 43, 44, 57, 60, 111;

Franco-Italian, 57, 60, 89, 92, 96, 103; French refusal to grant to Italy, 55; Great Britain accepts with U.S., 35-36; in capital ships, 74; in capital ships with Great Britain, 71; MacDonald and Stimson discuss, regarding cruisers, 69-70; method of determining, 29; air power and, 58; mentioned, 27, 28, 112, 147n19

Pax Britannica, 3

Peace societies, 12, 91

Phelps, Rear Adm. William W., 13

Philippine Islands: effect of acquisition on Japan, 2; Hoover's attitude toward, 148n18; Japanese threat to, 126; military value of, 2; and naval policy, 3, 77; neutralization of, 79

Plenary meeting, first, 64; second, 64-67; third, 67-68; fourth, 84-85; fifth, 104; sixth, 104

Pocket battleships (German), 60, 89

Portugal, 5

Pratt, Admiral William V.: meets with American delegates, 70; and naval advisers, 69, 82; on parity in capital ships, 74; supports treaty, 113, 166n21; mentioned, 58

Preparatory Commission: delegates to attend Geneva Naval Conference, 16, 17; and disarmament, 20, 27, 54, 55, 120; Gibson speech before, 24-25; and method of limitation, 68, 104; U.S. sends delegates to meetings of, 14; mentioned, 15, 29, 46, 51

Press: role of, 124; Stimson and, 158n54

Press reaction, British: to Dawes Society of Pilgrims speech, 33; to Gibson Geneva speech, 26; to Hoover-MacDonald meeting, 50; to London Naval Treaty, 106-107; to security pact, 96; to Stimson's "midnight statement," 98

Press reaction, French: to Anglo-American parity, 54; to Dawes' Society of Pilgrims speech, 33; to early developments at LNC, 69; on French naval position, 90-91; to Gibson Geneva address, 26; to Hoover-MacDonald meeting, 50; to London Naval Treaty, 105; to Stimson remarks on March 11, 94-95

Press reaction, Italian: to American proposal of February 4, 72; to Dawes' Society of Pilgrims speech, 33; to early developments at LNC, 69; to Gibson Geneva address, 26-27; to Hoover-MacDonald meeting, 50; to London Naval Treaty, 107

Press reaction, Japanese: to Gibson Geneva address, 27; to Japanese-American Compromise, 82; to London Naval Treaty, 118

Press reaction, U.S.: to Dawes' Society of Pilgrims speech, 33; to Gibson's Geneva speech, 26; to Hoover-MacDonald meeting, 49-50; to London Naval Treaty, 106, 114-115; to ratification of treaty, 117

Pringle, Rear Admiral J. R. P., 81

Privy Council, Japanese, 119

Public opinion: role of, 124. See press reaction, 119

Public opinion, British: on London Naval Treaty, 165n69

Publicity: rules regarding, 65

Rapidan Conference. See Hoover-MacDonald conversations

Ratification of treaty: provisions for, 105; in Great Britain, 119-121; in Japan, 118-119; in U.S., 109-118; mentioned, 125

Ratio: of aircraft carriers, 77; British conception of, 146n30; of capital ships, 61; defects of, 126-127; determination of, 67; Japanese position on, 15, 52, 53, 69; with Japan, 42, 51, 54, 62, 77, 79, 81; at Washington Conference, 6, 8, 122

Reed, Senator David A.: defends treaty, 112, 116, 158n48; and freedom of the seas, 75; negotiates with Japanese, 71, 77, 78, 79, 82, 118; and ratification of treaty, 109, 110, 117; urges reduction in cruiser demands, 72; mentioned, 58, 69, 118

Replacement of vessels, 87-88

Robinson, Senator Arthur H.: protests treaty, 113-114

Robinson, Senator Joseph T., 58, 72, 78, 109

Rodney, 71, 114

Roosevelt, Theodore: and Japan, 83; and modern American Navy, 1

Root, Elihu: on civil-military relations, 18; on submarine warfare, 86; on Washington Conference, 7; mentioned, 6

Russia, 2, 3, 83

Russo-Japanese War, 2

Saionji, Prince, 157n34

Saito, Admiral Viscount M., 17

Saratoga, 58

Schofield, Rear Admiral Frank H., 147n17

Scrappable age of ships, 39

Sea power: American concept of at Geneva Naval Conference, 19; British, 2-3, 6, 19, 43, 64; Japanese, 3, 6, 19, 53, 77; role of aircraft in, 76; United States, 1, 2, 125-127; World War I and, 4

Security: different kinds of, 122-123; Japanese, 53

Security pact: American position on, 89, 92, 97, 99; British position on, 94, 102-103; French position on, 19, 54, 55, 56, 61, 66, 88, 89, 90, 91, 92, 99, 123-124

Senate: and amendment to Immigration Act, 78; conducts hearings on treaty, 111-114; debates treaty, 115-117; influences on treaty, 45, 58; and Kellogg-Briand Pact, 22-23; and MacDonald visit to U.S., 31; members criticize Stimson "midnight announcement," 124; requests material bearing on treaty, 115; special session of, 114; submission of treaty to, 109, 111; and World Court statutes, 59; vote on treaty, 117; mentioned, 110, 113

Shantung question, 52, 83

Shearer, William B., 59, 110

Shidehara, Baron: explains need for higher ratio, 77; on Japanese public opinion, 160n34; reaction to American offer, 80; and treaty ratification, 119

Shipstead, Senator Henrik: on a consultative pact, 98; opposes the treaty, 113

Shotwell, James T., 91

Simonds, Frank, 108

Singapore naval base, 59

Sirianni, Admiral Giuseppe, 64, 107

Smyth, Capt. W. W., 81, 104, 158n43

Society of Pilgrims of Great Britain: Dawes' speech before, 31, 32-33

South Africa, Union of, 64

Spain: and Mediterranean Pact, 60-61, 102

Special vessels, 87, 105

State Department, 98, 117

Stimson, Henry L.: addresses plenary session, 65; on agreement with Great Britain, 73; on amendment to Immigration Act, 78; announces American proposal, 72; appointed Secretary of State, 23; briefs delegation, 59; on consultative pact, 91, 94, 96, 97, 100, 123, 162n1, 164n57; conversation with Italian delegation, 62-63; conversation with Tardieu, 90; cautions press, 160n39; entertains MacDonald, 47; and food-ship proposal, 49; and French security, 93; instructed to boast about treaty, 109; on Italian non-cooperation, 101; and Japanese agreement, 82; and Philippine Islands, 148n18; meets with General Board, 43, 58; "midnight statement" of, 97, 124; negotiations with Great Britain, 29, 38, 39, 41, 45, 74; negotiations with Japan, 52, 54, 80; pre-conference conversation with MacDonald, 62; presents agenda for Anglo-American conversations, 30; protests early conference, 35; and ratification of treaty, 109-115; reaction to Japanese attitude, 79; reaction to Japanese proposals, 77; refuses to furnish Foreign Relations Committee with correspondence bearing on treaty, 113; relations with the press, 158n54; reports agreement with Great Britain and Japan, 104; reviews Dawes' speech, 32; and security pact, 92, 99; and submarine warfare, 37, 86; submits new proposals to Hoover, 71; suggests four-power pact, 55; tenor of dispatches, 115; testifies before Foreign Relations Committee, 111-112; and two-power treaty, 81; urges Dawes to defend treaty, 114; and yardstick, 34, 42, 51, 69; mentioned, 44, 118

Stock market: collapse of, 156n98

Streit, Clarence K., 25

Submarines: abolition of, 37, 83; age and replacement of, 88; on agenda, 67; American position on, 71, 84; armament of, 85, 86; British position on, 72, 84; demands for at Geneva Naval Conference, 17-18; French position on, 55, 81, 84; general negotiation at conference on, 84-86; Hoover-MacDonald

conversations concerning, 48; Italian position on, 57, 85; Japanese position on, 51, 85; ratio with Japan, 77, 80, 81, 82, 112; regulations on use of, 84-86, 105; restrictions on building of, 84-86; mentioned, 65, 74, 105

Supreme War Council, Japanese, 119

Swanson, Senator Claude A.: on consultative pact, 92, 98; defends treaty, 116; not appointed delegate, 58; protests delay in cruiser construction, 37; and treaty ratification, 109; mentioned, 72, 110

Takarabe, Admiral Takeshi: criticized in Japan, 118; presents Japanese position on submarines, 85; supports agreement, 81; mentioned, 64

Tardieu, André: conversations with Stimson, 63, 90, 100; discusses German cruisers and Italian parity, 55; forms new government, 89; on method of limitation, 68; position supported in France, 56, 57, 69, 88; and security pact, 95, 101, 124; states French position, 66; supports MacDonald as chairman, 64; mentioned, 96

Three-power treaty: agreement on, 83; French threat to, 93; Great Britain and, 123; Hoover recommends, 90; Japanese demands and, 81; reasons for, 128

Tonnage, maximum, 68

Total tonnage, 56

Toynbee, Arnold J., 19

Trade: competition for, 4; naval threat to, 123

Train, Commander Harold C., 104

"Trained Reserves": and Anglo-French Naval Compromise of 1928, 21

Transactional proposal: described by Gibson, 68; Italian press reaction to, 69; on treaty agenda, 67

Transfer between categories, 67

Treaty for the Renunciation of War. See Kellogg-Briand Pact

Treaty, Four Power (Washington), 7

Treaty, Naval Limitation (Washington). See Washington Treaty

Treaty, Nine-Power (Washington), 7

Tsushima, battle of: effect of, 2; effect of upon Japanese demands, 69

Two-power standard, British, 2, 89, 123

Two-power treaty, 80-81

Underwood, Oscar W., 6

United States: demands at the Geneva naval conference, 17; renounces imperialism, 122

United States Fleet: establishment of, 146n3

Utah, 23

Versailles Conference, 108

Versailles, Treaty, 83

Vinson-Trammel Act, 127

Wakatsuki, Baron Reijiro: on compromise terms, 81, 104, 165n62; congratulated by Emperor, 119; explains Japanese position,

66; negotiation with U.S., 78; receives American proposal, 71; mentioned, 54, 64, 72

Walsh, Senator David I., 92

War Office (British), 14

War plans, 1, 79, 147n5

Washington Conference on Limitation of Armaments: account of, 5-10; French position at, 69; influence on American naval policy, 11-12; Japanese position at explained, 69; and the yardstick, 28; mentioned, 13, 36, 40, 53, 55, 61, 77, 86, 101, 108

Washington Conference treaties: effect of, 8-10, 53, 146n31; effect of U.S. navy, 11-12; effect on France, 15; provisions of, 6-7; reaction to in France, 8; reaction to in Italy, 8; reaction to in Japan, 8; reaction to in Great Britain, 7-8; reaction to in U.S., 7

Washington Naval Limitation Treaty: .British attitude toward, 147n19; Churchill contrasts with London Naval Treaty, 120; contingent modifications of, 46, 73, 76-77, 80, 89, 104; France fails to build to, 88; provisions of, 67, 122; mentioned, 13, 67, 106, 112, 114

Watson, Senator James E., 109, 110, 117

Weeks, John W., 12

Wester-Wemyss, Admiral of the Fleet, Lord, 7

Western Hemisphere, 126; role in U.S. military policy, 122

Wilbur, Curtis D., 20, 21, 147n8

Wilson, Hugh R., 63

Wilson, Woodrow, 4, 108, 126

World Court, 59, 74

World War I: and disarmament, 12, 122; general effect of, 3; influence of on Great Britain, 32; and submarine warfare, 84

Yardstick: attempts to formulate, 28-29, 33-34, 36, 38-39; Gibson's proposal for, 25, 27; and Hoover misunderstanding with General Board, 43-44; Japanese skepticism toward, 51; MacDonald urges, 37, 40; questioned by Stimson, 41, 42, 59; rejected by Stimson and MacDonald, 69-70; Stimson's suggestion for, 34; mentioned, 31

Young Plan, 164n43